'Over a hundred years, Joel Stephen Birnie's ancestors Tarenootairer, and her daughters Mary Ann and Fanny Cochrane, endured abduction, rape, enslavement, destitution, despair and disease, while their family and their world died before their eyes. But they were not broken, and Fanny Cochrane's voice comes to us still to declare their truth. A brilliant and harrowing recreation of lives once treated so cheaply.'
Emeritus Redmond Barry Professor Janet McCalman
AC, FAHA, FASSA

'In this bold and original book the author shows how one of Tasmania's best-known Indigenous families survived colonial policies of extermination and extinction. A tour de force.'
Emeritus Professor Lyndall Ryan
AM FAHA

My People's Songs

How an Indigenous Family
Survived Colonial Tasmania

Joel Stephen Birnie

MONASH
UNIVERSITY
PUBLISHING

My People's Songs: How an Indigenous Family Survived Colonial Tasmania
© Copyright 2022 Joel Stephen Birnie
All rights reserved. Apart from any uses permitted by Australia's Copyright Act 1968, no part of this book may be reproduced by any process without prior written permission from the copyright owners. Enquiries should be directed to the publisher.

Monash University Publishing
Matheson Library Annexe
40 Exhibition Walk
Monash University
Clayton, Victoria 3800, Australia
publishing.monash.edu/

Monash University Publishing brings to the world publications which advance the best traditions of humane and enlightened thought.

ISBN: 9781922633187 (paperback)
ISBN: 9781922633194 (pdf)
ISBN: 9781922633200 (epub)

Editor: Kerry Davies AE
Designer: Les Thomas
Typesetter: Jo Mullins

Cover image: Annie Benbow (1841–1917), *Tasmanian Aborigines at Oyster Cove Station* (c. 1900), crayon and watercolour on paper; 34 x 52 cm. Record ID SD_ILS:140803, W.L. Crowther Library, Tasmanian Archives, State Library of Tasmania, https://stors.tas.gov.au/AUTAS001124870148w800.

A catalogue record for this book is available from the National Library of Australia.

CONTENTS

List of Images vii

Glossary. ix

Introduction: A Song of Welcome xi

PART 1.   A Weeping Woman: Tarenootairer, c. 1806–1858 1
Chapter 1   Saltwater Country. 3
Chapter 2   Nummer-Lore (White Devil's Wife) 7
Chapter 3   A Token of Grief. 16
Chapter 4   "Black Man's Houses". 22
Chapter 5   Dinudară (Sarah) 35
Chapter 6   Her Feeble Pulse. 44

PART 2.   A *Femme de Chambre*: Mary Ann, c. 1821–1871 51
Chapter 7   A King's Island Daughter 53
Chapter 8   The Bride and Bridegroom 60
Chapter 9   "Your Humble Aborigine Child" 65
Chapter 10 Her Majesty, the Queen 78
Chapter 11 Uncle Walter's Hut 91
Chapter 12 Mary Ann and Her Countrywomen. 104
Chapter 13 Her Vital Spark Extinguished 114

PART 3.   A Vicissitude of Virtue? Fanny Cochrane, c. 1832–1905 121

Chapter 14 A Prison Nursery 123

Chapter 15 The Organ of Perception...................... 131

Chapter 16 Propaganda, Progeny and Prosperity 141

Chapter 17 Prove It or Lose It! 149

Chapter 18 Rituals of Captivity: Deconstructing Indigenous "Christianity" 159

Chapter 19 King Billy's Playmate 166

Chapter 20 Goodbye, My Father, Mother.................. .176

Epilogue 185

Notes... 193

Bibliography 223

About the Author 233

LIST OF IMAGES

Figure 1. John Skinner Prout, 1846, *Residence of the Aborigines, Flinders Island*, from the *Tasmania Illustrated* series 1844–1846. Colour lithograph. Accession Number 1700.8-5, National Gallery of Victoria, Melbourne. Gift of Dr Leonard Cox, 1966.

Figure 2. Ludwig Becker, 1852, *Aborigines of Tasmania [art original]*, portrait of (Sarah) Dinudara V.D.L. Pencil on paper. Identifier H24661/1, State Library of Victoria, Melbourne.

Figure 3. John Skinner Prout, 1845, *Shepherd's hut, Wybellinna [i.e. Wybalenna], Flinders, Feb. 1845*. Watercolour. NLA Object 134409624, National Library of Australia, Canberra.

Figure 4. Francis Russell Nixon, Bishop of Tasmania, c. 1858, *Walter George Arthur and Mary Ann Arthur*. Photograph. Item Number PH30/1/925, Tasmanian Archives, Hobart.

Figure 5. Charles Edward Stanley, 1847, *Natives at Oyster Cove, Nov. 1847*. Watercolour. NLA Object 134675801, National Library of Australia, Canberra.

Figure 6. *Tasmanian Aboriginals at Oyster Cove*. Copy of photograph made by John Watt Beattie c. 1890s from an original taken by Francis Russell Nixon c. 1850s. Item Number AB713/1/11693, Tasmanian Archives, Hobart.

Figure 7. Photographer unknown, c. 1860, *Tasmanian Aboriginals i.e. Aboriginal Australians, Oyster Cove; the Last of the Race. Wapperty, Bessy Clarke, Maryann* [sic]. Photograph taken c. 1860 and developed c. 1890 by J. W. Beattie. Accession Number H6550, State Library of Victoria, Melbourne.

Figure 8. Henry Frith, c. 1866, *Aborigines, The Last of the Race, Tasmania*. Photograph. NLA Object 139450014, National Library of Australia, Canberra.

Figure 9. Annie Benbow, c. 1900, *Tasmanian Aborigines at Oyster Cove Station*. Crayon and watercolour on paper. Record ID SD_ILS:140803, WL Crowther Library, Tasmanian Archive and Heritage Office, Hobart.

Figure 10. Photographer unknown, c. 1870s, *Portrait of Smith, Fanny Cochrane & Husband*. Item Number PH30/1/2846, Tasmanian Archives, Hobart.

Figure 11. Photographer unknown, c. late 1890s. *Fanny Cochrane Smith Wearing a Belt with Wallaby (?) Pelts*. Photograph. Record ID SD_ILS:616013. Allport Library and Museum of Fine Arts, Tasmanian Archive and Heritage Office, Hobart. https://stors.tas.gov.au/AUTAS001131821571.

Figure 12. Photographer unknown, c. 1899, *Tasmanian Aboriginal Fanny Cochrane Smith*. Photograph. Item Number PH52/1/18, Tasmanian Archive and Heritage Office, Hobart.

Figure 13. A. A. Rollings, 1903. *Fanny Cochrane Smith Recording Aboriginal Songs for Horace Watson*. Photograph. Item Number NS1553/1/1798, Tasmanian Archives, Hobart.

GLOSSARY

This glossary provides additional clarity on the most common terms encountered within this book (predominantly descriptive or categorical).

captive: defined by and relating to the Indigenous people living in the various Aboriginal establishments. None could leave without approval of the establishment administrators, and all were under the total control of the state. Just as if a prisoner escapes from penal authority, for an Indigenous resident to leave the establishments without permission was an act labelled as "absconding". Although it appears that a few had various degrees of mobility, especially in the later years of Oyster Cove Station (thus not categorised as "prisoner"), their lack of autonomy defines my utilisation of the term Indigenous "captive".

colonial and post-colonial: colonial refers to the period 1803–1901 and all documentation, policies and events that occur within this period. Post-colonial refers to the period from 1901 to the onset of World War One.

indigeneity: denotes the Indigenous identity of the main subjects and, specific to this work, their cultural identity.

Indigenous and **non-Indigenous**: with regard to this work, Indigenous refers to people born in the island nation of Van Diemen's Land (VDL, Tasmania, also known as New Holland) and its associated islands, whose ancestors previously lived on these islands for millennia. Non-Indigenous refers to the people and their descendants who emigrated to Van Diemen's Land from the late-18th century onwards, mainly from the United Kingdom. Although far more complex definitions or distinctions can be drawn, these two terms are used for continuity and narrative comprehension.

ontology: relates to the relationship between the subject's beliefs and their existence. For Indigenous people it embodies a form of "person-land-ancestral inter-relationship" (A. Rumsey, cited in Kenny, Anna 2013, "*Geist* through myth: revealing an Aboriginal ontology", in *The Aranda's Pepa: an introduction to Carl Strehlow's masterpiece Die Aranda- und Loritja-Stämme in Zentral-Australien (1907–1920)*, ANU Press, Canberra, p. 135). For example, Fanny Cochrane Smith's "spiritual and cultural ontology" refers to her personal relationships to these things, both past and present, and how it shaped her daily realities, or perception of them.

socio-cultural: relates to the relationship between a person's culture and their social or societal interactions (predominantly between Indigenous and non-Indigenous people).

socio-political: is used where there are evident interconnecting social and political factors, such as the dynamic between the captives and administrators at the Aboriginal establishments.

INTRODUCTION

A Song of Welcome

Tasmania's biographical pantheon is densely populated indeed. There are stories of Lady Jane, and Governor Arthur, Messrs Robinson and the Denisons, of notorious convicts and "pioneering" freeholders and, of course, of Truganini. Yet, unsurprisingly, the story of the most famous Indigenous family of the late-Victorian and post-Federation eras, colloquially known as the Smiths, is one scarcely told – a scant narrative rife with half-truths and pro-colonial propaganda.

Told as three comprehensive biographies, the ensuing tales form an unprecedented revision of the chronicle of a single Indigenous family. It begins with a girl named Tarenootairer (c. 1806–1858) and those very first fateful steps of British colonisation and incarceration on Aboriginal establishments. Her story is followed by those of her two surviving daughters – Mary Ann Arthur (c. 1821–1871), whose fight for autonomy laid the foundation for contemporary Indigenous politics, and Fanny Cochrane Smith (c. 1832–1905), who famously challenged the false declaration of Indigenous Tasmanian extinction. *My People's Songs* endeavours to rewrite almost a century of our history from the astute perspective of these individuals themselves – voices not often heard, or even known.

The paternities of Tarenootairer's known children have been the subjects of debate, misinformation and ill-conceived theory for almost 130 years. Such a sensitive topic would usually be relegated to a private discussion within a family, having little influence on cultural or historical events; however, Tarenootairer and her children have become significant political and scientific footnotes. The most famous and still-prevalent debate is over the paternity of her youngest daughter, Fanny Cochrane Smith – a debate that has raged from 1882 to the present day. Through these ongoing discussions, the life and legacy of Fanny Cochrane is predominantly reduced to theories about her paternity and whether or not she was indeed the "last full-blood Aborigine" of Tasmania (also known as New Holland and Van Diemen's Land, or VDL), dehumanising her existence and reducing her and her descendants to a mere colonial colour chart.[1] I have thoroughly researched the evidence indicating the paternity of Tarenootairer's children, and some of the familial relationships I have established are different from those generally considered accurate and espoused (erroneously, I contend) by colonial contemporaries including author and educator James Bonwick, and historians such as N. J. B. Plomley. In this book I refer to the paternities that I have established, and further details of my research can be found in my academic thesis, listed in the bibliography, for those interested in further reading.[2]

Victorian Crafters Gothic

The referendum in 1967 – ostensibly to include Indigenous Australians in the national census through an amendment of the constitution, although limited in its scope and questionable in its purpose – at the very least laid the foundation for a revolution towards Indigenous sociopolitical autonomy.[3] Following suit in 1971, the national population census recognised for the first time as "one group" people of both "full" and "mixed" Aboriginal descent, ushering in a new era in "identity" and "indigeneity" discourse.[4] Although constitutionally recognised,

INTRODUCTION

Indigenous Australians had little by way of rights to property and especially to land claims.[5] By the early 1980s, the fight had evolved towards the reclamation of culturally significant sites and, in Tasmania in particular, this battle had reached a political and public boiling point.[6] On 9 July 1983, my grandmother, Aunty Brenda Jean Campbell (nee Smith), now residing in suburban South Australia, petitioned then minister for Aboriginal affairs Clyde Holding.[7] Her main concern was the potential re-acquisition of a land grant awarded to one of her ancestral grandmothers, Fanny Cochrane, in 1889. Holding's deputy replied to her petition stating, "The Minister for Aboriginal Affairs ... has asked me to reply on his behalf to your further letter concerning recognition for Tasmanian Aboriginals. The Australian Government recognises that the descendants of Tasmanian Aboriginals are still engaged in a struggle for acceptance. It will support this struggle ..."[8] Yet progress was lagging.

In June 1986, my grandmother made another application, this time to the Australian Heritage Commission, nominating the famed "Aboriginal" Methodist church in the small country town of Nicholls Rivulet, her birthplace in south-east Tasmania, for preservation by the National Trust.[9] Aided by extended family and scholars, an exhaustive five years of historical research, condition reports and recommendations ensued. In October 1991, the Australian Heritage Commission finally approved her application on the provision it garnered no objections from the Tasmanian public, concluding with its expressed appreciation for her submission of this unique nomination.[10]

In 1994, I again visited Nicholls Rivulet as a teenager, with this iconic Methodist church my first port of call. Approaching it for the first time (in conscious memory), I immediately recalled a painting of this scene, rendered by my grandmother, of the road ahead as viewed from the seat of her dad's truck, the peak of the church roof emerging to the left from the near horizon. This simple and charming picture hung in pride of place in her kitchen – symbolically above the telephone, the conduit of family connection – embedding itself in my psyche and influencing my imagination of this place. The painting eventually received prime position along the front pews (with other artworks by relatives) at the "Service for Fanny" in 1995, the first service to be held in the church in many decades. Yet, at that moment, this famed wooden box was a mere shadow of its former "glory".

By the time of my visit, the modest building had lived many lives, and had in recent years been used as a hayshed. Nested among thickets of introduced weeds and native grasses, the broken windows and missing arches gave the appearance of eyes – large, hollow and tired. I was not alone. A cousin, who had generously acted as chauffeur, pried open the arched doors, the building now missing its original entrance. Forced to climb up through its splintered mouth, on entering this space the faint echoes of its former life soon awoke. The dark-stained Huon pine interior was barely faded and the original carved lectern was dusty but still standing at the ready, although the original organ had been apparently long ago "stolen". When the traces of those who came before us became visible to the eye, such as the faint groove in the door frame that many decades of familial hands had worn down, a richer experience was certainly evoked.

We visited the surrounding areas, such as the old sawmill of my great-grandfather Gus, and his father (or grandfather)[11] Joseph before him, now barely visible piles of sawdust reclaimed by nature; the house my grandmother was born and raised in, burned down in the 1960s and now only concrete foundations, with a rusted woodfired oven to mark the spot; and, of course, the ominous Oyster Cove Station, the former Aboriginal establishment now an eerie place of still waters, haunted forest and the unmarked empty graves of our captive ancestors.

Yet a series of question marks now hangs over my reminiscences of this day.

Why were a plot of land, a place, a building left behind two decades before so vital to preserve in that present?

How influential had some scripted "orthodox" history of my heritage been on my own perception of this experience?

And how much of what people think they know – about the past, about culture, about family – has been manipulated or wholly invented to sell a new paper, a book or a film?

"Decolonising" History: Stage One

It is said that history repeats itself, and traversing a family archive comprising generations of suppressed voices, dispossession and violence it appears variably true. From the "caste debates" of the late 19th century to genocide denialists in the early 21st century, there is a seemingly endless confrontation of scholastic dissension, with little regard for the human subjects. The three main subjects of this book have, for over 150 years, been victim to westernised narratives of their lives, cultures and identities, and with *My People's Songs* the goal has been to utilise a foundational process of "decolonialism" – to re-examine the evolution of colonisation and its effect on our social, cultural and political history, and subsequently rewrite this narrative.

"Decolonialism" is, at its core, a process of eradication – of eliminating colonial fictions to find the authentic voices within. It is a long and arduous process that can be painful, confusing and at times very confronting. It has taken me into dark places hidden within our history I did not know existed. Unfortunately, the lies that were incubated long ago have shaped the truths of today, and one must understand that unravelling more than a century of misinformation can be disturbing, even heretical, to some in the present. However, the demand for a decolonised history cannot be achieved when one is afraid of, or forced to hide, the results. When seeking the truth, we must be prepared to accept the answer. From truth comes genuine understanding; perhaps from heresy comes healing.

Our ancestors are not puppets for the present nor static representations of past presumptions; they were and are human. Biographies are not about elevating them on some "saintly" pedestal, but about embracing their flaws, and their fears. The knowledges, or perspectives, used to sketch these individual profiles are sourced from every available public archive, frrom the bureaucratic databases of births, deaths and marriages to a wealth of colonial documenters, newspaper articles and police gazettes, as well as published oral histories and academic texts. These are all necessary to assist both in verifying old knowledge and affirming that newly discovered. Yet we are forced in many, if not most, cases to extract the truth from the lie, the fact from the fantasy. We are unable to take what we see or read at face value. Instead we are faced with a challenge of filtering the colonial or imperial archive of text, images and artworks in order to come to some semblance of conclusion and understanding.[12]

The published works on colonial-era Indigenous Tasmanian history are, although extensive, unbalanced and lacking in Indigenous perspectives. The most prominent of all the post-colonial publications is Plomley's exhaustive research, delving deep into the archives of George Augustus Robinson, the so-called "Chief Protector of Aborigines" on the Flinders Island settlement, and giving indispensable (if selective and biased) access to the lives of the captured Indigenous Tasmanians.[13]

INTRODUCTION

And it is Robinson's accounts of this era – such as of the Bass Strait "slave trade", famously noted as "the African slave trade in miniature" – that have informed the so-called orthodox narrative of our pasts.[14]

A desire to re-evaluate early colonial relationships between Indigenous Tasmanians and settlers appears to have, at its heart, cultural survival and the concern that the concept of slavery denotes a loss of "culture and identity".[15] However, the few decades of "slavery" in the Bass Strait were never long enough to eradicate the culture from Indigenous women and children; in fact, it provided their very sustenance and procured the produce that fed the industry of the "straitsmen", the sealers and whalers who worked the strait. The only period of cultural eradication, or cultural genocide, was during their incarceration on the various Aboriginal establishments, yet here, still, the colonisers were unable to completely curb the millennia-old traditions of the captives.

Academically, I do not wish to define the Indigenous experience by "white" or western definitions. Examining all records that pertain to my earliest ancestor, her chronology and personal narrative, only validated her own "slave" identity. I support my ancestor's portrayal as a slave only because that is the narrative *she* inferred – abducted from her family by straitsmen at approximately 12 years of age and taken to an island from which there appeared no escape. Her abductor kept her neither as wife nor even for labour, selling her directly in exchange for skins to another, who then sold her to another. The next 12 to 13 years of island captivity was an endurance of forced labour, beatings and birthing multiple children to a man 40 years her senior, her first child likely born within a year of her initial abduction – surely a definitive example of both the enslavement and trade of a human being.

Adding to Tarenootairer's own statements, an embedded slave identity is found at the heart of the cultural and social politics of her two surviving daughters, Mary Ann and Fanny Cochrane, giving further emphasis to their, and their mother's, personal identification. This, too, has bled across generations to become a source of mutual identification for many descendants of these women, specifically my own family (I only speak on their behalf) – a personal well of emotional and psychological strength for those who have also found themselves victims of a violent patriarchal society.

* * *

Part of the decolonising motive has been to maintain the broadest degree of accessibility in the presentation. The language of the period can be very confronting (for example, the words "natives", "blacks", "Aborigines", "half-castes"), yet in this book it has been retained for historical authenticity – essential to historical biography. This has also has affected the use of Indigenous language and terminologies within the text. For example, one of the primary examples of colonial shifts in power is the predominance of matriarchal lineages and their cultural survival. And those familiar with Indigenous Tasmania and related discourse will notice that throughout this book I have avoided referencing colloquial terms like "palawa" or "pakana" (originally meaning a male or boy).[16] This is merely a personal choice to neutralise as much as possible the conflicting use of these terms among the broader community, and to avoid the use of patriarchal terminology, especially in a work primarily regarding Indigenous women.

While engaged in the research, I took the opportunity to extract the fragmentary records of the Cape Portland language from the journals and language lists of G. A. Robinson, to which Tarenootairer was a known partial contributor. After extracting it from lists and

INTRODUCTION

journals, the language was to play three vital roles: to restore the known language to its cultural purpose as a tool for communication; to tell as much of Tarenootairer's story as possible in her own language, acting as a *symbolic* representation of decolonialism; and to provide a useful tool for tracking various cultural changes among subsequent generations over the next century as words dropped out, were replaced and were then reclaimed and reused. However, the complexities of language research require a more thorough analysis than the scope of this book allows. As such, the use of language at this stage distracted from the intent of Tarenootairer's initial historical biography, and as a consequence had to be reserved.

* * *

A decolonising methodology is a complex one of stages, influenced by the availability of documentation and the varied approaches necessary to examine and interpret the stories they tell. As much as I wanted to provide complete biographies, and complete examples of decolonised historical biographies, my intent was usurped and dominated by the need to correct old historical tropes. I realised no single project can achieve all aspects of decolonialism, and that this correction was the most arduous and necessary first step, to lay the foundation for the next.

This stage, which I believe to be the only *fundamental* stage in the process of decolonisation, can be broken down into three main steps: the deconstruction of colonial materials and the narrative they have informed; the extrication and contextualisation of the Indigenous perspective from this material; and a reconstruction of the original narrative from this perspective. In short, the intent is to turn the majority of statistical information into the descriptive, to recontextualise what is known, and to re-examine these events by installing an essential Indigenous perspective on the source material.

Decolonisation involves not telling our ancestors about their lives but allowing them to tell us. It is about stripping back two centuries of layers and, in doing so, enabling a renewed understanding of our history, where the Indigenous voice can be at the fore. When I approached this topic from the subject's perspective, individual stories emerged that enabled me to find my ancestors' own voices among the saturation of colonial, religious and contemporary agendas that permeate Indigenous Tasmanian historiography. Perhaps only by examining individual narratives first can an honest picture of Indigenous communities and history as a whole be obtained. Each community, family and individual has their own unique story of, and relationship to, colonisation, shaping historical and traditional knowledges and alternative Indigenous identities. No two islands are the same, no two communities are the same, no two families are the same and no two people are the same.

* * *

I have chosen to name this introduction "A Song of Welcome". The title derives from a traditional song sung by Fanny Cochrane herself and recorded by Horace Watson on phonograph in 1903. Present was an unidentified journalist who recorded and recounted this particular moment:

> Accompanied by some of her friends … she [Fanny Cochrane] accepted the invitation of Mr Horace Watson to meet him in his private ethnological room. While there … she lost all feelings of restraint, clapped her hands and cheerfully sang and spoke

INTRODUCTION

into a home phonograph … Her "Song of Welcome" was most heartily given.[17]

The article, clipped from the paper and pasted into Watson's photo album of ethnographic curiosities, further states that the "Song of Welcome" was sung at the arrival of spring, "when the bush re-echoed with the music of the birds, and the trees were in full blossom". On hearing her own voice played back to her, Fanny Cochrane is alleged to have exclaimed, "Ah! Those are my people's songs, my poor, poor race, my mother Tanginootara's [sic] own song, and all are gone." Over the decades since its recording, the song's title has varied from "A Song of Birds and Flowers" to the "Spring Song"; however, I've settled on "A Song of Welcome", for it acts as a positive invitation from my ancestors, and myself, welcoming the reader to discover, with an open mind, the extraordinary stories within.

PART 1

A Weeping Woman:

Tarenootairer, c. 1806–1858

Chapter 1

SALTWATER COUNTRY

> … about Cape Portland and at every boat harbor
> along the whole line of coast the bones of the
> murdered aborigines are strewn over the face of the
> earth and bleaching in the sun.
>
> *George Augustus Robinson, 24 August 1831*[1]

Tarenootairer's[2] clan was likely the Pinterairrer of the north-eastern coastal plains of the main island, in what is present-day Cape Portland, and the Mussel Roe River, which is also referred to as "layrappenthe", roughly translating to "saltwater country".[3] The layrappenthe landscape was made of windswept sandy beaches and significant bird sanctuaries, set among freshwater lagoons and open grassland. For millennia this area had supported an estimated 400–500 people, comprising some 10 to 11 clans, with staple seasonal foods of seals, shellfish and birds such as mutton, ducks and swans.[4]

The clans of the Cape Portland nation had experienced sporadic contact with explorers, whalers and sealers from France, Holland and the Americas since as early as the mid-17th century.[5] But in the decade of Tarenootairer's birth, the British Empire had declared *terra nullius* and officially, forcibly, laid claim to the whole of the island.

Tarenootairer was believed to be born around 1806, but little is truly known of her "traditional" cultural life. A general examination merely provides a fragmentary overview of pre-colonial subsistence. From what can be ascertained, her language, songs, dances and day-to-day living were presumed, like most cultures, to be centred on geography, marriage customs, seasons, astronomy, spirituality and, of course, food – of which much traditional knowledge has been successfully retained.[6]

Sketches by settlers and commissioned colonial artists, ranging from French contact in the early 1800s to Thomas Bock's portraits of the 1830s, showcase (with usual speculation) the similarities in traditional dress among various eastern clans. They show women sparsely adorned in sinews, skins and shell necklaces, with closely cropped hair or entirely shaved heads,[7] and men with shimmering red-ochre locks, medicinal bones hung from their necks and armed with obligatory spear in hand. Both men and women from multiple nations were etched with extensive and decorative scarifications.

Theoretically, the decimation of the Indigenous coastal nations by all manner of settlers potentially explains the lack of reliable information regarding their pre-histories, and their fates. Overwhelming accusations pointing to the sealers and whalers inhabiting the neighbouring Bass Strait confirm they indeed played their significant part, but they were just one fraction of an ensemble cast of perpetrators.[8] In fact, so notorious were the straitsmen that deciphering fact from fantasy is all but impossible, the men themselves, and the press of the day, feeding their mythology for decades to come: "In the words of one sealer," reported *The Voice*, "As we stole the dams we killed the cubs."[9]

By the early summer of 1816, Tarenootairer was approximately nine to ten years of age, and the Cape Portland nation was estimated at a few hundred individuals (likely an amalgam of its various clans) and led by the "chief", Tolobunganah. Captain James Kelly, then engaged among the eastern strait trading in kangaroo and seal skins, narrated his remarkable coastal encounter with Tolobunganah and his "tribe", giving rare insight into Tarenootairer's elusive childhood mores. He wrote:

> Tolobunganah asked Briggs not to go away until they had a dance. The whole mob of them, about three hundred in number, formed a line in three divisions – the men and women forming two of them, and children another. Tolobunganah then gave the signal to commence the dance, and it was a most singular one. The women in the centre division began a song, and joining their hands, formed a circle, dancing round the heap of dead seals. They then threw themselves into the most grotesque attitudes, beating the lower parts of their bodies with their hands, and kicking the sand over each other with their feet. The loud laughter of the men and children evidenced their gratification with the sport, and the women having sat down, the children went through a similar dance. The men then commenced a sort of sham fight with spears and waddies, dancing afterwards round the heap of seals, and plunging their spears into them as if they were killing them. The dance lasted about an hour. Tolobunganah then informed us it was over.[10]

This record of the "seal dance", likely a general hunting dance that would be performed to celebrate any successful bounty, shows a symbiosis between the settlers and Tarenootairer's people, and a clear account of mutual trade between the straitsmen and the Cape Portland nation. Some, like a man named Thompson, were reportedly much admired by the Cape Portlanders and described as "nearly the only one with whom the natives now had friendly intercourse".[11] Yet such examples are the exception.

Though there had been contact and exchange with European explorers, traders and settlers for a century or more, the functionality of traditional Indigenous life was now truly changing, and for the worse. At the behest of a new colonising government, a culture of extermination had begun. The result was the brutal era known as the Black War, one of the most devastating and documented accounts of colonial conflict in recorded history.

Chapter 2

NUMMER-LORE (WHITE DEVIL'S WIFE)

The eastern nations of the island were famously volatile, and the 1810s marked a distinct rise in tumultuous relations between the encroaching settlers and the northern and central coast clans.[1] Yet it is suggested that at the time of Tarenootairer's infancy a complex system of human trafficking, specifically of women, had been established.[2] "These poor women," lamented Captains Kelly and Hobbs, "were mostly purchased off their parents, either for carcasses of the seal, or for hunting dogs."[3] Though this statement may perhaps be a gross exaggeration, it does indicate a form of slavery had indeed become gainful business. And it is clear from those whose narratives were documented that the majority of traded or abducted "sealing women" heralded from Tarenootairer's nation in the north.[4] Some of these women, especially those among the western islands, came to be known as "nummer-lore" among the Cape Grim and Robin's Island language groups, translated at the time to mean "White Devil's Wife".[5]

As the use of women for bartering had become prevalent, dwindling food supplies and the decimation of natural resources likely instigated desperate acts of abduction.[6] No longer seasonal visitors, the sealers were now permanent residents in the strait and their personal survival, as well as that of their businesses, depended on these stolen women, some of whom were just children.[7]

According to Captain Kelly, the straitsmen had turned their necessity into industry, acquiring up to five "wives" per "master", that quota being the only law among them. It was a limitation conceived not relative to any morality, "but to prevent any of them securing a monopoly of the catch through owning too many seal-catching wives".[8]

Although the circumstances surrounding her abduction are conjecture, documentary evidence of the straitsmen associated with Tarenootairer's early captivity does allow insight.[9] In 1831 she herself orated to the "conciliator", George Augustus Robinson, that she "was forcibly taken from her country when a girl by James Parish … says that Parish sold her to John Smith for four seal skins and that Smith afterwards sold her to George Robinson on Woody Island".[10]

For clarity, by her own alleged testimony Tarenootairer was abducted by Parish from coastal layrappenthe country around 1818 to 1819. Parish was then a resident sealer on Hunter Island in the west of the strait, and was likely accompanied by a party of boatmen or sealers raiding for women.[11] These "North" women relayed to G. A. Robinson that, when the sealers captured them, they tied their hands and forced them into boats, transporting them to their island bondage.[12] With such notoriety, the settlers and straitsmen's success in the subjugation of Indigenous women and children was evidently won through violence, the sealers themselves making "free use of their firearms" – though not without a rain of spears falling upon them in retaliation.[13]

Yet armed force was not the only method. A more complex narrative can be gleaned from the account of a sealer known as Duncan Bell, who utilised "his woman" as a decoy to procure others from her clan to the beach, where the next day his party "could capture the gins".[14] Although his particular recount ends in total rebellion and the slaughter of Bell's entire sealing party, it suggests, controversially, that some of the women already enslaved in the strait were themselves becoming active participants in the abduction of young women.

It can never be known if Tarenootairer saw the boat coming – if the attack was conducted by surprise or sheer trickery. Whether stalked and ensnared like the mammals they hunted, sold to Parish by her own nation for little more than a hound or perhaps lured, like a mythological siren, to the vulnerability of the open coast and to her sorry and violent future, Tarenootairer was indeed "forcibly taken", and she was a mere 12 to 13 years old.

* * *

With her hands bound, Tarenootairer was ushered by Parish across the shark-infested waters to the western islands, and to the makeshift huts and cottages of the resident straitsmen.

On King Island, the largest island in the western strait, we learn about the early community of sealers through Francois Peron's encounter with them in 1802 – their culture perceived as rustic, inevitably requiring them to live off the land, "making clothes out of seal and kangaroo skins", their homes like "shanties constructed with pieces of wood driven into the ground" and roughly hewn bark filling in the gaps.[15] Here, Parish encountered a man named John Smith, to whom he sold his child captive in exchange for said skins.

Smith, a temporary resident on King Island around 1818–1821, did not, however, possess Tarenootairer for long, swiftly selling her to his neighbour, George "Geordy" Robinson, in approximately 1819. A sealer and whaler, Geordy Robinson (not to be confused with the much better-known G. A. Robinson) was aged about 53 years (c. 1820) and "the oldest man in the Straits" according to G. A. Robinson's journal.

A five-foot, nine-inch Scotsman from the Clyde, of fair complexion, brown hair and blind in one eye,[16] he had emigrated first to Sydney and then to Bass Strait some 22 years earlier as a free man.[17]

Geordy Robinson's cottage, "replete with a neat garden", was near Sea Elephant Harbour, on the island's central-east coast, so named for the large gatherings of sea elephants that seasonally beached themselves there.[18] The most abundant of the species, the elephant seal was specifically hunted for its oil, from which those like Robinson derived their main incomes.[19]

Although dubbed "not a cruel husband", the mere sight of Geordy Robinson was said to induce a state of fear in some of the women.[20] By her own accounts, Tarenootairer's role was to "get skins for her master, which he sold",[21] and a retrospective account of the Indigenous women's mode of hunting was relayed in detail in a newspaper article from 1892:

> We [the sealers] gave ... the women each a club that we had used to kill seals with, and they went to the water's edge and wet themselves all over their heads and bodies, which operation they said would keep the seals from smelling them as they walked along the rocks. They were very cautious not to go to windward of them, as they said a seal would sooner believe his nose than his eyes than a man or a woman came near him. The women all walked into the water in couples ... There were about nine or ten seals upon each rock, lying apparently asleep. Two women went to each rock with their clubs in their hands, and crept closely up to a seal each, and laid down with their clubs alongside. Some of the seals lifted up their heads to inspect their new visitors and smell them. The seals scratched themselves and lay down again. The women went through the same motions as the seal, holding up their left elbow and scratching themselves with their left hand, taking and keeping the club firm in their right hand

ready for the attack. The seals were very cautious, now and then lifting up their heads and looking round, scratching themselves as before, and lying down again, the women still imitating every movement as near as possible. After they had lain in the rocks for nearly an hour, the sea occasionally washing over them (as they were quite naked we could not tell the meaning of their remaining so long), when all of a sudden the women rose up to a sitting posture, their clubs lifted up at arm's length, and each struck a seal on the nose and killed him …[22]

In servitude, life for Tarenootairer was inescapable and violent, and she declared that Geordy Robinson "was in the habit of beating her with sticks".[23] For many girls, escape from the clutches of their masters was impossible and, for some, attempts to do so would result in sickening punishments if caught.[24] Although not all island narratives entail brutality and slavery, accounts of atrocities committed by some of the sealers, given especially by the captive women of the western strait, are truly shocking and paint an undeniably hellish picture.[25]

The sealers gave the women derogatory names such as Black Poll, Dumpe and Jumbo, and by this time Tarenootairer had been given the nickname Tibb, the predominant name by which she would be referred over the next two decades. Her new moniker meant an unfaithful woman of "low or loose character", a "cant name for a strumpet" in Shakespearean times.[26] In the play *Pericles, Prince of Tyre*, the name Tibb is symbolic of "wanton-ness" – an allegorical term for female sexual promiscuity;[27] and by the 17th century Tibb had also become a famed shapeshifting witches' familiar.[28]

Tarenootairer's eldest known daughter, Mary Ann, was to be born to Geordy Robinson some time between 1819 and mid-1821.[29] Many children were born from cohabitation with the sealers, either with their "masters" or by being prostituted around the islands for the price of skins and food,[30] though by the month of Mary Ann's birth, Tarenootairer was practically still a child herself, at approximately 13 or 14 years old.[31]

***

In the heart of the Bass Strait whaling industry, glimpses into life on King Island show a relatively "each man for himself" existence where only the most industrious survived. Those who succumbed to its unpredictability were remorselessly left behind – quite literally left for dead – and Geordy Robinson proved no exception. G. A. Robinson's search party discovered the wreck of a whaleboat replete with sail, oars and clothing "embedded in the sand" along the Leven River. "This makes eight boats … lost on this coast," he noted, and further:

> About half a mile from where the boat lay was found the skeleton of a man, little doubt but it was one of the boat's crew. Ordered the same to be buried … My coxswain said that she belonged to a man named George Robinson who had formerly lived thirteen years at King's Island and who was on his return to that island – at least the sealers at the Hunters said they expected him.[32]

Geordy Robinson himself spoke of "two men who were murdered on Kings Island [sic] for their women",[33] and took an opportunity to narrate to the *Hobart Town Gazette* how the mid-1820s were degenerating into a time of violent unrest:

Saturday 1st July 1826
King's Island.

> We have the pleasure in being able to communicate the following anecdotes of this island, gathered from George Robinson, who resided on it thirteen years. This old man, at the age of 67 [sic], has been compelled to quit the cottage and garden which he had

constructed there, in order to escape from the outrages of the desperate characters who appear to be daily gaining strength in those parts ... Robinson raised culinary vegetables of all kinds, and his crops of wheat were very productive ... Robinson says the Kangaroos are scarce, though he acknowledges having killed about 60 every month ... Robinson visited Flinders' Island about a month ago, on which he says there are 20 white men, with native women and children.[34]

An additional news report affirms Geordy Robinson's own narrative of this time, stating his desertion of King Island was due in no small part to "the frequent attacks and robberies of the straggling boats".[35] The western strait was indeed becoming a dangerous place to live.

In November 1825, Geordy Robinson was formally removed from his abode by the master of the *Governor Sorrell*, J. H. Skelton. At the request of Captain Whyte, Skelton was conducting a "search and inquiry", scouring the strait and capturing the growing criminal population taking refuge among the seemingly lawless isles. This excerpt from the original newsprint was written by Skelton himself in February 1826:

> From Western Port I went to King's Island, and took off a free man named George Robertson [sic], who had been on the island 13 years. He was attended by a man. He had also a black woman with him, and a child. I brought him to Preservation and there I left him.[36]

The most significant knowledge in Skelton's article is that, unlike Geordy Robinson's own recollection, he places a "black woman" and a child with him at this time. These two are most likely Tarenootairer and Mary Ann (although there can be no certainty as to which child is referred to).

In this increasingly precarious period, Tarenootairer had by now given birth to at least two known children, and most likely more. Motherhood in these times, and under such circumstances, is scarcely contextualised. Tales of infanticide and forced abortion, premature mortality by malnutrition and introduced disease are juxtaposed with rare accounts of attentive fathers and adoring mothers.[37]

Robinson's abandonment of King Island and subsequent relocation to Preservation Island was short-lived, lasting an approximated three years, before he resettled again on the adjacent Woody Island in about 1828.[38] Woody Island consisted of dense tea-tree and she-oak woods, and was home to abundant moorhens, rats, wombats, quail and magpies, with light but rich soils where luxuriant "wild indigo" and "indigenous geranium" grew among immense mutton bird rookeries.[39] By the account of G. A. Robinson's visit on 10 November 1830, Geordy Robinson's life here appeared almost idyllic, set among the documented brutality that populated the surrounding islands at this time. His new home was populated by "several dogs and cats", with "fowls, pigs &c" and, noted G. A. Robinson, "[He] showed me the bacon he had made: was very good and the first made in the Straits. Gave me some hen's eggs, two large pieces of crystal and some beads."[40] Despite the blistering sand thrown up by the wind, Robinson's various plots resembled the humble crofts of his native Scotland[41] and cultivated "wheat, potatoes, onions, cabbage &c." of notable quality:

> ... the wheat appeared very fine and was as high as my head, and the potatoes were excellent. The way the land is cultivated renders the place quite romantic, from the rocky place he has been obliged to cultivate in patches: you pass by winding walks through some underwood and then come to a beautiful cultivated spot and from thence to another ... He was very civil.[42]

NUMMER-LORE (WHITE DEVIL'S WIFE)

Among this romanticised image of quaint picturesque orchards, we find possibly Tarenootairer with a new son (name undocumented, but likely to be Duke), and Geordy Robinson now in "possession" of a second woman. Notes G. A. Robinson:

> Told him I should take away one woman and as he was so advanced in years should leave him one to assist him, but told him to use her well. This woman was named Ploorernelle and by her he had one little boy, a fine child. The woman I brought from Woody Island is Toogernuppertootenner, sister to Mannerlelargenner [sic] … Told him … it was well for him I came here or he would be cleared off the land.[43]

In her own accounts, on entering adulthood Tarenootairer hinted at a newly defiant attitude towards her captivity and her ageing "master". However, this oddly temperate time in her life was not all as it appears in G. A. Robinson's journal, as she herself recounted incidents of the wanton cruelty of the sealers on Woody Island.[44]

Now in her early 20s, Tarenootairer had experienced and witnessed extraordinary violence committed against her body and her people. Having been born to presumed cultural autonomy in the early 1800s, she was stolen from her family to become no more than a slave – a living commodity to be bought and sold like the animal pelts they coveted, for the pleasure and survival of colonising settlers and exiled criminals. It is narratives like Tarenootairer's early years that have influenced the oft-cited claims of "the African slave trade in miniature".[45]

Chapter 3

A TOKEN OF GRIEF

By 1830, the Black War of Van Diemen's Land was in full effect. Despite the intensity of the violence and destruction reaped upon them, Indigenous Tasmanians attempted to ease tensions with the settlers. There are accounts of inviting the "white man" to participate in "corroborees" situated around a large partroola (fire) where "they would sing to them"; others speak of "the Aborigines" helping lost settlers, such as, "if you passed their camp at night by the roadside, the women would show you home with torches of stringy bark".[1] These are but a couple of examples of Indigenous groups aiding their new colonisers and extending invitations to conciliate. Yet such gestures of accommodation and friendship were wholly in vain. Just like the native carnivores that were perceived as threats to the colony's farms, the Indigenous Tasmanians, too, now had a price laid on their heads – £5 an adult and £2 a child – "to encourage colonists to bring in live captives", although it seems the dead later garnered an equal bounty.[2]

The destruction of the Indigenous population was so severe that the new colony, governed by Sir George Arthur, enlisted a conciliator to try to negotiate with those who remained. The aforementioned George Augustus Robinson – a successful builder and secretary, and highly religious – was appointed with the task.[3] Robinson was sent on a mission to locate and capture as many remaining Indigenous

Tasmanians as possible and relocate them to a proposed but still unprepared settlement in Bass Strait.

Despite Governor Arthur's claims to the contrary, an attempt at creating a settlement on Bruny Island in the south was an abject failure. An assessment of a few of the outer-lying islands, such as King Island in the north-west and Maria Island to the east, was also unsuccessful, with King Island and Maria Island deemed unsuitable due to large settlements of uncontrollable settlers.[4]

* * *

Regardless of their agreement a few weeks earlier (that Geordy Robinson, now 63 years of age, could keep Tarenootairer), her initial abductor, James Parish, landed on Woody Island; at G. A. Robinson's behest, he was there to finally remove Tarenootairer, and other captive women in the strait, from the enslaved life he had sold her into.

At the stroke of midnight, with six other emancipated island women, she landed on her home soil of Cape Portland, possibly for the first time since she was a child: "… they are all fine young women", noted Robinson. "Parish said the men did not offer resistance."[5]

On encountering the camped roving party, Robinson recorded each woman Parish had brought to him. When he had first met Tarenootairer on Woody Island, Robinson referred to her as Ploorernelle, a name possibly relating to the sun and translated as meaning "sunshine"; yet on this second encounter she was known as Tarenootairer, and Tibb. What is known is that her new, or preferred, name of Tarenootairer correlates to the bitter act of weeping, quite literally, "to sit down and sway the body in token of grief".[6] After almost 13 years in captive "service" in the strait, after birthing multiple children, still living or dead, her new name is surely a poetic reflection of her physical and mental condition at this time.

The relief of the newly freed was palpable and bittersweet.[7] For Tarenootairer, the irony of being emancipated from the restraints of her servitude under Geordy Robinson by the very man who had placed her there was surely not without notice, and her life was to dramatically change from that moment.

Confronting the devastation reaped upon her clans and the drastic action called for by the colony, Tarenootairer soon joined Robinson's conciliation party and was to play a vital role in ensuing events.[8]

* * *

Much to Robinson's benefit, Tarenootairer became a great asset to his cause of "rescue by round-up".[9] She accompanied her contemporaries on conciliatory missions to the coastal Furneaux Group "in search of other sealing women"[10] and, between the close of May and December 1831, she assisted further missions spanning the north-eastern districts of the main island most affected by the Black War. Her movements were followed by the newspapers, such as the *Courier*, which quickly relayed these so-called "missions" for their eager readership:

> Mr G. A. Robinson, with his domesticated Blacks is now exploring the region round George-town and Cape Portland with the same conciliatory views, and we have great hopes that his endeavours will be successful.[11]

What we know of Robinson's endeavours come from his own journals. Through Robinson's eyes we are presented with both a joy displayed by the so-called free Indigenous Tasmanians when meeting his party, appearing almost relieved to have been found before the other white man got to them, and glimpses of the "mission Aborigines" showing signs of regret at their actions and taking opportunities to plot their escape. Robinson was in persistent fear that, when they went on their daily hunting sojourns, they would abscond and never return. We see touching scenes among them, with descriptions such as "the natives pluck the flowers from the heath and stick them in their hair", as well as infighting and tensions erupting: "Tom it appeared had quarreled with the aboriginal female Tibb [Tarenootairer] and had sent her back [from the mission] with Woorrady [sic]." So, too, we see Robinson collecting creation stories, language and tools, for example: "Tibb made me a grass rope such as the black women climb trees with."[12]

By July, Tarenootairer was once again joyfully hunting with other women who participated in the missions near her native Cape Portland.[13] For Robinson, Tarenootairer's knowledge of the north-eastern nations was essential in locating remnants of once-large clans. Despite abduction as a child, her knowledge of her homeland remained astute:

> Tibb said there was two tribes, one about Waterhouse Point and another near Port Dalrymple, where they always stop, and that they are savage people. Said there is no natives down the east coast, and that with those tribes there are three of Mannalargenna's people.[14]

As an evidently skilled tracker, Tarenootairer had now travelled from the northern islands to the dense bush of the central-east nations, ever closer to her home country, and back to the eastern strait. One of the most famous missions was the attempted capture of Umarrah, a notorious leader of the Indigenous resistance and a prized capture for Robinson – though it is said the people who participated were ostensibly as eager not to locate him as G. A. Robinson was hopeful to find him.[15] Tarenootairer's future husband, Nicermenic, which means red or fire tail bird, a Parperloihener man from Robin's Island in the north-western nation, was also captured about this time.[16] He had joined the infamous group led by a female resistance warrior called Walyer, known to Robinson as "the Amazon".[17] The hesitation of Tarenootairer and others from these missions to locate the free could be respondent to the rise of Indigenous resistance fighters at this time, like Umarrah and Walyer, who, once captured, would label Robinson's roving party as traitors to their people.[18]

For Tarenootairer, her time among Robinson's missions was not entirely in desperate or fearful search and rescue. She would also get a taste of their future subordination at the Aboriginal establishments, and by 3 October she was to find herself in Launceston, where her daughter Mary Ann had been living in domestic service. Here, Robinson was visiting the Indigenous captives being held in prison. Two days later, to impress the visiting governor with his authority and influence, we find the "whole of Robinson's natives" now being utilised as waiters.[19]

By the close of 1831, Robinson's mission group had grown significantly, taking them, and Tarenootairer, on yet another assignment to capture the still-allusive "Big River People". The cast list was impressive:

> Robinson set off from Campbell Town on 15 October 1831 in search of the Big River People with thirteen mission aborigines – the youths Richard, Timmy, Lacklay, and Pevay, the couples Tom and Pagerly, Woorraddy and Truganini, Mannarlagenna and Tanleboneyer, and Umarrah and Wollaytopinneyer, and the sealing woman Tibb. He also had three servants, his son George, a clerk, and seven dogs and a horse.[20]

Huddled by the mission's fires with her contemporaries, freed from the slavery of the sealers and tasting the air of her homelands once again, Tarenootairer was now, assuredly, contemplating her next move.

A TOKEN OF GRIEF

By now, the infamous Black Line – a vain attempt by the colonisers to drive the most resistant to settlement from "the settled districts [down] to the Tasman Peninsula" – had failed to capture any substantial numbers.[21] The concept was both bewilderingly naive and, with the involved participants – many of whom were responsible for the frontier violence – surely doomed to fail.[22]

Those who were captured by Robinson's mission or the Black Line were kept imprisoned in various temporary institutions. The experimental settlement on Gun Carriage Island was a disaster.[23] The island itself was too small and too hostile to sustain any population for an extended period of time,[24] and the Indigenous captives lamented their traditional lives, initiating a fatal melancholy.[25] A new settlement was desperately needed, and Flinders Island, the largest in Bass Strait, became the prime contender.

During her year among the famed roving party, evidence suggests Tarenootairer had begun a relationship with a young Indigenous man, a whaler named Edward Tomlins. The son of Poolrerrener, Tomlins grew up on Kangaroo Island and was the brother of Bullrer (alias Louisa), Tarenootairer's friend and contemporary while among G. A. Robinson's party. Now, likely pregnant, Tarenootairer abandoned Robinson's mission and joined the new Bass Strait establishment, then known as The Lagoons (c. February 1832), where her life was to drastically change yet again.

Chapter 4

"BLACK MAN'S HOUSES"

> We have been removed since the 1st of February down to this place, which is Paradise compared with the other, and which I have named Wybalenna, or Black Man's Houses in honest English. We have an abundance of water, an excellent garden, and every comfort a rational man can want.[1]
>
> W. J. Darling, 6 April 1833

Initially, The Lagoons – deceptively sold to the remaining Indigenous populace as a place of refuge and negotiation – became a prison, partly because it was difficult to escape from Flinders Island. For Governor Arthur this was to be a place of drastic cultural colonisation: "[E]very endeavor should be made to wean them from their barbarous habits, and progressively to introduce civilized customs among them," he sanctioned.[2] On being shipped to this ill-equipped refuge, for Tarenootairer, the "mission Aborigines" and the newly captured mainlanders, life here would be as hard for them as anywhere.

The island itself was deemed suitable for the new Aboriginal settlement due to its initial abundance of wild food and predominantly fine weather, despite the ever-persistent winds and poor agricultural soils. The pros and cons of Flinders Island were laid out in a report to the surveyor general in 1832 detailing its supplies of usable woods, such as blue gum, she-oak and tea-tree; and its abundance of wild land game, such as kangaroo, wallaby, echidna and possums, with black swans, ducks, quail and mutton birds rounding out the "feathered tribes".[3]

To the administrators the settlement gave the appearance of impending "success". With the construction of a terrace of small brick houses replete with thatched roofs, which could fit up to two small families each, gone were the days of sitting under half-moon-shaped boughs of tied-together bark. The initial abundance of wild foods provided the bulk of everyone's diet; however, the rationing of European supplies was encouraged over native produce, a method used to control the Indigenous captives.[4] This was to become a major problem. While cargoes carrying barrels of the island's abundant mutton birds, kangaroo, possum and seal skins were shipped off to the colonists, the captives of the settlement were given salted meats, mutton and a sparse supply of poorly grown vegetables.[5]

Even at its very inception, the Aboriginal establishment became not just an island prison, but a disease-riddled death camp for its new prisoners. Many of the captives expressed a desire to be sent back to the relative freedom of the mainland despite the warfare inflicted against them and feared greatly being under the so-called guardianship of the pleengenner (white man). This was especially so for those who had formerly lived among the ferocity of the sealers. The women who had chosen to be emancipated from the clutches of their "masters" were still no safer on the grounds of The Lagoons.[6] These men, some of whom had formerly been "owners" of the women and resented them being taken from their control, were now asked by Governor Arthur to act as guards to the new settlement, an ill-fated decision to say the least, and, "far from the eyes of the Governor, [they] began to maltreat their subjects".[7]

MY PEOPLE'S SONGS

Figure 1: John Skinner Prout, 1846,
Residence of the Aborigines, Flinders Island (Wybalenna).

* * *

Soon after the establishment of The Lagoons, the acting officer in charge, Sergeant Wight, was replaced by Lieutenant Darling, who changed the settlement's name to Wybalenna, meaning "black man's houses". His goal was to strictly impose British civilisation.[8]

The settlement duties were eked out to the captives from the onset. Men were to procure food, log the local woods and build fences. Women were to learn domestic hygiene, gather wattle and native grasses for bedding and thatching, and learn sewing and lacing. All parties were now expected to go to school for Bible lessons and to learn their letters. Failure to adapt to this regime instigated punishments such as imprisonment in the makeshift jail or the stifling of rations.[9]

Gradually and reluctantly, Tarenootairer and the other captives were forcibly clothed according to the European standard. The clothing itself began contributing to disease, especially pneumonia, to which they were particularly susceptible.[10] Made of brick and thatched roofs, the houses at the settlement became damp and unhealthy. Death by disease was exacerbated by a great despair. With their confinement to this island prison, the devastating effects on their lives and cultures became apparent all too quickly. Even the plethora of Indigenous languages and dialects became difficult to retain as the death rate dwindled the number of fluent speakers to but a few.[11]

The journal of Quaker missionary James Backhouse, recorded in the early summer of 1833 to 1834, gives direct insight into the regime of Europeanisation at the Wybalenna settlement. "After breakfast the Aborigines were assembled before their huts in their Sabbath garments," he begins, "with their tin plates and pannakins, and as such had them with knives and spoons." Further in the journal:

> The men were in clean duck frocks and trowsers, except a few, who's [sic] washing the women had neglected ... The women were arrayed in stuff petticoats, checked bed gowns, and aprons. Most of the women had handkerchiefs on their heads, and about their shoulders some we had given them as shawls. The men had those of the like kind about their necks.

In the "shed of boughs" (being used as a chapel), writes Backhouse, they sat on the ground "with the white people" listening to the "tract of the Sabbath"

> ... with great quietness and attention, though being little capable of understanding anything more than the general object of our meeting ... I could not help feeling some emotion this morning when we met, at the thought that nearly the whole of the remainder of the aborigines of Van Diemen's Land were before us, their countenances fine and expressive.

The following excerpt expresses a romanticised sentiment at the loss of their culture, as well as the hardships that had befallen them:

> It is surprising how much clothing appears to affect the countenance. Men do not look the same in face when naked and when clothed. About one-fourth of the aborigines died here of acute inflammatory disease of the chest in the last rainy season, and about one-third on the west coast of VDL. Diseases of this kind make great havoc among this people very frequently.

Yet Backhouse finishes the lament with a justification in the perceived "successes", no matter how minute, of the British colonial agenda:

> The appearance of the aborigines is greatly improved since we were last here, and there is an evident increase of civilization among them. This is most conspicuous in those who have been longest on the settlement.[12]

* * *

The bulk of knowledge about life at the Aboriginal establishment also comes from the journals kept by George Augustus Robinson, who replaced Lieutenant Darling as appointed chief commandant in July 1835. However, his journals are distinctly void of relevant information regarding the cultural lives of the Indigenous captives. Instead, Robinson, at times in melodramatic fashion, records their so-called primitive behaviours and his struggles to "Europeanise" them.[13] It is interesting to note that Tarenootairer, significant during Robinson's conciliation missions, is absent in any great detail from the majority of his journals at the settlement, suggesting an avoidance of contact on Tarenootairer's behalf, or a mere lack of interest on Robinson's. In fact, an examination of any of the records of this era reveals that accounts of daily life for Tarenootairer in the earliest years at Wybalenna are wholly incomplete and highly speculative.[14] So, too, the absence of birth announcements, which directly affect Tarenootairer's own narrative, hint at a lack of interest from the administration when rare births occurred. Instead, establishment journals, like Robinson's, are rendered dedicated diaries of post-mortems and dismembered corpses as keepsakes.[15]

The best that can be scribed is the knowledge that Tarenootairer, within her first year at Wybalenna, had given birth to a daughter, Fanny Cochrane, likely her initial reason for abandoning Robinson's roving party, and was at least briefly reunited with her son, Duke. He had been in the care of a soldier's wife while Tarenootairer was employed by Robinson, before being swiftly escorted by the commandant himself to the King's Orphan Asylum (later renamed the Queen's Orphan Asylum and also known as the Orphan School) in Hobart, never to return.

There is little documentation pertaining to Tarenootairer's children in these early years, and it appears her time as a new mother was relatively short-lived. We do know that Fanny was placed in the care of establishment catechist Robert Clark, who advocated the severing of cultural and familial bonds.[16] And, like her elder siblings, she was eventually taken to the Orphan School in New Town, further dislocating Fanny from her mother's influence.[17] This apparent dissolution of their maternal relationship at such a crucial early time caused an inevitable disconnect between mother and daughter in the following decade.[18]

Tarenootairer's earliest years at the settlement also saw a reunion with her eldest surviving child, Mary Ann, herself sent to the establishment in approximately 1834. The first mention of the two together is found in Robinson's journal of 19 February 1836, when he wrote, "Mary

Ann a halfcaste girl of fifteen years has a class and is very attentive; she instructs her mother who is in her class."[19]

Tarenootairer's newfound relationship with her daughter would prove highly fruitful. Buoyed by her colonial education, unshakable will and marriage to would-be activist Walter George Arthur in 1838, Mary Ann was to become a strong matriarchal figure in the lives of her mother and her siblings.

Sarah

A couple of "Sarahs" pop up throughout various journals.[20] However, from January to September 1836, Tarenootairer was still known by the name of Tibb, as recorded in a census of "Aborigines at Wybalenna" in September by Charles Robinson. Around 1836, George Augustus Robinson gave Tarenootairer the name Sarah.[21] These name changes were apparently instigated at the request of the sealing women, who considered their previous monikers given by the sealers a reminder of the lives they had endured under their control.[22] However, a positive view on these name changes must be met with some scepticism. The renaming of individuals was a distinct strategy often "adopted by slave owners" to Europeanise their subordinates and to break down affiliations and custom.[23] For some, like Truganini, these names were condescending, to say the least, and engaged a sense of imperialist mocking:

> Truganini was renamed Princess Lalla Rookh, Little Jacky became Bonaparte, Big Jemmy became Alphonso and Wongeneep was renamed Queen Evelene [and Ryenrope was re-named Cleopatra].[24]

Tarenootairer's new name was of similar reflection. Formerly a title meaning "princess", Sarah derived from the black Egyptian slave or servant girl whom French legend claims accompanied Mary Magdalene,

"BLACK MAN'S HOUSES"

Mary Jacobe and Mary Salome to the coast of France, landing at what is now called Saintes-Maries-de-la-Mer (where she became the "saint" of the Rom of Western Europe).[25] Despite this, one simply cannot deny it was an improvement from the derogatory Tibb.

* * *

Her possible relationship with Tomlins now over, he having abandoned Bass Strait in 1836, at Robinson's behest Tarenootairer was "married off" to Nicermenic, who was renamed Eugene.[26] These marriages were just another example of colonial control and Robinson's attempts to remove the prisoners from their former culture, to introduce Christian ideological social structures into their lives and, in a vain attempt, to curb what he believed was deviant behaviour at the settlement. In essence, the very purpose of Wybalenna itself.

A few years her junior and a keen pupil, Nicermenic was an alleged former warrior and appears a volatile personality during these times.[27] From what little there is to draw on, Nicermenic's time at Wybalenna appears to have been consumed by hunting and fighting, for example:

> The sergeant of the detachment and the aboriginal woman Sarah, reported to me that there was a riot in the square, and that Frederick [a fellow captive] was murdering her husband. I directed the sergeant at once to take his men and interfere, and when he expressed himself afraid of so many black people in such an excited state, referring to the successful resistance little more than double their number had made to the whole military and civil force of Van Diemen's Land, I armed myself and entered the square, but all violence had ceased, and [after Sarah had told Frederick that Henry Jeanneret, Robinson's successor, was about to shoot him] Frederick was away.[28]

The two newlyweds were conferred their own house (house number four) along with the other couples[29] but little of their life together is detailed.

Whether coerced or consensual, Tarenootairer's marriage to Nicermenic produced two more known children and possibly another. The first, named Adam, was born about 1837; a second, unnamed, son was born on 7 June 1838.[30] Collectively, these births elevate Tarenootairer to one of a mere handful of women at the establishment who managed to give birth to reasonably healthy children.

As already established, little can be gleaned from records regarding the early relationship between the Indigenous parents and their children. It is obvious that both Tarenootairer and Nicermenic had little autonomy at Wybalenna when it came to parenting, both being under the administrative control of the colonial authority.[31] Like Fanny, Adam would be sent to live with the family of catechist Robert Clark.[32] However, far from the watchful care of their parents, time with the Clarks was fraught with rigid routine and often abuse. The treatment of the children was increasingly brutal, causing both siblings to rebel and be intermittently placed into the care of their sister Mary Ann:

> Eugene and his wife, the father and mother of Fanny and Adam, being asked if they were willing that their children be sent back to Mr. Clark, said they were not. Fanny being asked if she understood the nature of an oath answered "No", and the doctor explained it. Fanny said she did not wish to return to Mr. Clark.[33]

In light of Tarenootairer's children being subject to poor conditions and ill-treatment, the justification that they were better off in the care of the Clarks than of their own parents is confounding.

"BLACK MAN'S HOUSES"

* * *

Towards the close of the decade, life at Wybalenna had become truly fragile. More than half of those brought to the island settlement had died from disease, with approximately 68 deaths occurring between 1832 and 1836.[34] By 1838, the rapid death rate of the Indigenous captives was making morbid news, declared the *Cornwall Chronicle*:

> "[T]hey die", says our friend, "at the rate of twenty per cent per annum, without any births to supply the loss. Ninety are all that now remain of the various and large aboriginal tribes of Van Diemen's Land, so that the utter extinction of the race is hastily approaching."[35]

Even the governor's wife, Lady Jane Franklin, was lamenting their plight in poetic prose: "How the stories trickle in, of a people hungry for their homeland," she wrote, "what visions do their eyes spin, as they stare across the water, blue as truth; as far and final as the hangman's noose."[36]

By March 1839, Tarenootairer's then youngest son, known only as "Sarah's child", at a mere eight and a half months old and culturally not yet old enough to be attributed a name, would tragically succumb to the fate of many others.[37] The child's death followed an outbreak of influenza that had been raging in Hobart since December 1838 and had made its way to Wybalenna by January. In February, Robert Clark wrote to G. A. Robinson, who was stationed in Port Phillip pending his permanent residency there as "Chief Protector of Aborigines": "[O]wing to the epidemic of influenza now affecting them," he states, "several of the sick natives had removed to the bush … said there was an abundance of medical comforts but Walsh [the doctor] did not give orders to issue them."[38] In fact, Walsh's neglect of the Indigenous captives during the epidemic was so bad that it was a direct cause of his dismissal.[39]

For Tarenootairer, the death of her child was met with grief and the following of tradition:

> Interred three of the deceased natives, viz Phillip, G Robinson and Sarah's child, in the same grave in the afternoon. The child had been decapitated by the mother for the purpose of keeping as a relic.[40]

The tragic death of "Sarah's boy" was not in vain. His tiny body was to be utilised as both spiritual and physical "medicine". The retainment of skulls, jawbones, forearms, teeth and so on was a standard traditional practice. Either kept whole or powdered, these bones were believed to relieve headaches and other ailments, with some naming these appendages as "the doctor".[41] According to Robinson's journals, many of these objects were bartered for and so, too, unbeknown to the Indigenous captives, heads were being decapitated from the newly deceased at the request of eager collectors.[42]

* * *

Disease and despair remained their prime enemy. An irregular and poor diet diminished their fragile health: "… rice with plums and sugar was served out for dinner in the absence of mutton; the boisterous weather and want of men prevented the boat going out for sheep", noted Robinson.[43] As farming adequate crops was too difficult to foster in the island's sandy soils, and European food supplies from Launceston were unreliable, native foods were the only supplement, reducing wild game numbers to an unsustainable level.[44] Their native produce had also become a marketable commodity by which to finance the establishment. A "native" market begun by Robinson was held on Tuesdays, where their meagre produce was to be given away for preserves and a pittance. Skins, shell necklaces and baskets became a cottage industry to procure money for the settlement.[45]

As rigid routines under Robinson and Clark were established for the dwindling population of children, so, too, life for Tarenootairer and the women of Wybalenna was equally harsh under the control of Robert Clark's wife. Despite inevitable opposition, a weekly regime of European domesticity such as cooking, cleaning huts, washing clothes and sewing occupied their increasingly desperate days.[46] For Robinson, their sewing became a marketable example of his influence. "[T]he French net [made by the women] is a superior art; several specimens have been manufactured into D'Oyleys, and which, together with specimens of worsted knitting, are herewith forwarded for the information of his Excellency the Lieutenant-governor," he boasted.[47]

Vain attempts to convey acceptance of their new colonial culture saw the captives reciting obligatory Bible readings, taking tea in the bush or at the homes of the officers and visiting the settlement houses to sing hymns "to fine effect".[48] Yet, against all odds, the Indigenous Tasmanians would retain a strength of tradition. Even better, those who were surviving their confinement were finding ways to balance and combine their colonial duties with those of their own culture.[49] The unique culture of the Bass Strait island women and children that Tarenootairer both retained and adapted as a proverbial "nummer-lore" (white devil's wife) was the source of her very survival at Wybalenna.

Regardless of their best efforts, the daily routines were by now as much to blame for the despair experienced by the Indigenous captives as the poor living conditions. Despite attempts to appease the administration and adapt to their new regimes, both cultural and spiritual, little came by way of improvement in their health or wellbeing.[50]

* * *

The new decade of the 1840s would usher in a new administration. The succession of Henry Jeanneret as superintendent, followed soon after by Joseph Milligan, would see little change. The remaining Indigenous captives' attempts to take control of their lives, to curb the daily violence and disease that had become commonplace, went unheard by the masses or, if heard, largely ignored.[51]

For Tarenootairer, her husband Nicermenic and their surviving children, the endless miseries of Wybalenna were to endure with their relocation from Flinders Island to a new settlement along the southeast coast of the main island, known as Oyster Cove.

Chapter 5

DINUDARĂ (SARAH)

The chosen site for the new settlement was a decrepit former convict station that had apparently "become available because it was thought to be too unhealthy for convicts to live there".[1] Poor finances, an untrustworthy administration and an uncontrollable death rate were noted as reasons for the move.[2] On 15 October 1847, the schooner *The Sisters* carried Tarenootairer, her husband and their children, as well as Wybalenna's remaining captive Indigenous population – now totalling 46 in all – to the new establishment. It was a move that initially brought great opposition from the island's colonists.[3]

The new settlement shared many traits of the Wybalenna constructs. Their huts were now made from timber slabs with unpaved, muddy earth surrounding the obligatory chapel, mess room, hospital, a cookery or bake house, and "a dozen wooden cells formerly used for solitary confinement".[4]

Despite the poor conditions of the new settlement, without the suffocating governance of George Augustus Robinson, or Henry Jeanneret, who succeeded him, the Indigenous Tasmanians were allowed more cultural autonomy. Restrictions became a little more relaxed, but only a little, remarked local resident George Davis: "[T]he Blacks at Oyster Cove like to come to Bruni and go around for a few days seeing their old haunts. They felt at home."[5]

The Oyster Cove residents would be allowed an annual (although some reports say biannual) "holiday" from the settlement. For this, they preferred to journey up the Huon Valley to a place known as the Hermitage.[6] However, it was less than a holiday, with the group instead carrying bags for collecting rations and other supplies.[7] The collection of donations was now increasingly essential. Accompanied by her beloved dog Rover, Tarenootairer and her contemporaries would use these charity drives to escape their torments and at least gain some semblance of their previous selves.

As well as allowing them to visit the landscapes of their beloved nations, these external sojourns became a useful tool for the colonial authority to relieve fears the Indigenous residents posed a threat to the civilians, and so, too, their visits to Hobart became amusements for the curious, a type of "entertainment … for colonists to enjoy".[8] This was never more evident than when Tarenootairer and her family were invited to the home of the governor, then Sir William Denison, in December 1847, becoming a Christmas spectacle for invited guests and inquisitive locals.[9] Under the headline "Christmas Festivities", stated the *Courier*, "The greatest novelty was the appearance of the remaining 'aboriginal inhabitants' of the colony, who, occupying two cabs, were driven about the city."[10]

* * *

Despite an apparent loosening of the reins, the colony had by now tightened its grip on the finances of the Aboriginal settlement, the £2000 annually dispensed by the government reputedly "pocketed by officials long before it reached the Aborigines".[11]

DINUDARĂ (SARAH)

Money was not the only reason for the colony tightening its grip on their lives. New and stricter "racial" policies were being implemented. Coinciding with other settler colonies, the new government decided that the "able-bodied" Indigenous residents should be made to work, and it was recommended that Mary Ann and other "half-castes" of the establishment be expelled from government care.[12] Tarenootairer's children were now becoming pawns in the colony's new political and racial ideologies and, once again, most of them were removed to the Orphan School.[13]

Alternatively, instead of expulsion, Mary Ann, with her standard education and her stable (although reportedly abusive) colonial marriage to Walter George Arthur, was to be used as a suitable surrogate for the few children who remained.[14] Walter went one step further, petitioning for more Indigenous autonomy at Oyster Cove to care for his family.[15] His request was granted, and he was provided with a job, a salary and a block of land, where a three-roomed bush-hut was built to house himself and his wife, her siblings and his mother-in-law.[16]

Unfortunately, ill-treatment by settlers continued to plague what was left of the resident Indigenous Tasmanians and little was done to remedy this abuse.[17] If the move to a former convict station, abandoned for its "failure to meet convict health standards", was intended to curb the high mortality, it was certainly to no avail.[18] Following nearly four decades of death and despair, little joy remained of a once-vibrant culture and people.[19]

A few "traditional" family groupings were seemingly maintained among them.[20] Yet, with dwindling numbers, tighter funds and fewer administrators, all the Indigenous residents were now being encouraged to work off the settlement for their bread and butter.[21] The boys, such as Tarenootairer's son Adam, William Lanne and Moriarty, were apprenticed aboard fishing and whaling ships.[22] The girls, like Fanny, were utilised as house maids or were married off to white men at their earliest convenience.[23]

For Tarenootairer and her contemporaries, Oyster Cove would at least prove to have greater cultural benefits. Unable to stifle the death rates instigated by poor European rations and disease, the Indigenous residents were allowed to resume their traditional methods of hunting native fauna.[24] It is in these activities that we find at least some accounts of a betterment in their quality of life.

Native foods, so depleted on Flinders Island, were now more abundant and were wholly sought out over lesser quality colonial produce. Stated Mrs Benbow, "[We would] cultivate a little strip of potatoes on northern side of creek; [the] government supplied them with spades and hoes; but [they] were very lazy, had not been brought up to it, and liked hunting and fishing [better]."[25]

"Tabelty ningina moomera proberry partroola!" (go get wood, put [on] fire) would be heard as bundles of wood were collected to make fires for cooking and heat, carried on their backs with a coil of rope tied around the waist.[26] They had their own "lunna-bunna" (a native potato, also called black man's potato or kidney potato) found under a delicate flower. Fish, mussels, oysters, "loetererlepeene" (freshwater crayfish), eels and native grubs were cooked by traditional methods, in the hot ashes of an open partroola. Meat, such as "metubbener" (possum), "truhanner" (kangaroo) and, for a few, "plentenner" (snake) were also prepared in this way. Possums were caught by climbing trees cut with notches and "shifting it [themselves] up" using bark loops around the trunks as a kind of rope, until the sleeping possums were within reach. Oysters along the coasts of Bruny Island were collected by feeling around the water with their feet.

English trout and salmon had been introduced into the nearby streams and inlets along the D'Entrecasteaux Channel, and could be caught simply by "tickling them" with a hand. Swan eggs, a favourite, were collected along the inlets seasonally. Staple flora and vegetables consisted of the succulent "worerutterer" (pigface, aka dead man's fingers), fresh "lacra" (bracken fern) shoots and a fungus, "tooreela" (native bread), would be dug up from a few inches under the earth. There was "willila" (wild oat type flower), kangaroo apple, wild cherries and "mulla" (blueberries). The soft, brown, sour-tasting "punk" from within a log, used to carry burning embers, could be eaten also. Herbs were both flavoursome and medicinal. Medicines made from lacra and white-gum sap continued to be consumed to combat stomach upsets. The cooked fat from snakes would be used for skin infections.[27] The spiritual and medicinal use of human bones from deceased loved ones was here, too, used to cure headaches, bites and other ailments.[28] However, just like at Wybalenna, these were becoming much sought-after artefacts for the curious and scholarly.

This bountiful native produce was not to last. By the early 20th century what remained of the traditional wild game in the island's south-east had been drastically reduced. Tarenootairer's granddaughter Flora lamented the loss of traditional fauna since the devastation of colonisation. "[A] strange thing," she noted, "that since the blacks died God has not populated the country with animals; used to live with wallaby and kangaroo; opossums would come to your door to eat and now have to hunt to find one."[29] This statement further emphasises the ongoing spiritual connection to native fauna.

The elder women continued to rebel against colonial customs. By the time they were at Oyster Cove, their woollen or hand-sewn chemises had been replaced with harsh, dense layers of black fabrics, "women's clothing a thick petticoat or skirt and blouse of thick material like a 'bluey' [blanket], and red caps".[30] These clothes, which had contributed to spreading the diseases that destroyed them, would be wilfully discarded whenever they could. "[They] seemed to vex the women more than anything and would tie their clothes into a bundle and kick them up into the air."[31]

Photographs from the station, taken predominantly by Francis Nixon between 1858 and 1862, show the women in a uniform of scrapped, knitted or hessian-style garments fashioned in typically Victorian styles, sporadically decorated with printed head wraps and bon-bon-adorned berets and beanies, with their men dressed in "moleskin trousers and jackets".[32] Unfortunately, Tarenootairer is not present in these photographs; in 1858 she was likely at the home of Fanny awaiting the birth of her first grandchild.

There is, however, one sketch of Tarenootairer rendered during her time at Oyster Cove Station, drawn by German illustrator Ludwig Becker in 1852 on his visit to the establishment.[33] Becker was well known for his naturalist illustrations for encyclopaedias, yet more famous for his death during Burke and Wills's doomed Victorian expedition.[34] This delicate portrait, in classical Becker style, is little larger than a playing card and titled *Dinudara (Sarah)*. Likely positioned face to face with Tarenootairer, Becker drafts her in contemplative pose, wearing the famed bluey and smoking a small clay pipe. The equally delicate watercolour version further brings her likeness into living colour, yet conflicts with oral history anecdotes. These sketches were initially rendered only in pencil and painted at a later date, a

DINUDARĂ (SARAH)

likely explanation for why her famous red hair is not depicted. "[O]ne woman, Sarah had a red head. Fiery red – I've seen Irish men with hair the same colour. The only one that I ever saw – not with red ochre – it was natural," quipped Mrs Elmer in 1910.[35] Regardless of this alleged inconsistency, this silent portrait remains the most vivid likeness of Tarenootairer in existence.

Figure 2: Ludwig Becker's portrait titled *Dinudara (Sarah) V.D.L.*, Oyster Cove, 1852.

***

Despite a brief era of cultural reprieve, despair, poverty and the lure of colonial vices began inducing some at Oyster Cove into alleged prostitution to support themselves.[36] Many were succumbing to alcoholism. Young women such as Mathinna, Pangernowidedic and Mary Ann had become victims of alcohol-induced violence, and some died. So, too, alcohol would embed itself into Tarenootairer's legacy. Her granddaughter (and namesake), Sarah Laurel Smith, states, "Now Billy my gibli [drink] fine one … my grandmother [Tarenootairer] would say this on approaching a public house."[37]

Their resident doctor, William Smith, would also have a unique impact on Tarenootairer and her family. Akin to Wybalenna, Oyster Cove would prove a poisoned prison. Smith was fond of prescribing vast quantities of alcohol and mercury to treat all manner of abdominal and respiratory complaints.[38] However, it was not only the medical treatments issued that were cause for concern. Under the management of Joseph Milligan, suspicions would be raised regarding the "bad water" being supplied at the establishments. Their poor quality of living paralleled the scarcity of children being born at the settlements and for the captives, and even a resident surgeon, the "bad water", as well as their poor medical treatments, would be identified as the culprit,[39] fuelling the belief that the colony was deliberately hastening their extermination by sterilisation and poisoning.

Tragically, in May 1849, aged only about 40 years, Tarenootairer's (now seemingly estranged) husband Nicermenic died suddenly from "catarrh, with abdominal disease".[40] As the Indigenous population dwindled, so too did public interest. The establishment overseers, protectorates and so-called doctors would gradually retire from their duties and eventually return to their motherlands, where they were rewarded with sturdy pensions and academic praise. In 1851 their former "conciliator" and "protector", George Augustus Robinson, paid one last pitiful visit to his former "natives" at Oyster Cove before returning, with his family in tow, to England.[41]

* * *

In 1855 there were only 16 Indigenous Tasmanians living at the station, including Tarenootairer and Mary Ann. Fanny Cochrane had married a former convict sawyer and was running a boarding house with her husband in Hobart, before living on various leases around North West Bay.[42] Collectively, Tarenootairer and her daughters, and the remaining captive Indigenous population, sat confronted with a land now wholly bloodstained, both literally and figuratively.[43] By these years, the oral creation stories of stars, people, animals and spirits had become muddied with horror stories of frontier violence that would echo throughout subsequent generations. Stories of the wanton murder of men, women and children were never to be forgotten by the Indigenous or the non-Indigenous.[44]

Chapter 6

HER FEEBLE PULSE

Through her youngest daughter, Tarenootairer (and contemporaries such as Truganini) would enjoy regular recess at her various homes. Both Fanny Cochrane and her husband went to great lengths to accommodate her kin:

> While the natives were alive they were constantly with Smith and his wife [Fanny], who, at great expense to themselves, provided them with every comfort it was in their power to give. Therefore, it will be seen that instead of Smith [William Sr.] marrying his wife with any monetary view, the Treasurer was quite correct when he said Smith married her for love, and to join their lots together. I will just remark that all travelling expenses of the natives, in going from the station [Oyster Cove] to visit him, wherever he lived, either at Hobart or Irish Town, were borne by William Smith, Fanny's husband.[1]

Yet, this period was marked by another shocking tragedy – the precipitous death of Tarenootairer's son Adam on 10 October 1857, aged only 20 years, a greatly felt loss to both the family and the community.[2] At Fanny Cochrane's home, Adam, struck with fever induced by influenza, which he had contracted during a whaling apprenticeship, was lovingly tended to by his mother and sisters.[3]

Following this sorrow, Tarenootairer found herself in a bittersweet scenario. She was about to be one of the few Indigenous residents of the station to become a grandmother.[4] Eight months after the death of her son, in the isolated marshy forest of North West Bay, about seven miles from Oyster Cove, a grieving Tarenootairer was present at the birth of her (presumed) first grandchild, William Henry Smith Jr.[5] Born on 1 August 1858, inside the humble wooden cottage of her daughter, it had been years since a child "had been born to any of the captives".[6] William Jr's birth was a great cause for celebration for the Indigenous Tasmanians at the establishment and genuine pride for his grandmother. "He is a fine, healthy-looking child, of whom they and all the blacks are very proud," it was declared.[7]

* * *

Yet, despite these few tender moments of joy outside of her life at the Aboriginal station, Tarenootairer could not escape the fate that had befallen most of her contemporaries. Back in the decrepit huts of Oyster Cove, a recent "cold wind" carried with it the dreaded influenza, the wretched disease that had all but wiped out the majority of the captives, and at least two of Tarenootairer's known children. Sick and assuming the worst, she approached her impending expiration without fear.[8]

It is no surprise that, for a people for whom death had come to define their daily lives, the traditional mysteries surrounding the spiritual rituals of the afterlife remained solid, active and continuous. Death is just another continuation of existence; the dead are never far away.[9]

The last week of Tarenootairer's life is documented in the Oyster Cove Visitors Book, recorded by the establishment's appointed surgeon, Dr William Smith, giving devastating details of her final hours.

On 23 September, Dr Smith entered the station and found most of the inmates afflicted and Tarenootairer "suffering from great debility", coughing and with "little appetite". As usual, his prescription consisted of alcohol such as wine or brandy, either pure or mixed with a raw egg, arrowroot and beef tea. Two days later, he found his cure-all was to little avail. By now she could hardly move:

> [T]here is great difficulty in getting her to sit up even for the purpose of taking anything, her relatives state that she starts in her sleep and raves considerably; the tongue is brown and dry and the teeth – covered with scales [?]; pulse feeble.[10]

On 27 September, a false sign of improvement was observed. Her pulse appeared stronger and her mobility had improved, yet severe dehydration was still evident. The night raves also became chronic, disjointing her sleep and maintaining her weakness until the month's close.

Though influenza was declared the guilty condition, what is not documented among these entries is the possible correlation between Tarenootairer's symptoms and that of mercury toxicity.[11] Mouth ulcers and insomnia are believed to be classic signs of the presumed "unintentional" poisoning that would assist in claiming the lives of many captives at the establishment.[12] Furthermore, her symptoms collectively appear to parallel the long-term and final-stage effects of inappropriately treated syphilis.[13]

Despite continuous care, without the appropriate medicines and dry, hygienic living conditions to both stave off and cure the sickness, nothing could be done. Dr Smith's final entry scribed on 3 October 1858 states, "Visited the Establishment and found Sarah had died early this morning."

Following her grandson's joyful birth only two months earlier, Tarenootairer was now dead, aged around 52 years.[14] For her family, the wake was held in traditional Indigenous fashion. Befitting her very name, they awoke that morning to find the remaining residents of the establishment camped outside their home, wailing in song and grief at their tragic loss.[15] In contrast, her death was solemn but minor news to the colony, stated the *Courier*:

> We regret to state that several of the aborigines have been suffering from influenza, and that Sarah died a few days since at the estimated age of 65 [sic], of a low fever of typhoid type. The deceased was the mother of Mary Ann, the wife of Walter, now the head man of the feeble remnant of what was not many years since a powerful race.[16]

Despite the melancholic sentiment, Tarenootairer's death had brought the colonists one step closer to a much-anticipated closure of an embarrassing colonial era, fraught with shame.

On the cusp of her passing, educator and occultist James Bonwick allegedly paid a visit to Oyster Cove Station. Here he spoke with Mary Ann and Walter Arthur, painting with words a lamentable picture of the sorry state of the residence. Through her attributed nickname Tibb, Tarenootairer's era – at least her first violent encounters with the white man – began with a derogatory Shakespearean reference and, through Bonwick, it similarly closed. Described like a certifiable coven of Macbethian witches, of the captive elder women he wrote:

> They lived wretchedly in dirt and neglect. Their food was cooked in a pot from which I saw the dogs allowed to eat. They lay in their clothes, with a dirty blanket in the cold season. They could not read, and they were never read to. They cared not for prayer, and had no one to pray with them. They bartered food and blankets with disreputable neighbours to obtain drink. They sat about on the ground with their mangy dogs, smoking their filthy pipes, and cackling over stories of their past.[17]

Though Bonwick's contempt is palpable, for me, this closing image renders one of great defiance – of a group of extraordinary women who had survived the tidal wave of brute force, disease and incarceration that the dreaded ships and their devil's cargo had brought to their shores, to spend the last hours of their lives as they chose – smoking, eating, drinking and laughing.

Eulogy

Possibly the most famous figure of Indigenous Tasmanian survival is Tarenootairer's contemporary, Truganini. On Tarenootairer's death, she would take it upon herself to become a surrogate matriarch to Tarenootairer's family, dividing her time between Mary Ann at Oyster Cove and the home of Fanny Cochrane in what is now Nicholls Rivulet (formerly Irish Town). Her surrogate maternity was of such strength that some of Fanny's eventual 11 children, never knowing Tarenootairer personally, would cite Truganini as their grandmother, affectionately calling her Lally. She would take them on much-recited hunting trips, shocking them with stories of the horrors she had witnessed throughout her harrowing life.[18]

So, too, like Truganini, Tarenootairer's death is possibly not the end of her story. In the next few decades, the remains of many who were interred in the mapped but incomplete graveyard of the Oyster Cove establishment were to be exhumed, examined and sometimes exhibited. As in life, they were stolen from their homelands and held captive once more.

Almost all the administrators of both Wybalenna and Oyster Cove were guilty of varying degrees of "grave robbery". At the time of Tarenootairer's passing, Joseph Milligan was an instigator and advocate of collecting Indigenous Tasmanian skeletons.[19] During his sporadic tenure as medical officer between 1843 and 1855, he understood the value that Indigenous Tasmanian remains had to "metropolitan anatomical and anthropological circles", himself acquiring specimens.[20]

The acquisition of remains was apparently no great effort. In 1863 Tasmanian governor Thomas Gore Brown noted there being "no difficulty in procuring skulls ... Several gentlemen have promised to exert themselves to obtain specimens for me".[21] By 1908, museum collections globally had acquired a substantial graveyard: "the crania catalogued in museums as Tasmanian ... which have been studied and described by anthropologists", noted Sir William Turner, "are seventy-nine in number".[22] This estimate proved wholly deficient. Post-publishing by the Royal Society of Edinburgh, Turner's paper instigated further exhumations, and in 1910 he wrote:

> Messrs Harper and Clarke ... reported that they had disinterred nine skeletons of Tasmanians in a burying-ground adjacent to Big Oyster Cove, where a settlement had been provided for the last remnant of the natives. They stated their intention to publish shortly a description of the interesting relics of this extinct race.[23]

Although no certainty can be claimed that her remains suffered this fate, such knowledge renders the closure of Tarenootairer's remarkable tale as perhaps incomplete. One can scarcely guarantee that even in death she was able to rest undisturbed.

In closing her biographical chapter, it is difficult to truly comprehend the extraordinary life of Tarenootairer. It is a violent tale from slavery to captivity, of subjugation and endurance. If anything, Tarenootairer's greatest achievement was her very survival – her extraordinary ability to withstand the onslaught that followed the British colonisation of her country. Therefore, her greatest legacy is not drawn from her actions or achievements, but from her influence, providing vast and eternal inspiration for her two surviving daughters and the many generations that have followed.

PART 2

A *Femme de Chambre*:
Mary Ann, c. 1821–1871

Chapter 7

A KING'S ISLAND DAUGHTER

Mary Ann Robinson[1] was born in a small cottage at Sea Elephant Harbour when her parents were situated on remote King Island, sometime in the years between 1819 and 1821.[2] She was likely the first child of Tarenootairer, still on the cusp of her teens, and her so-called master, the Scottish sealer and whaler named George (Geordy) Robinson.

Two decades prior, King Island had been a political prize sought by both the French and the English.[3] Sea Elephant Harbour (or Bay), on the island's central east coast, was the premier spot of anchorage for explorers and became sporadically documented in the journals of captains Baudin, Hamelin and Robbins.[4] It was also the millennia-old home of sea elephant colonies, their desired fats and skins the principal income for Mary Ann's father. They were, even then, under threat from overhunting.[5] Charles-Alexandre Lesueur sketched Mary Ann's childhood landscape in 1802, igniting visions of an infant girl scampering among abundant coastal eucalypt thickets, and slumbering seals on kelp-covered beaches.[6]

Yet the 1820s are depicted as a period of great instability and lawlessness in the strait. The first possible record of Mary Ann's existence is of being forcibly removed with her mother and father from their modest King Island croft by Master J. H. Skelton on board the *Governor Sorrell*, landing on Preservation Island around December 1825.[7]

By the close of the decade, the famed "conciliator", George Augustus Robinson, was scouring the strait demanding that the sealers and straitsmen "give up their women".[8] This provides the most logical scenario for Mary Ann's removal from her family at the time, yet this may have occurred much earlier. Instead of being "rounded up" by G. A. Robinson's search party and sent to the experimental Aboriginal establishment, she was placed by her father into the care, or "service", of the Aylwin family, who were stationed in Launceston, the major trading hub of the sealers.[9] It is here, at the approximate age of nine years, that Mary Ann's story truly begins.

A Chambermaid

George Aylwin was a merchant of whale oil and a tallow chandler (candle manufacturer), thus dealing directly with the sealers and whalers of the strait. At the time, candles were produced with animal fats, and the boiled blubber of whales lit the colony's lamps. "The highest prices for Rough Fat and Tallow", Aylwin advertised, meaning that he paid a good price for the primary produce.[10] Within the burgeoning township of Launceston, Aylwin's business was highly profitable, exporting quality oils throughout the colony and back to London;[11] in fact, his subsequent influence was so substantial he was elected District Constable there in 1826.[12] Aylwin was of a notable character too. The drama of the Launceston wharfs on a violent New Year's Day had *The Hobart Town Courier* painting him no less than a hero, and it is here we first meet a young "black girl", no doubt Mary Ann:

> We regret to state that the squalls and high winds which prevailed last week were attended with several serious and fatal accidents. On Christmas day Mr. Gordon, as Coroner, held two inquests on the bodies of the unfortunate men who were drowned. The one

was on Robert Dudlow, a free servant of Mr. Aylwin. The boat had scarcely left the shore when the black girl, whom he is bringing up, ran to him saying the boat had gone down, which he discovered floating under water. Assisted by Mr. Chipman he succeeded in rescuing Brown, the man who had charge of the boat, and at the imminent risk of his own life dashed through the breakers and dived and brought up his assigned servant, who had sunk to the bottom, and by proper care was ultimately restored to life. The unfortunate Dudlow, however, it would appear, when he had quitted his hold of the vessel had been seized by a shark, as his remains were much mutilated.[13]

The *Courier's* heroic saga did not escape the notice of George Augustus Robinson, making him aware of a young Mary Ann long before she was to meet him.[14]

By 1831, Aylwin had taken over the licence of the Ship Inn, situated in Launceston's main hub of Charles Street – a relatively luxurious property with a dwelling-house, two parlours, a bar and bakery, malting and brewing houses, and replete with stables.[15] It was the perfect setting for Harriet, George Aylwin's wife. A keen seamstress, within a year of her marriage in 1826 she had opened a shopfront in Sydney where she advertised to the desired market her new "Dress-making and Millinery line". As relayed in the *Sydney Gazette*:

> Mrs. A. flatters herself, that, from her knowledge and experience in the above Business, having been in some of the first Houses in the West End of London, she will be able to give ample Satisfaction to those Ladies, who may favour her with their Commands.[16]

If the above advertisement is any clue, being a high-fashion woman of means was a keen interest in Harriet's married life. A news article from 1829 gives direct insight into Aylwin's highly coveted fashionable elite of the period, and the subordinate roles "black children" were given among them:

> It is now the prevailing taste in Paris, closely imitated in London, to have a black woman for a cook, a black boy or girl for a femme de chamber, and another for a lacquey. If this fancy continues there might be some chance of disposing of a few of our aboriginal blacks, if we could manage to produce them for sale about Park lane or Bond street.[17]

Under the à la mode influences of Mrs Aylwin, Mary Ann would have adopted her mistress's classic Victorian-era accoutrement, albeit one reflective of her position in the household. Like an immutable doll, her elegant side curls, popular in the 19th century to give an oval frame to the face and likely combined into a coiled chignon at the base of her neck, was a style she maintained well into her adult years in the 1860s.[18] Yet, regardless of any willing appropriation of colonial costume, Mary Ann would not, or could not, ever be accepted as equal. Britain's global colonies at the time held an estimated 800,000 slaves, and both demand for them and a fear of their revolt were a hot topic of the times. In the parlayed article, it is clear the prospect of slavery was an open discussion in Van Diemen's Land and, coupled with her mother's captivity in the strait, the spectre of future enslavement hovered over Mary Ann's childhood from her very first breath.[19]

Servitude to a white mistress would be a recurring role for Mary Ann Robinson, a fate shared by many Indigenous girls.[20] By the 1830s there were a number of Indigenous children, mostly the daughters of sealers, sent to work in Launceston as domestic servants and to gain so-called educations.[21] Though seen as a legitimate form of so-called gentrification or reform, few of these children would have access to any genuine social advancement, their place as equals among this "newly emerging society" stoically denied.[22]

George Aylwin's professional relationship with the straitsmen would have meant sporadic, or even regular, contact with Mary Ann's father. Of this relationship little can be gleaned, yet she herself recalled him fondly. In contrast to her mother's narrative of abduction, forced labour, cohabitation and violence, Mary Ann's recollections of her father appear quaint. This is not unusual. The children born of slave owners and their subordinates were given opportunities other black children were often denied, such as higher positions within a household, access to education and even money or assets bequeathed to them on their fathers' deaths.[23]

Her relationship with her mother during this period cannot be ascertained; however, a possible close encounter occurred in September 1831. George Augustus Robinson, with his famed "mission Aborigines", including Tarenootairer, had arrived in Launceston. The Launceston Gaol was situated on Patterson Street, just around the corner from the Ship Inn (on Charles Street), where Robinson was visiting the Indigenous prisoners temporarily detained there.[24] It cannot be known if Mary Ann knew her mother had joined the so-called Friendly Mission; however, the presence of Robinson and the roving party, as well as the headlines they were making, were colliding their realities and bringing the Black War directly to Mary Ann's doorstep:

> The Aborigines – Mr. G. A. Robinson … (who came to Launceston yesterday morning) … has been for some time in pursuit of the natives on the eastern coast, and has been following their track backwards and forwards … had the good fortune to come up with and capture, between Forrester's River and the Little Piper, the fugitive Yumarrha [sic] … Yumarrha is very communicative, and

stated to Mr. Robinson that they would not have committed so many murders as they have but on account of the women being kidnapped from them by the Sealers.[25]

Less than two years later, Mary Ann's time in service to the Aylwins ended. The reasons for them placing her into the Queen's Orphan School on 8 August 1833 are unspecified, and a number of scenarios can be viably drawn. The date (although no certainty can be placed on Orphan School record dates) of Mary Ann's entry coincides with four potential events that give due cause for her admittance. First, her father Geordy Robinson had possibly died by this time (estimated between October 1832 and July 1834), rendering the Aylwins no longer obliged to care for her, and validating her classification as an "orphan" replete with the description of "parents dead" in the entry notes. Second, the imminent birth of George and Harriet's second daughter, born on 6 August 1833, approximately two days before Mary Ann's admittance, and whom they subsequently named Mary Ann. Third, the establishment of the Aboriginal settlement on Flinders Island around 1832 and a plausible recommendation that she now be sent there would mean her placement in the orphanage was a transitory measure.[26] And last, one cannot ignore the coincidence between the timing of Mary Ann's abandonment by the seemingly class- and image-conscious Aylwins and both public and political protests in the United Kingdom (published in the Van Diemen's Land press from 1831 onwards) against slavery in the British colonies, leading to the passing of the *Slavery Abolition Act* by the British Parliament on 28 August 1833.[27]

* * *

There is no indication of exactly how long she spent at the Orphan School, constructed in 1828 to house the growing population of abandoned, orphaned or even abducted children.[28] Overseen by a head matron and two schoolmistresses, the female wing was but a suffocating regime of industrial tuition and religious studies, a "teacher of psalmody" closing the day in melodic "miserere".[29] Here, Mary Ann would certainly have been reunited with (or even met for the first time) her young brother Duke, who had been living in the male wing since October 1832. At the cost of £12 per annum, the treatment of both Indigenous and non-Indigenous children admitted was relatively the same.[30] However, with overcrowded dormitories causing soiled and sickly conditions, and soulless superintendents with their notoriously cruel punishments, most agree that the Orphan Schools were no safe haven for either.[31]

After approximately one year or more, leaving all in her wake, Mary Ann was conveyed to the newly named Wybalenna Aboriginal establishment on Flinders Island, arriving some time around 1834. By now, she was a young teenager trained to be of service to the patriarchal establishment, but possessed of an intellect eager to challenge it.

Chapter 8

THE BRIDE AND BRIDEGROOM

At Wybalenna Mary Ann was to be reunited with her mother, yet was immediately sent with other girls "to live at the storekeepers house".[1] Having spent the bulk of her young life under the tutorship of the Aylwins, and with brief instruction from government institutions, Mary Ann, even at this early age, was able to be of service to the commandant's household as well as the new school.[2] When aged about 15 years, she became the first Indigenous teacher at the establishment, conducting her own class as well as assisting the Robinson family in the Sunday school – with Tarenootairer an early pupil.[3] Though the period is little documented, this moment would evidently herald the beginning of Mary Ann's matriarchal role in the lives of her own family and of the establishment's melancholy captives.

***

Despite her obvious education and burgeoning determination, Mary Ann's captivity at Wybalenna offered no genuine liberty.[4] Outside the school, life at the establishment was a mere repeat of her subordination in Launceston. Seeking any form of escape at hand, she had begun turning to gibli (drink), caught "red handed" by George

THE BRIDE AND BRIDEGROOM

Augustus Robinson "secreting" liquor in "a tin pot in the passage".[5] Opportunities for autonomy, such as her marriage at age 16 to Walter George Arthur – son of Rolepa, a Ben Lomond "chieftain" and himself a teenager – proved volatile.[6]

It is possible the two had met earlier in 1833, when Walter and Mary Ann were each resident at the Orphan School. So, too, they could have earlier encountered one another on the streets of Launceston, where Walter, then known as Friday, was living a so-called Dickensian childhood, employed as a 12-year-old thief, or pickpocket.[7] In 1835, the pair were reunited again when, at Robinson's behest, the children of the Orphan School were brought back to Wybalenna.[8] Like Mary Ann, denied the liberty of living with his own family, Walter was placed in the household of the catechist.[9]

Although a promising student, Walter was considered "resistant", "inattentive" and "disorderly", so, believing responsibility would curb his behaviour, G. A. Robinson promoted him to Sunday school teacher, eventually granting him his own class.[10] Walter and his contemporary, Thomas Brune, began the *Flinders Island Chronicle*, the first Aboriginal newspaper,[11] where, under the watchful eye of the superintendent, acting as editor, they would preach Christianity and write about "the benefits of the white people's way of life".[12] Yet, despite their high hopes, the propagandist newsletter was inevitably choked by the limited readership of those who were literate.

After a brief and fruitless pairing with a much older woman known as Flora, in December 1837 Walter's involvement with the *Flinders Island Chronicle* ceased upon him being discovered in Mary Ann's bed.[13] George Augustus Robinson was incensed and both were swiftly reprimanded.[14] Jailing Walter as primary punishment, Robinson and his authoritarian behaviour did not, however, go unchecked. "Mary Ann very saucy to me today," he penned. Either by will or by force the juvenile pair were duly engaged.

Mr and Mrs Arthur's Wedding Day

Robinson's journal entry for the pair's colonial wedding on Friday 16 March 1838 paints a unique picture of Indigenous engagement in European customs. No other wedding at the establishment was celebrated quite like this one. Although it renders an image of jovial celebration, which no doubt it would have been to all participating, an undercurrent of colonial propaganda, as opposed to it being an act of any serious cultural or spiritual indoctrination, is evident.[15] The Arthurs' wedding marks the first incident of many where Mary Ann and her marriage would be used as tools for the colony's socio-political agendas.

"This morning early preparation making for the marriage of Mary Ann and Walter G Arthur," begins G. A. Robinson's memoir of the proceedings. By early afternoon, he records, "a large party of the native women … who had their heads decorated with chaplets or garlands of flowers and dressed in their best habiliments, formed in procession". Robinson and the clergyman "walked first", followed by the bride herself, "with a headdress of ribbons and ostrich feathers and a gilt chain round her neck and other garish ornaments", he mocked, followed next by King Alfred (a fellow inmate) and the party of women "two and two". Held in the forest to the rear of the commandant's quarters, the bride and groom were introduced within a circle of oval boards "laid on the ground for tables" with "grass on each side for the natives to recline upon in the ancient custom", with Robinson noting, "the natives were perfectly silent and attentive to what was going on during

THE BRIDE AND BRIDEGROOM

the ceremony". The ceremony was performed "after the manner of the Scottish Church", and on its conclusion all were

> regaled with a good dinner of mutton, vegetables and rice. Four bottles of port wine was given to them to drink the health of the happy couple ... The afternoon was spent in mutual good humor and hilarity. Mr. Clark played the flute and the natives danced first in imitation of the whites ... and then their own country dance. Several of the native boys run in sacks, and the whole was a day of much festivity, enjoyment and pleasure to the natives.[16]

However, though much mutual reverie had evidently been enjoyed, the administration ultimately segregated the dining. "The natives took tea in the forest. The officers dined with me," concluded Robinson.

Immediately after Mary Ann and Walter's nuptials, their induced marriage proved the antithesis of George Augustus Robinson's high expectations. Despite their apparent complementary personalities – young, colonially educated and eager to advance – their marriage could be viewed as merely another colonial prison for each of them.

* * *

The couple were allowed to become residents of the wind-blown Chalky Island.[17] Here the establishment's herd of sheep were stationed, and Walter was trained to be both manager and shepherd.[18] When Robinson visited the relatively isolated pair on 13 April 1838, he commented on the state of the young marriage he had enforced:[19]

> I had very bad accounts of Walter. He ill-used his wife, was very idle so much so that he was said to do little else than lie in bed from morning to night and too idle to make his own bread. His wife complained much of his conduct.[20]

In June, the commandant reported the couple having almost burned down their hut.[21] Though most likely accidental and not attributed to their volatility, this incident does appear to have prompted their move to Prime Seal Island for a further five months, until January 1839.[22]

Regardless of his initial disappointments, George Augustus Robinson had greater plans for the new couple. By now, buoyed by his ego as Tasmania's great "conciliator", he was keen to assist in pacifying the raging Victorian Black Wars[23] and overt in his desire to amalgamate the Indigenous Tasmanians with the Port Phillip communities for what he believed would be their very survival.[24]

Figure 3: John Skinner Prout, 1845, *Shepherd's Hut, Wybellinna* [i.e. Wybalenna].

Chapter 9

"YOUR HUMBLE ABORIGINE CHILD"

Relocating the remaining Indigenous Tasmanian captives to the colonial state of Victoria was not a new concept. "We would remove by degrees," noted the *Courier*, "… both the people now here with Mr. Robinson and those at Flinders' Island to an easily accessible convenient station in New Holland." In mindless, mythical prose the *Courier* continued:

> A peaceful halo would play around such an establishment, and gradually, under the guidance of a prudent, active, superintending hand, its civilising and missionary influence would be felt in the remotest corners.[1]

Despite initially meeting the idea with unease, the colonial administration eventually acquiesced to Robinson's Victorian mission. He was declared "Chief Protector of Aborigines" at Port Phillip on 12 December 1838, and to accompany him his new "family" of "mission Aborigines" were additionally appointed.[2] Despite their aforesaid marital conflicts, as Robinson's premier example of successful colonial appropriation, the Arthurs, especially Walter, were at the forefront of his selection.[3]

Mary Ann's role at Robinson's new post was made crystal clear by Robinson himself. "[A]s female servants cannot be procured she may be useful," he wrote to his wife.[4] As per his instructions, she left

Flinders Island for Port Phillip a few months after her husband, on 30 March 1839,[5] aboard the cutter *Vansittart* as one of four servants with the "Lady of G. A. Robinson Esqr, Chief Protector, and family … and an aboriginal woman and child", arriving on 3 April.[6]

There are no specific records regarding Mary Ann's daily life in Port Phillip outside those showing her developing a deep friendship with Kalloongoo, alias Charlotte, a 28-year-old New Holland woman whom Mary Ann had worked with under the Robinsons.[7] Kalloongoo had arrived at the Wybalenna establishment in mid-1837, and had up until then been interchangeably known as both Windeerer and Sarah. Akin to Mary Ann's mother, she had been "forcibly taken from her country" by the sealers James Allen and Bill Johnson,[8] spending many years on Kangaroo Island, off the coast of South Australia, before being transported to the establishment, where Robinson renamed her Charlotte. With her young son Johnny Franklin in tow, Kalloongoo had been safely returned to her homelands by Robinson's "mission".[9]

As provisions were initially scarce, Mary Ann and her husband were allowed to build themselves "a grass hut to live in",[10] yet domestic set-ups were short-lived.[11] It would quickly become apparent that the Indigenous Tasmanians who had accompanied Robinson were of little use to him, and he appeared desperate to be rid of them.[12] After a failed attempt to have them returned to Wybalenna, he requested that the colonial secretary aid in "disposing" of the "Van Diemen's Land Aborigines" across Port Phillip,[13] a move surely instigating the elder Indigenous Tasmanians to rampage across Victoria's vast and violent interior.[14]

Some of them were successfully employed and "several were loaned out to work for Robinson's sons" as well as other settlers.[15] With his novice experience shepherding on Chalky Island, Walter George Arthur, and a 25-year-old man named Maulboyheenner (alias Small

Boy, Timmy and Robert), accompanied Alfred Langhorne, droving 800 head of cattle to South Australia.[16]

In 1840, an Aboriginal "agricultural" establishment was set up by Robinson and his assistant protector, William Thomas, at "Narre Narre Warren". Under the instruction of Mrs Robinson, vain attempts at schooling were instigated for the adults and children he was hired to procure.[17] Mary Ann's role as the first Indigenous colonial teacher at Wybalenna, and under the direct employ of Mrs Robinson, meant she would have been instrumental in this particular endeavour, aiding communication with Robinson's new "captives", which would have dominated her time on the mainland.[18]

A Conflicting Return, 1842–1847

After three years in Port Phillip, Mary Ann, now around 21 years of age, was to reluctantly return with her husband to Wybalenna.[19] On 23 July 1842, laden with a plethora of gifts from Robinson to be handed out among the "Flinders natives", Walter, Mary Ann and Davey Bruny prepared for a journey back to their former island captivity.[20] Arriving at the wharf only to disconcertingly find that their ship had sailed earlier that afternoon, the trio were temporarily stranded, with little alternative but to make camp on an icy mid-winter beach at Williamstown, prematurely returning to the Robinson household on the following day.[21] Finally, on 30 August, the group officially left Port Phillip for the downhearted journey back to Flinders Island. Attended by Robert Clark, a brief interlude with the governor awaited them on their homecoming:

> [O]n the afternoon of yesterday the four aborigines lately arrived on their way from Port Phillip to Flinders Island … had the honour of waiting upon Lady Franklin, to whom they were introduced by

> Dr. Officer. Her ladyship conversed with them for upwards of an hour, when she was joined by his Excellency the Lieut. Governor. Both Sir John and Lady Franklin appeared much pleased with the natives, particularly with Walter George Arthur, chief of the Ben Lomond tribe, and his lubra (wife), Mrs. Arthur.[22]

George Augustus Robinson's journal of the period mentions no due cause for their return; however, their return to Wybalenna did not signal a relapse to their previous subordination.[23] By now Henry Jeanneret had been appointed commandant of the Wybalenna establishment and his tenure was evidently fraught with conflict from the onset. How much of this was made known to both the Robinsons and the Arthurs is uncertain, yet a letter from George Washington Walker to Jeanneret's wife, Harriet, does give direct insight.

Dated 16 September 1842, Walker's letter sheds light on the Arthurs' desire not to be sent back at all, stating, "a feeling of aversion towards residing again on Flinders Island has been induced", with the Arthurs (according to Robinson) expressing a "wish to return to Launceston".[24] Yet Walker's letter was mostly a word of caution to the Jeannerets, a direct warning, in fact, of the Arthurs' impending return:

> I will now briefly advent to the subject which forms the more immediate occasion of my writing. There is a vessel in the harbor with a number of Aborigines on board, destined for Flinders Island. They have been for some time resident at Port Phillip; and I find that they have imbibed, from what sources I know not, impressions unfavourable as regards the present system of treatment of the Natives on Flinders. It may be wholly without just cause: but if their minds have become in any way prejudiced, it is better that you, and especially that the Doctor, should be aware of it; so as to avoid in every allowable way, administering food to such prejudice; which he might unwittingly do ... The Aborigines have received the impression, that the present mode of treatment

"YOUR HUMBLE ABORIGINE CHILD"

on Flinders Island is rigid and severe, and that, especially in regard to allowance of food, a considerable abridgment has taken place.[25]

To the administrator's dismay, the trip to Port Phillip had inspired, in the youth especially, a newly found desire for choice, to "assert their rights" in both reclaiming their position as the island's original inhabitants and holding the colony to its still-empty promises.

Immediately, they became a vocal opposition to the authoritarian governors.[26] From this moment onward, through their united literacy, Mary Ann and Walter became the voices of their captive people and, in doing so, established their own voices in Indigenous Tasmanian history.

Henry Jeanneret's conduct disregarded George Washington Walker's further advice: "I need hardly remind the Doctor," he wrote, "of the absolute necessity that exists, in all dealings with the Aborigines, of winning their confidence and good-will by kindness." Jeanneret's regime of child removal, endless work for no more than rations, and solitary imprisonment as punishment was abhorred by the captives, who could no longer suppress their anger.[27] News of his conduct had evidently reached the Arthurs on their return to Wybalenna, and by December 1843 their registered concerns were ratified when Jeanneret was dismissed and replaced with Dr Joseph Milligan.

For Mary Ann there was a deeper involvement than mere rations and general humility. The incidents involving Dr Henry Jeanneret had at their core gross abuses of the establishment's Indigenous youths, yet Jeanneret himself was not the protagonist. There were growing reports of the Clarks' brutal treatment of the children in their care, and the charges against them were led by Mary Ann's little sister, Fanny Cochrane. On 5 August 1846, Henry Jeanneret wrote directly to the colonial secretary:

> Sir, I have the honour to acquaint you, for the information of the lieut.-governor, that in consequence of complaints from all the female aboriginal children of cruel treatment by the catechist, and having separately inquired of each, and finding they do not materially vary in their statements, which are corroborated by concurring circumstances, and Mary Ann Arthur also declaring that she had ineffectually applied to Mr. Milligan on the subject, I have considered it my duty to commit Fanny Cochran [sic] (about fourteen) to the care of her sister Mary Ann Arthur ...[28]

Fanny swore of Mr and Mrs Clark's punishments, such as "flogging on the table naked, chaining [and] gagging". Her brother Adam iterated, "I told Dr. Jeanneret Mr. Clark had beaten me. The mark on my face was made by a stick. Mr. Clark struck me. Mr. Clark put me into Fanny Cochran's box. I was also flogged across the table. I had opened the gate and let the cow out."[29]

As well as removing them to government institutions, Jeanneret, at Mary Ann's request, placed some of the children into her personal care; however, the promise of "remuneration" for her services, if "she and her husband Walter Arthur conducted themselves well, cooked and washed for the children, and kept them tidy and orderly", was disobligingly denied.[30]

Having yet again returned to her role of chambermaid, this time to the Clarks' household, Mary Ann was privy to the daily lives of these children.[31] According to Jeanneret, she initially expressed great concern about their welfare, especially that of her sister, and is purported to have stated:

> I requested Mr. Milligan to let me have my sister to live with me, as she was all covered with sores. I asked Mrs. Jeanneret:

"*Mamma*, why does not *Papa* take Adam [her half-brother] away from Mr. Clark?"

They have almost killed one of my children.[32]

Despite Mary Ann's obvious concerns, she appeared to backtrack and denied both her own and her sister's claims, eventually siding with the catechist. So, too, after an independent investigation by Lieutenant Matthew Curling Friend, the Clarks themselves were eventually reprieved.

The reasons for the conflicting statements allegedly made by Mary Ann remain unclear; however, documented conversations in later years reveal her deep paternal relationship with the catechist Robert Clark. Also, Clark and Jeanneret had evidently much to defend themselves against and their statements concerning Mary Ann's claims, especially those made by Jeanneret, must be viewed with some scepticism. To this is added the precarious position of Mary Ann and her family, being at the very epicentre of actions and accusations against the administration, and having the most to lose if the jury did not swing in their favour.

* * *

A primary example of the new era of Indigenous self-empowerment at Wybalenna is evident in the following petition against Henry Jeanneret's proposed return in 1846. Led by the Arthurs, the petition was addressed to Queen Victoria, the figurehead of their misery, and presented to "Queen Victoria's Secretary of State for the Colonies".[33]

The petition was written in the belief that the Indigenous captives actually had the power to seek change in their relatively impuissant lives:[34]

Petition to
Her Majesty Queen Victoria, 17 February 1846

The humble petition of the free Aborigines Inhabitants of V.D.L. now living upon Flinders Island, in Bass's Straits &c &c &c.

Most humbly showeth,

That we Your Majesty's Petitioners are your free Children that we were not taken Prisoners but freely gave up our Country to Colonel Arthur then the Govr. after defending ourselves.

Your Petitioners humbly state to Y[our] M[ajesty] that Mr. Robinson made for us & with Col. Arthur an agreement which we have not lost from our minds since & we have made our part of it good.

Your Petitioners humbly tell Y.M. that when we left our own place we plenty of People, we are now but a little one.

Your Petitioners state they are a long time at Flinders Island & had that plenty of Supd'ts & were always a quiet & free People & not put into goal [sic].

Your Majesty's Petitioners pray that you will not allow Dr. Jeanneret to come again among us as our Supdt. As we hear he is to be sent another time for when Dr Jeanneret was with us many Moons he used to carry Pistols in his pockets & threaten'd very often to shoot us & make us run away in a fright. Dr. Jeanneret kept plenty of Pigs in our Village which used to run into our houses & eat up our bread from the fires & take away our flour bags in their mouths also to break into our Gardens & destroy our Potatoes & Cabbages.

Our houses were let fall down & they were never cleaned but were covered with vermin & not white-washed. We were often without Clothes except a very little one & Dr. Jeanneret did not care to mind us when we were sick until we were very bad. Eleven of us died when he was here. He put many of us into Jail for talking him because we would not be his slaves. He kept from us our Rations when he pleased & sometimes gave us Bad Rations of Tea & Tobacco. He shot some of our dogs before our eyes & sent all the other dogs of ours to an Island & when we told him that they would starve he told us that they might eat each other. He put arm into our hands & made us to assist his prisoners to go to fight the Soldiers we did not want to fight the Soldiers but he made us go to fight. We never were taught to read or write or to sing to god by the doctor. He taught us little upon the Sundays & his Prisoner Servant also taught us & his Prisoner Servant also took us plenty of times to Jail by his orders.

The Lord Bishop seen us in this bad way & we told H[is] L[ordship] plenty how Dr. Jeanneret used us.

We humbly pray Your Majesty the Queen will hear our prayer and not let Dr Jeanneret any more to come to Flinders Island. And We Y.M's servants & Children will ever pray as in duty bound &c &c &c.

Sgd. Walter G. Arthur, Chief of the Ben Lomond Tribes King Alexander, John Allan, Augustus, Davey Bruney, King Tippoo [sic], Neptune, Washington.[35]

Despite alleged manipulation by European hands, the petition's accusations ring through and reflect the dire situation and brutal treatment the Indigenous Tasmanians were utterly entrapped in. Jeanneret's dictatorship would prove their fiercest "Post-Black War" battle, and one believed to have the potential to be their greatest success.[36] It is unclear just how far the petition journeyed or whether it ever reached Queen Victoria herself. Despite being "taken seriously in the Colonial Office", even regarded as no "finer case for the House of Commons", the concerns of the petition were subsequently ignored.[37] Jeanneret was reassigned by the British Government to his post as surgeon, commandant and justice of the peace until the settlement's close a year later, in 1847.[38]

Jeanneret was deeply incensed at this episode and the besmirching of his name.[39] In his own words, there was not "real cause of complaint against me" and he claimed that it was instigated by both Milligan and Clark.[40] For 17 days Walter was imprisoned in retaliation by the superintendent;[41] and many of the Indigenous signatories retracted their claims once the petition became known, on the intimidating behest of its newly reappointed accused.[42] Each, with the exception of Walter, claimed little involvement in the writing of the petition and cited coercion by Clark, Milligan and the Arthurs.[43] Even non-signatories were interrogated by Jeanneret, and persuaded to sign declarations of coercion.[44] However, Jeanneret's collected statements are themselves a coerced testimony, and thus cannot be regarded as fact. Mary Ann, whose husband was imprisoned, surely had little option but to recant her claims. For example, "I take my husband's rations," she conceded. "… My tobacco was never stopped but once; that was for refusing to give up a dog. It was my mother's dog …"[45]

Reflective of this time, John Skinner Prout's watercolours of Wybalenna observe an unnerving silence, a lonely, windswept and barren place void of activity. His rough graphite portrait of Mary Ann, titled *Mary Ann, Kings Island*, shows her barefoot, dressed in a snug knitted shoulder shawl and a shell necklace, with her tight ringlets framing her youthful but melancholy expression – a potent depiction of joyless endurance.[46]

"We do not like to be his slaves …"

The captives' petition to Queen Victoria contains one missing link.[47] From the very words of her husband in supporting letters of protest to

"YOUR HUMBLE ABORIGINE CHILD"

the governor-general, we see clearly Mary Ann's direct involvement in the writing of this famed petition, yet her name is omitted from the initial signatories.[48] This deliberate omission is further evidenced when Walter wrote to the colonial secretary soon afterward, affirming:

> I did nothing to make Doctor Jeanneret put me into Jail but because I was one of the people who signed the Letter ... and because my wife put her name down in it both Doctor Jeanneret and Mrs Jeanneret Called her a Villain ... All I now request of his Excellency is that he will have full Justice done to me the same as he would have done to a white man.[49]

So, too, her involvement in the petitions is evinced by Mary Ann herself. Responding to Jeanneret's return and his wrath, from her island cottage she wrote her own follow-up to the colonial secretary in direct protest. Fighting the administration with its own weapon of choice, this time in her own name, she set down:

Van Diemen's Land, 10th June 1846

> I thank my Father the Govr that he has told us black people that we might write him & tell him if we had any complaint to make about ourselves. I want now to tell the Govr that Dr. Jeanneret wants to make out my husband & myself very bad wicked people & talks plenty about putting us into jail & that he will hang us for helping to write the petition to the Queen from our country people. I send the Gov. two papers one from Dr. Milligan & one from Mr. Robinson of Port Philip [sic] to tell the Govr that they know us a long time & had nothing to say bad of us but Dr. Jeanneret does not like us for we do not like to be his slaves nor whish our poor Country to be treated badly or made slaves of. I hope the Govr will not let Dr. Jeanneret put us into Jail as he likes for nothing at all as he used [sic] he says he will do it & frightens us much with his big talk about our writing to the Queen he calls us all

liars but we told him & the Coxswain who Dr. Jeanneret made ask us that it was all true what we write about him. I remain, Sir, Your humble Aborigine Child, Mary Ann Arthur.[50]

As the only letter of protest written by an Indigenous woman at Wybalenna, the significance of Mary Ann's letter cannot be stressed enough, yet there is more to survey. With so much at stake, the fear in her words is palpable, yet so is her desperate desire for autonomy. Her "humble" position is a deliberate bid to win favour, and one that could be applied to paternal relationships throughout her life, referring to all men in authoritarian positions as father, and even here the colonial secretary. Her politics centre on references to captive slavery and the accountability of the colonial administration, holding them to their promises of concern for both their welfare and that of her country, even furnishing character references and supporting documentation to validate her claims.[51]

So, too, her character as matriarch among the Indigenous captives became solidified from this period onward. No longer willing to be a mere "femme de chambre" to the administrators' households, she was attempting to seek personal independence from paternalistic governance. Her sense of empowerment at this time even saw her attempting to reclaim money bequeathed to her by her deceased father in the early days of the establishment, which was clearly never received: "poor Walter & Mary Ann are making inquiry for it now as it came to her by rights," noted Clark.[52]

* * *

"YOUR HUMBLE ABORIGINE CHILD"

After extensive inquiry and much protest from all sides, by 1847 Jeanneret was yet again dismissed and Dr Joseph Milligan reinstated with the charge of relocating the remaining captives to the mainland.

Regardless of their collective petition's success, or lack thereof, the Arthurs' battle for their captive contemporaries, and for their own liberties, would continue with the move to the new Oyster Cove establishment.

Chapter 10

HER MAJESTY, THE QUEEN

Once at the Oyster Cove establishment, Walter was hired to manage the boats and attend to the mail-bags, for which he received one shilling a day.[1] The Arthurs had also been granted a small acreage on which to accommodate themselves and their in-laws and run a dairy farm for the establishment.[2] They were granted one more additional hectare of land to grow produce for self-sufficiency – the aim of lessening expenses being at the foreground of administrative decisions at the new settlement.

With enough land to cultivate, now totalling 15 (or possibly 20) acres in all, the couple would be provided with a more superficially independent lifestyle than was afforded their contemporaries at the adjoining station.[3] However, none of this came without obstacles. The dubious characters who inhabited the surrounding forests were a constant hurdle to their progress, attempting to claim the land given to Walter for themselves or issuing petty complaints.[4] The prospect of an "Aborigine" leasing property as well as being in charge of "white men" caused at least one abject protest. "[T]he two white men that I charge with assisting the natives [in allegedly stealing shingles, two bullocks and a cart] are in the employ of Walter George Arthur, aborigine," spat an incensed neighbour.[5]

"The 'bad white fellows' often came up in their talk," recalled James Bonwick. "[They] haunted them still, stealing their clothes, and making them drunk … No fence enclosed their ground, and the wide Bush was theirs for wanderings."[6]

The high mortality rate that had so affected their residency at Wybalenna was to devastate them at Oyster Cove also. According to Milligan, of the 46 captives who were initially sent to the establishment, at least 10 were dead within the first year.[7]

* * *

It is believed that Mary Ann and Walter did not produce children of their own, although this is not conclusive. It should be noted her supposed infertility was a possible side effect of congenital syphilis, contracted from her mother during pregnancy, when, prior to the Aboriginal establishments, treatment was not available.[8] Regardless, family life in their small but liveable hut would prove a little cramped. In the later years of Wybalenna, Mary Ann had become mother not only to her youngest sister, Fanny Cochrane, and intermittent "orphans" such as William Lanne, but also to a mysterious boy named Little George, maintaining this relationship at the Oyster Cove establishment. To quote Colonial Secretary J. E. Bicheno:

> … the youngest boy George should be left another year or so upon the Aborigines' Establishment under the care of Mary Ann a half caste woman who is much attached and very attentive to the child … the fifth girl "Fanny Cochrane" almost a woman might remain with her half-sister "Mary Anne" – indeed I can scarcely say how otherwise she could be satisfactorily disposed of.[9]

Due to poor administration during Joseph Milligan's tenures at both Wybalenna and Oyster Cove, there are no known records as to the parentage or birth date of Little George. There is substantial cause to presume that George is an additional child born to Mary Ann's mother, Tarenootairer (who was now living with the Arthurs), and her husband Nicermenic, at Wybalenna around 1845. George vanishes from the Oyster Cove records around 1851, either presumed dead or, as the above recommendation notes, removed from the establishment and into the unknown. As matriarch to the establishment's children, Mary Ann had an especially deep maternal bond with her siblings, even referring to them as her own children.[10] For Mary Ann and Walter, whether as biological or surrogate parents, after the myriad Georges involved in the Arthurs' lives – from Mary Ann's own father to their so-called conciliator – Little George evidently meant a great deal to the pair and had been named after prominent colonial progenitors, the closest to their own child the pair would know.[11]

* * *

Their first year at Oyster Cove would see a drastic social change in their lives. The remarkable photographs, artworks and reminiscences relating to the pair belie sentiment of a sweet married life in Victorian times, albeit manufactured for colonial consumption. As early as 1847, Mary Ann and her husband were not just at the foreground of sociopolitical activity but also in the front row as visual representatives of the last "remnants" of the island's original peoples.

The colony, desirous of images of the depleted Indigenous captives, were now using the new science of the photographic lens. The first known photograph of Indigenous Tasmanians ever taken, a daguerreotype attributed to Thomas Browne (c. 1847–1848), showcases a staged studio portrait of the three youthful critics of the establishments.[12] The photograph depicts Walter George Arthur, standing regally replete with wallaby pelt and spear; Mary Ann subordinately positioned gazing up at her husband, and so too clothed in wallaby pelt and seed necklace; and a young Davy Brune, standing behind the pair with neatly shaved beard, a slightly blurred spectre gazing down on them. It is unknown whether Browne was compelled or commissioned to capture them in presumed "traditional" pose, as the classic "noble savage". One can only imagine the feelings shared between Mary Ann, Walter and Davey – three of the younger generation moulded since childhood into becoming propaganda for the colony's Europeanisation of its new subjects – to now be dressed, or undressed, in representation of the very culture the colony was determined to wipe out.[13] Though it drew obvious amusement, wrote Denison:

> The only thing that moved these men [a party of six Indigenous men] to laughter, was our showing them some daguerreotype likenesses of those of their countrymen who were up here at Christmas. None of those who came yesterday were the same, but they recognised the individual likenesses very cleverly, and were much amused with them.[14]

The Governor's Christmas Party

During the Christmas period of 1847, Sir William Denison, the colony's then appointed governor-general, was harangued into accommodating a small group of the Oyster Cove captives during his annual Christmas celebrations for the upper echelon of Van Diemen's Land society. The group consisted almost entirely of Mary Ann's own family, with the distinct exception of Fanny Cochrane. To quote Denison:

> There were four men; their names, Walter (who calls himself a chief, but is not as great, evidently, in the eyes of his companions as in his own), Eugene, Nomy, and Neptune; three boys, Billy,

Adam, and Moriarty (the last, I imagine, named after Captain Moriarty, the port officer). Of the women, the most remarkable character was Marianne, the chieftainess, Walter's wife: an immense, stout, masculine-looking creature, apparently a person of far more influence than her husband. I could not catch all the women's names: there was one called 'old Sarah', Marianne's mother; two called Martha and Nanny, whom I did not learn to distinguish from one another, and two girls called Methinna and Hannah.[15]

This event, however, was not entirely innocent. The initial visit of the captives to Hobart was for the purpose of handing over some of their children to the Orphan School, or coercing them to do so. Having been driven around Hobart Town in cabs, "in order to let people see how perfectly inoffensive they are", the captives were ushered to the governor-general's home in New Norfolk.[16]

To dine, their guests were kept in a separate tent from the whites until cordial dining was over and festivities such as sports, smoking and curious banter could officially commence. William Denison's own journal gives rich detail of the sheer spectacle that this unique event became:

> December 27, 1847. – We had the most amusing afternoon with our black guests: we had fixed their dinner hour for two o'clock, in order to give us time to return from church before their arrival ... the white ones ... were well advanced in their meal before it was announced that the blacks were coming. In they came, fourteen of them, packed in two carriages, sitting on one another's knees, or squatted at the bottom of the vehicles, evidently not caring how, in the intense delight and novelty of their visits. W_____ and I received them at the hall-door, shook hands with them, and walked before them to their tent, where we very soon got them all seated. Spreadborough and Parkinson

carved for them, and we all (the children included) helped to wait on them. It was comical to see their evident effort to remember what had been, before their arrival, duly impressed upon them, as I afterwards heard, viz.: that it was not considered good manners to eat with their fingers; but they handled their knives and forks very cleverly, on the whole; and their appetites certainly seem almost boundless. After they had devoured immense quantities of beef and plum pudding, we gave them pipes and tobacco, for which both men and women have a great relish; but some of them appeared to think that half the virtue consisted in the length of the pipe, anxiously picking out the longest of those presented to their choice, and contemptuously rejecting the shorter ones. Meantime the children, who did not smoke, were regaled with abundance of fruit and lolly-pops. While this was going on, W____ and I made a short digression to the labourers' tent, to enable W____ to drink "a merry Christmas and happy New Year" to them all, a toast which was received with great applause; but we did not stay there long, for the black tent was evidently the great attraction, and thither went all the white visitors, when their own meal was concluded, to watch the goings on. Hither, too, came half New Norfolk, or more than half, I should think. We asked all our own acquaintances to come down and look at our festivities; and the rest of the inhabitants of the township had asked themselves, it seems, and got in somehow or other in the bustle, the great object with all being to see the blacks, whose coming had created a great sensation. However, all were quiet and orderly: no one was rude to the blacks, and they, I think, were rather gratified than otherwise at being the objects of so much attention. When they had smoked and eaten fruit for some time, we began distributing our presents amongst them; shawls, coloured handkerchiefs, and bead necklaces to the women and girls, cloth caps and coloured worsted comforters to the men and boys. Most of these articles of finery were instantly put on over their other clothes; and then the sport began. A rope, hung between two trees, served for a swing, which amused them much for a little while; but the great delight was when we gave them a ball, and set them to play at rounders, a game which they are accustomed to play, and in which they certainly excel. Men, women, and children, all played together, and all equally well; and I scarcely knew which to admire most, their skill in aiming the ball, or the dexterous and extraordinary twists of their bodies and limbs, by which they avoided it, when aimed at them. Then, their unwearied energy, and unfailing and intense enjoyment of the game, their extraordinary shrieks of delight, and their perfect good humour over it all, made it a really pleasant as well as amusing scene; and the invited and uninvited white population of New Norfolk formed a large and admiring circle round them, and seemed never tired of watching them. But you will want to know something of the names, appearances, &c. of our guests … They spoke a very comical sort of broken English: one very favourite expression of theirs is "gammon", a word whose meaning they are quite aware of; and they have not the least hesitation in applying it to anything you tell them, which seems to them at all surprising, or difficult to believe. They were a little inclined to think of was "gammon" when they were told that W____ was the Governor, whom they had come to see, because, as they remarked, he had not got a cocked hat on; and one or two other facts which we told them (real facts, for we had no intention of taking them in), were unhesitatingly pronounced by them to be "gammon". The word "fellow" is also very common, and applied to both sexes indiscriminately; thus, in the course of the evening, old Sarah gave it as her opinion that Mrs. S____ was "a fine fellow"; and when I asked Marianne the age of one of the girls, she at first shook her head, intimating that she did not know, then assured me in general terms, that the girl was "old fellow", and afterwards answered my question through the medium of Dr. M____ [Milligan] (who has for some time had the care of these blacks, and who was with them), by naming to him certain events which had happened about the time of the birth of this girl, from which he deduced for me that the said "old fellow" must be about thirteen or fourteen years old. Our guests departed about six o'clock, in the same order in which they had come. We shook hands all round, and promised to pay them a visit some day at Oyster Cove, and they drove off, having, I really believe, thoroughly enjoyed themselves.[17]

To round off this veritable circus, they were invited to attend the theatre and yet again made the headlines. "[O]n Monday evening these natives were also treated to the play, where they seemed much amused," relayed the *Hobarton Guardian*.[18]

It would appear that, by now, Mary Ann and family were becoming accustomed to their morbid celebrity, yet the novelty soon wore thin. The governor-general did indeed pay a visit to Oyster Cove Station but, by January 1849, the bitter cold and ever-pervasive sickness was leeching their strength. "They were delighted to see me," he wrote, "but complained a good deal of cold, which was surprising, as I found them, in the middle of summer, sitting over large fires; the rooms very close, and themselves wrapped up in the thickest blanket wrappers you can imagine."[19]

Denison's lamentable trip was in stark contrast to Robert Clark's initial musings on the establishment. As Clark corresponded with Bonwick:

> They are now comfortable; have a full supply of provisions; are able to till their gardens, sew [sic] peas, beans, and potatoes; anxious to earn money, of which they know to a certain extent the value. They are thankful to the Lieutenant-Governor and the Colonial Secretary for removing them from Flinders Island, and to Dr. Milligan for all the trouble he has taken … Their houses are comfortable and clean. They are as contented as possible.[20]

If Clark's description is to be believed, their comfort was evidently a short affair. Of the 38 individuals resident in 1848, by April 1851 only 30 were listed.[21] In that month, George Augustus Robinson paid his one and only visit to the Oyster Cove establishment, making notes and compiling a census of the remaining population he had barely met (the list given him by the storekeeper). Over the course of a few days, the few captives he spoke with, including Mary Ann and Walter, expressed a desire to return to Wybalenna, describing their living quarters as "damp" and "unhealthy", the Antarctic winds like a "funnel". He made additional notes emphasising their poor health and labelling Walter, Mary Ann and Jack Allen as "fat". He was given a shell necklace by Mary Ann and Fanny (alias Plonoopinner), the manufacture of which was both a new cottage industry as well as a parting tradition.[22] The official closing scene to Robinson's exploits with the Indigenous captives – to whom he would become forever, inextricably tied – sees him farewelled aboard a whaleboat by the Arthurs, Frederick, Flora and "child".[23]

"… of sterling character …"

By now the captives at Oyster Cove were charitable party guests, described in newspaper reports as "the last of a race, fast hastening from the face of a land once their own, [who] must not be forgotten. To pass them bye [sic] in the general festivities, would be a disgrace to the age, and to the colony especially."[24] Mary Ann's role as "matron" was becoming well recognised and of much admiration. She was of "sterling character", recalled Joseph Russell to the *Mercury*.[25] Denison's Christmas party, and the ensuing daguerreotype, were clear examples of Mary Ann's image, as well as her marriage, becoming fodder for public propaganda.

Figure 4: Francis Russell Nixon, Bishop of Tasmania, Oyster Cove, c. 1858, *Walter George Arthur and Mary Ann Arthur.*

MY PEOPLE'S SONGS

Parties of the curious and "pleasure seekers" were now being ferried past the establishment, sometimes allowed to dock and pay visit to the "savages". A significant example of this occurred on 6 December 1853. This day marked a visit to Oyster Cove from an excitable party of Quakers.[26] Their visit was relayed in detail in the *Colonial Times*:

Pleasure Trip to Oyster Cove and the Channel. – The Aborigines

The second pleasure trip by the steamer *Culloden* took place on Saturday afternoon. The day was beautifully fine, and the number of pleasure seekers unusually large: so much so, that many were unable to obtain passage … After proceeding along the channel a few miles, a most magnificent view of mountain scenery was obtained. We stopped a short time to allow a party of gentlemen an opportunity to visit the aborigines settlement in Oyster Cove. Some dozen got into the boat, and as tide was very low, a difficulty occurred in landing. This it was proposed to obviate by the rowers carrying the passengers ashore. The first gentleman was rather unfortunate, his bearer being a little man, while he was tall and weighty. The consequence was that the bearer stuck fast in the mud, retaining hold of his charge, who was almost precipitated into the water, but managed to reach the landing place by only going knee deep. Some ten minutes walking brought us to the settlement, a quadrangle, with a range of wooden buildings on three sides. The first person we saw was "Mary Ann," the Queen, a fine, portly, smiling lady about thirty years of age. The King stood close by. He is stoutly built, and about five feet and a half high. Only four men were visible. We saw some half dozen ladies, but with the exception of Her Majesty they had all passed their prime. Some youngsters we caught taking a survey of us through a partly opened door, but when our eyes were turned that way they beat a retreat.[27] The men were all neatly dressed. The women wore a sort of sack made from blue woollen [sic]. Only one wore a printed dress. One of them wore a very neat sort of woollen dress, fastened round her waist by a bright leather strap. Most of them had for their head-dress a tall conical woollen red cap. One lady had a silk handkerchief bound round her head inside of which, above her left ear, was stuck the well-worn pipe ready in case of need. They asked for tobacco – cigars they would not smoke – and complained of their own tobacco being bad. Mary Ann, it appears can read with fluency, and asked for books. She wanted "something lively". She had read "Uncle Tom's Cabin" and pronounced it "very much true". Books were promised her. Our stay was cut short by hearing the "bell pealing" and after many bows and shaking of hands with the ladies we finally took ourselves off accompanied by His Majesty ...

Published in 1852, *Uncle Tom's Cabin; or, Life Among the Lowly*, was one of the most popular and influential novels of the era. Still highly controversial, it is considered to be among the first of the "protest literature" and anti-slavery works.[28] The author, Harriet Beecher Stowe, born into a highly religious family and herself the wife of a theologian, set her novel in America's Deep South, concerning herself with the plight of three main slave characters and their respective fates. Despite being pro-abolition, she is accused of being still very much pro-colonisation, treating her black characters as "childlike" and in need of strong European leadership.[29] Through the character of Uncle Tom, Stowe implies that a form of saintly martyrdom can be achieved through their suffering; through Eliza, who escapes her slavery to Canada, Stowe emphasises salvation through the assistance of Christian kindness (of which the Quakers play their premier role). Stowe's novel influenced the image of Quakers as activists and abolitionists as well as propagating many black stereotypes of the following century.

The Quakers' reference to "Mary Ann, the Queen", along with exaggerated personifications of Her Majesty and His Majesty, recall the black caricatures within *Uncle Tom's Cabin*, and harken back to George Augustus Robinson's renaming of the captives at Wybalenna. Stowe's novel falls on racial stereotypes to convey her slave characters, such as Topsy the "pickaninny", Uncle Tom as the pious and passive slave, and the rotund and demure "Mammy".[30] These very stereotypes are wholly evident in the Quakers' recollections of their encounters at Oyster Cove and specifically of Mary Ann and Walter, characterisations that would stick to their respective profiles in the ensuing decades, particularly in the "recollections" of James Bonwick.[31]

The Quakers' article does, however, offer a unique example of the "guestbook" version of Oyster Cove. If the encounter is accepted as authentic, this information is significant in strengthening Mary Ann's identification with the politics around slavery and the anti-slavery movements imbued in *Uncle Tom's Cabin*, as well as the fracturing of black families in colonial nations (of which she knew all too well),[32] and it shows an express desire to comprehend, endure and overcome her own captivity through literacy.

Chapter 11

UNCLE WALTER'S HUT

As previously explored during their time on Flinders Island, Mary Ann and Walter's great influence and gusto in challenging authority at Wybalenna, although appearing defeated by the second half of the century, gained a minor second wind at Oyster Cove Station.[1] Walter continued to appease the colony with displays of his European Christian "civilities", yet also grated on them with his desire for independence for both himself and those who remained of his fellow captives.[2]

One cannot deny the presence of Christianity enforced upon the Indigenous captives at both establishments, with regular religious services provided by the resident administrators. The Oyster Cove Visitors Book (1855–1869) provides prolific entries from the official chaplains, whose mission was to provide the "natives" with "Divine Service".[3] The clergymen would boast of "well attendance" by the captives; however, according to one administrator's recollection, the neighbouring gentleman "was unpopular; and whenever his horse was seen on the hill, it was a signal for general dispersion".[4]

Walter would allegedly boast of his devotion to the Christian doctrine, claiming to "read a chapter of the Bible to his family every night", yet no certainty can be given to this statement.[5] The couple's alleged belief in Christian teaching becomes overshadowed by their remarkable attempts at using Christianity to both please their colonisers and expose their hypocrisy.[6]

Contemporary historians have emphasised that the appropriation of Christianity, especially by the youth, served a greater purpose than mere spiritual salvation.[7] The persistent presence of Christianity in the remnants of the Arthurs' written works began at Wybalenna. At the beginning of 1846, the Arthurs formed The Flinders Aborigine Bible Society, with the official subtitle of Auxiliary to the British and Foreign Bible Society in London. Although this was surely pleasing to the administration, the Arthurs did not want their society known to the superintendent, with whom they were "not friends", instead appealing by letter directly to the governor himself. Here they express a desire for their society to be officially authorised by both the governor and the Hobart Town Bible Society, and hint at a deeper purpose than religious recognition. Drafted by Robert Clark and addressed to the prominent Quaker George Washington Walker, Mary Ann and Walter dictated their request for both official acknowledgement of their group and its patronage by the lieutenant governor, appealing for books and "to make [an] application in their name". As well, Clark noted the impending conflict about to erupt at the establishment and his desire to avoid it (although he would become wholly embedded in it), concluding this request on behalf of the Arthurs with a reaffirmation of their complaints against Jeanneret: "I feel for my poor people," he writes. "They are treated as slaves."

For the Arthurs, understanding Christian doctrine to be at the very foundation of contemporary western European civilisation and law may well have been a tool for understanding the Europeans' swift success at subjugating the Indigenous Tasmanians. Christianity became a distinct socio-political tool that gave Walter and Mary Ann the "confidence" to deal with the administration and aid their own needs.[8] One cannot overtly state the couple were genuine spiritual appropriators of Christian doctrine, but they were utilisers of its deeply embedded social, cultural and political influence. "I have this day visited the [Oyster Cove] Station and find all well. All the Aborigines were out hunting except Mary Ann with whom I had a Spiritual conversation," jotted the resident chaplain in 1856. This entry denoted a lust for knowledge, or at least curiosity, on Mary Ann's behalf in matters of spirituality.

To colonial Christians, such as James Bonwick and George Augustus Robinson, the appropriation of Christianity represented proof of successful cultural colonisation and divine salvation, yet the Arthurs were clearly "clever political strategists", deliberately "flattering" the pious colonial authoritarians in an attempt to advance their unprosperous lives.[9]

From a direct conversation with Mary Ann in 1859, James Bonwick solemnly quotes her as saying: "We had souls at Flinders ... but we have none here ... we are thrown upon the scum of society. They have brought us among the offscouring of the earth ... Nobody cares for us."[10] As the administration rapidly retired or even passed away, replaced by contracted and increasingly disinterested overseers, so, too, Walter lamented, "[W]e are now few in number to have a strange man attend to us in our old age. I beg, to your Excellency, to remain your most obedient servant."[11]

Mary Ann walked with Bonwick in the squalid grounds of the establishment, exposing to his horror the decrepit state in which they were forced to live. On encountering the ruined former quarters of the now-deceased catechist Robert Clark, who died aged 60 of "disease of the heart" on 29 March 1850,[12] she was allegedly reduced to tears:

> "Here," said my weeping companion [Mary Ann], "here poor Father died," she sobbed. After a little silence the sad story was resumed ... "I attended him," said she, "along with his daughter,

night and day. But all the people wanted to do something for him, for all so loved him. And then he would talk to us, and pray with us. He would tell me what to read to him from the Bible, when too weak to hold the book himself. How he would talk to us! When he thought he was going to die, he got the room full, and bade us 'Good-bye.' He held up his hands and prayed for us. He did love us. And then he said, while he was crying, 'Mind you be sure and all meet me in heaven!'" … The poor creature could not tell me anymore, but fairly sobbed aloud. I tried to comfort her, saying that God had kindly allowed him to go to his wife in heaven, and to the good Blacks who had died before him, and who would be so glad to see her there. If only Walter and she would keep his counsels, they might yet see him again. She shook her head, and mournfully, and yet with bitterness, replied, "No one cares for the Natives' souls now that Father Clark is gone."[13]

Figure 5: Charles Edward Stanley, 1847, *Natives at Oyster Cove, Nov. 1847*. Little George and Mary Ann second and third from left.

94

Bonwick and Clark were evidently friends and this excessively sentimental scene, and the language used, must be approached with caution. However, what this professed recollection exposes among its saccharine sentiments is the overtly Christian attributes of the captives' interactions with the colonial authority, as well as an additional loss for Mary Ann not often acknowledged. In the battle of Indigenous people versus colonisers, the relationships developed by the captives with those who came to "rule" over them (some, like Clark, for approximately 15 years) can be easily overlooked. Clearly, for Mary Ann, the loss of the administrative, religious and political influence of Clark, with whom she had lived and worked for the majority of her captivity, was as painful as the loss of any biological family.

Bonwick Comes to Tea

A strategically placed Bible in their "bush cottage" is the scene that met James Bonwick when he was invited to tea by the pair at Oyster Cove in 1859. Bonwick was an educator and historian with a keen interest in esotericism.[14] In 1870, he published recollections of his visit in *The Last of the Tasmanians: or, the Black War of Van Diemen's Land*, one of the first significant commercial publications on the subject. Looking beyond his evident mocking, a touching experience with the famed couple, and a rare insight into the later years of Mary Ann's married life with Walter, can effectively be witnessed.

Written like a sequel to the Quakers' visit of 1853, the scene is painted as if lifted directly from Harriet Beecher Stowe's very description of Tom and Aunt Chloe's modest cabin. Bonwick recounts:

> His Majesty took me into particular favour, and invited me to a banquet in the palace – or tea in the hut … Arrived at the door of a neat three-roomed Bush cottage, I was received with many

smiles by the buxom Maryann, who introduced me within. There I found my royal host conversing with a Sydney half-caste, who had come on a friendly visit. The room into which I was brought had many tokens of civilization and gentility wanting in most of the country cottages of England. The furniture, though homely, was suitable and comfortable. A carpet covered the floor. Not a particle of dust could be seen. A few prints adorned the walls, and books lay on a side-table. The Bible occupied a conspicuous position. The daily newspaper was there, as Walter was a regular subscriber for the press. The table was laid with quite a tempting appearance, and a thorough good cup of tea was handed round by the jovial-looking hostess. It was about the last evidence of civilization to be witnessed in connexion with the interesting race of Tasmanians. I have elsewhere described the gift of some Flinders Island diamonds from poor Walter. I was to receive a parting remembrance from his wife. He had given me what was most valuable in his eyes. She presented me with what was pleasing to hers. It was a charming necklace of the smallest and most brilliant polished shells I have ever seen. Even then I felt the delicacy of her nature, as she said putting the glittering object in my hand; "Give that to your daughter". I thanked her, and inquired if my lassie should wear it as a necklace. "No," replied my poor friend, "let her wear it on her back hair as the Indian women do." Ten years have passed; but I never see my daughter adorned with this pretty wreath without thinking of Maryann the half-caste.[15]

Akin to Aunt Chloe's "Mammy" profile of the "round, black, shining face" prepping supper for her household – to quote Stowe, "her whole plump countenance beams with satisfaction and contentment"[16] – so, too, James Bonwick's "Maryann" is the genteel and buxom hostess, jovially preparing a "tempting spread" for their allegedly prestigious guest. "She was unquestionably a woman of weight in the country," Bonwick proclaims, "bringing down upon the floor as she walked a pressure of some seventeen or eighteen stone. There was not only vigour of intellect, but a strength and independence of will, stamped upon her expansive features."[17]

Additionally, his Walter is a character of "superior" and "civilised" dignity. As he states, "Walter was far above the rest of the people … his eye was of even unusual expressiveness. His general aspect was one of seriousness and melancholy."[18] It is a profile undoubtedly reflecting a comparative appropriation of Stowe's Uncle Tom; says Stowe, "There was something about his whole air self-respecting and dignified, yet united with a confiding and humble simplicity."[19]

James Bonwick would include an artist's sketch of the couple for his seminal publication. Instead of using existing photographs of the pair, he used a fabricated sketch lifted from a famed 1864 group photograph (replacing William Lanne's image with Walter's). Here, Bonwick prefers to represent the couple akin to his own imaginative manufacture, a quintessential Victorian commemoration of regal, pristinely clothed characters.

Mary Ann, no stranger to the artist's pencil, had by now become a subject of many new artworks and photographs. One of the last known photographs depicts her in a dark Victorian gown, splitting and fraying at the sleeves, a felt scarf wrapped atop her head, her face framed by those trademark curls (see page 102). Two other women beside her are dressed in cardigan and bluey, noted by Bonwick as "holiday attire, such as may be seen in the photograph taken by the Bishop [Nixon]".[20] There is another photograph, attributed to Nixon, of the Arthurs in archetypal marital pose in front of their cottage, with Mary Ann now seated in the station's uniform of billowing chemise and knitted cardigan, Walter stiffly standing beside her in men's attire replete with his boatman's cap (see page 87).

Figure 6: Photograph titled *Tasmanian Aboriginals at Oyster Cove*.
Mary Ann seated centre with Truganini leaning on her knee (second from left).
Copy of photograph made by John Watt Beattie c. 1890s from an original
taken by Francis Russell Nixon c. 1850s.

In most of the photos taken at Oyster Cove between 1858 and 1862, Mary Ann is dressed distinctly from the other women, yet this couple's portrait presents her clothed in standard Oyster Cove costume. Closer inspection makes obvious that her outfit is not her own, the cardigan ill-fitting to say the least, its minute size barely able to be stretched over her ample chest, inferring staged costuming by the photographer. However, despite latent manipulation, this photograph remains the only authentic image of the famed pair towards the end of their remarkable, pioneering marriage.

Missing at Sea

Having established, together with George Washington Walker, the Hobart Town Total Abstinence Society, as well as the Van Diemen's Land Total Abstinence Society (c. 1846), James Bonwick's stance on alcohol consumption was wholly evident, and he concluded an account of his 1859 visit to the Arthurs with a warning on the evils of alcoholism.[21] The record of his brief sojourn to their home, though rare, is typical of the often-recited denigration of the pair's marriage. "[T]he curse had already been felt in their little homestead," he bemoaned, "for Walter had already fallen to the drunkard's stage."[22]

The influence of alcohol on the establishment was nothing new. From the very beginning, the Arthurs' marriage was fraught with abusive behaviour, and would further disintegrate and continue to be scarred by alcohol-induced abuses, wholly affecting their endless struggle for autonomy.

By 1858, it was reported that Walter had "relapsed into his old habits of drinking, neglecting his duty and indulging in violence".[23] Threats to have his wages stopped until he and Mary Ann sobered themselves were met with apparent resentment at being "interfered with" by the administration.[24] Regardless of the state of their relationship, the pair believed it was their right to endure it as they chose.

To invoke even more melancholy, Mary Ann was witnessing a new and more industrious life for her younger sister, Fanny, who, on her marriage to a former convict, had been granted permission to leave the establishment. Bonwick noted:

> After a marriage of five years, she gave birth to a child. The Government had made the pair a grant of one hundred acres of land, though not to be sold. Maryann had, at the time of her conversation with me, recently received a letter from her sister, stating that she was then living perfectly happy with her husband in Hobart Town.[25]

Such correspondence with Fanny would, no doubt, have come with a bittersweet sting. The same year she became Aunt Mary Ann to Fanny Cochrane's first child, the pair took turns in caring for their ailing mother and finally bade her goodbye towards the close of 1858.

Although minor attempts were made to change their ways, Walter continually reverted to his poor habits of intoxication and violence. In September 1859, Dandridge reported to the colonial secretary that Mary Ann was unwell due to "injuries caused by ill-usage".[26] Walter would "abscond" for weeks on end, retreating on sporadic whaling voyages to escape both his behaviour and its potential consequences. With little option, the Oyster Cove administration, after more than a year of his absence, threatened to cut his wages altogether until he returned to the station and his wife. However, such threats fell short, with Walter again shipping out aboard the whaling ship *Sussex* for a good 18 months.[27]

What effect this period had on Mary Ann is unknown but a side effect would be the instigation of ever-persistent ill-health, which would never subside.[28] So, too, as Mary Ann's volatile marriage was disintegrating, her relationships with the other captives at the station appeared to be affected also,[29] and it is apparent that she was participating little in cultural traditions with the others. Of the entries in the Oyster Cove Visitors Book relating to the Indigenous captives leaving the establishment on various hunting tours, she is almost never mentioned.

In 1861, Mary Ann would receive her biggest blow. The alleged poetic "hymns sung by the women to their guardian spirits to protect their absent husbands [on the whaling ships] and to bring them home in safety" now echoed unheard.[30] Friend and contemporary Jack Allen returned to the establishment from a voyage with the news that her husband was dead:

> Fatal Accident to An Aborigine. – On Saturday night between eight and nine o'clock as two of the few remaining aborigines at Oyster Cove, known by the names of "Walter and "Jacky Allen" were returning to the Cove in Mr. Bridge's boat, when the boat was off Sandy Bay Point. "Walter" accidentally fell overboard, and although every assistance was given from his own boat, and from the river craft, coming up at the time, the unfortunate native was lost.[31]

Walter's untimely death was deeply felt. Hospitalised with measles, Mary Ann's grief manifested in great periods of sickness, not helped by the dubious cures inflicted on her.[32]

She was now a widow living in a decrepit home, and Walter's demise signalled a silence in Mary Ann's once powerful voice. She was now a widow living in a decrepit home.[33] Formerly one of the most prolific voices of Indigenous Tasmanian captivity, from Mary Ann there were now no more letters of defiance to be found, not even lamentations of loss to the visiting curious to be obtained.

Figure 7: Photographer unknown; taken c. 1860 and developed c. 1890 by J. W. Beattie. Photograph titled *Tasmanian Aboriginals, Oyster Cove; "The Last of the Race"*. Wapperty, Bessy Clarke, Maryann [sic].

Mary Ann's significant role as matron for the station's children was, too, by this stage utterly void. The boys, like William Lanne, who had lived with the Arthurs since leaving the Orphan School, were now young men and, following in the footsteps of Walter, relishing their freedom on whaling ships:[34]

> Those who take an interest in the unfortunate remnant of an unfortunate race, will be surprised to learn that the last man of our Tasmanian aboriginal population, has shipped as a seaman on board the whaling barque *Aladdin*, and is about to brave the perils of the briny deep in the whale fishery. This resolution on the part of our sable friend is, to say the least of it, highly commendable and shows an energy of disposition above the general average of his race. We trust that when he returns to us, he will be entitled to a substantial lay.[35]

Yet these coveted voyages left some, like her youngest brother Adam in around 1857, fatally succumbing to exposure and disease. The young girls at Oyster Cove had left or died, like Mathinna, who was found drowned in a puddle while allegedly drunk.[36] The ominous Orphan School had become a dormitory of death for Aboriginal and non-Aboriginal children alike, and by 1862 all the Indigenous children who had resided there were dead too.[37]

Chapter 12

MARY ANN AND HER COUNTRYWOMEN

With Walter buried and Mary Ann in mourning, William Lanne took over the reins of protest on behalf of their people, "lodging official complaints" about their feeble conditions "as late as 1864".[1] As the ageing captive population of Oyster Cove was thinning, now comprising a total of six individuals, the "nostalgia" for the Tasmanian Aboriginal race was increasing, and the remaining captives "were once again paraded through Hobart".[2] Yet again, this procession would reach all the way to the top of the social hierarchy:

> [O]n 25th August 1864, four of the six Aborigines then alive were present at a ball at Government House, and their photograph there was taken as an official record by H A Frith. On this visit they also went to the theatre.[3]

One of the most famous photographs of Indigenous Tasmanians during the 19th century is this commemorative portrait of the "prestigious" event, instigated by their pre-empted "extinction".[4] The neo-classical composition and Romanesque pillars, designed to give an air of Victorian nobility to the image, are no distraction from the expressions of despair and distrust on the faces of its subjects. Flowers and ribbons adorning their hair, wearing hand-sewn ball gowns made by Mrs Dandridge, ill-fitting and frumpy, the women stare at the camera with anger and discomfort. William Lanne, now the only surviving male at the station, is slumped in his chair in sheer indifference.

This photograph, titled *Last of the Tasmanians* – a popular caption for all pictures of the surviving Indigenous captives at the time – is a commemoration of their role as puppets for colonial amusement, to be dressed up like dolls, used and discarded when the colony outgrew its barely existent guilt.

The morbid intent of this photograph, and an example of the celebrity that Mary Ann and her family had acquired, can be found in Frith's own advertisement in the *Mercury* of 1865: "Now Ready, for this Mail – Photographs of the Last of the Aborigines of Tasmania. Copies of the Original Picture Photographed for the Government."[5]

Two years later, in May 1866, the remaining five were invited to the Queen's birthday ball, where their presence generated a grand degree of excitement:

> They were dressed in new ball dresses, and were apparently pleased with the attention paid to them. The card of the invitation described them as "Mary Anne, and her Countrywomen".[6]

They didn't even get to keep their finery. The Tasmanian Exhibition of the same year, exhibiting the usual examples of Indigenous basketry, shell necklaces and bracelets, included "Head Dresses worn by the Aboriginal Women at the Government House Ball on the Queen's Birthday. J. S. Dandridge, Oyster Cove".[7]

On 5 January 1866, a widowed Mary Ann entered into a new marriage to a local Englishman named Adam Booker, a labourer aged 63 years and himself a widower.[8] Booker proved an uncouth personality[9] and Mary Ann remained a victim of alcohol-fuelled domestic violence. "Drinking and smoking and knocking about were what killed Mary Ann," declared a Mrs Davis in 1908.[10]

The new couple continued to live in the home she had shared with Walter, where she was able to be in "continuance of the occupation license" over the land that had been granted to her late husband.[11] However, the many issues with surrounding pastoralists would plague the new couple, with their hut broken into on 19 May 1869 and a "blanket and rugs stolen".[12]

* * *

The celebrity afforded Mary Ann and the captives would more ebb than flow, but reached its zenith in January 1868, with an invitation to an elite royal event:

> Amongst the many attractions upon the Regatta ground yesterday, not the least for the curious, were three out of the four remaining aboriginal natives, King Billy, Queen Mary, and Lalla Rookh [Truganini]. They were brought up from Oyster Cove to be presented to the Duke of Edinburgh yesterday had the opportunity afforded. We understand the Presentation will take place before His Royal Highness leaves the colony.[13]

Although all three were in attendance, only Lanne and Truganini were formally presented to the duke on the steps of the pavilion. For them at least it did not end there, with invitations extended to participate in the day's proceedings, such as handing out awards to the various winners.[14]

If Mary Ann was presented to the duke, it remains undocumented. The royal visit closed with gifts for the duke of two photographic portraits, one of Lanne and the other of Truganini, as well as an obligatory shell necklace.[15]

MARY ANN AND HER COUNTRYWOMEN

The regatta would appear to be the last of their famed engagements and, as public interest waned, "scientific" interest reigned. Regular lectures by self-proclaimed scholars of the day included hosted discussions on the various languages and customs of the "natives", supposedly scientific reasons for their impending "extinction", and where they fit into the Darwinian evolutionary schema of the human race.[16]

Figure 8: Henry Frith, c. 1866, *Aborigines, The Last of the Race, Tasmania*. From left, Bessy Clarke, William Lanne, Mary Ann, Truganini.

Mercury and Dr Smith

The last decade of Mary Ann's increasingly despairing life at Oyster Cove was marred with chronic ill-health. Of the 15 years of entries in the Oyster Cove Visitors Book, comprising mostly chaplain notes and the surgeons' visits to ever-poorly patients, the bulk that refer to Mary Ann detail her constant illnesses. For more than a decade, from 1856 to 1867, she suffered from chronic influenza, undiagnosed abdominal pains, colic, partial paralysis, boils and both constipation and bilious diarrhoea. If her susceptibility to colds was not debilitating enough, the treatments prescribed by the establishment's doctors, most specifically the "surgeon" Dr William Smith, were to contribute directly to her physical undoing.

In the 19th century, most were unaware of the irreversible effects of mercury poisoning. Mercury was prescribed mostly in the form of "calomel", a common treatment for skin infections, syphilis and to promote internal "evacuations".[17] On 1 September 1860, Mary Ann was diagnosed by Smith with "some affection of the liver" and recommended to have a "grey powder of Mercury, three grain[s] twice daily followed by 'salts of senna'".[18] Coupled with this poisonous prescription, according to the many entries in the Visitors Book, Smith's treatment of choice was vast quantities of alcohol. In February 1863 she was prescribed "beer twice a day" for general debility and partial paralysis.[19] A terminal pain in her kidney was treated with a wine glass of gin and a pint of beer daily.[20] In 1865 her liver and bowels were still affected, with back and abdominal aches combined with persistent constipation.[21] In 1866 she was suffering from boils on her legs, which she attempted to cure herself with a bread poultice.[22] Her constant bouts of ill-health instigated preparations for her possible demise.[23]

Like her mother before her, what is most tragic about Mary Ann's chronic ill-health over the course of two decades is that many, if not most, of her illnesses were likely the result of the disparate treatments she received. Her internal debilities, such as headaches and muscular weakness, incessant kidney pains, difficulty urinating, poor appetite and variegated bowel disorders, as well as "the precipitant on her tongue", were collectively signs of mercury poisoning.[24] Her trundling obesity, noted with such mocking by Robinson and Bonwick, was exacerbated by the excessively prescribed alcoholic "cures" for the aforementioned conditions. Her fragile health did not stand a chance.

Two "Truly Distinguished" Women

At the close of the 1860s, Mary Ann, chronically unwell and trapped in another volatile marriage, was witnessing the final degrading chapter of Oyster Cove Station. By the end of the decade both she and Truganini were to be the station's only official Indigenous residents. William Lanne, believed to be the only surviving male of the captive Tasmanians – beloved by both his people and his fellow seamen, as well as the public at large, who, in the poorest of taste, placed him on a metaphorical throne as the new "King" of his race – was to depart this life at the mere age of 34 years.[25]

In February 1869, Lanne returned from a whaling voyage on the *Runnymede*, bloated and "complaining of sickness", with a bout of choleraic diarrhoea. Checking himself in at the Dog and Partridge Hotel, Lanne attempted to "dress himself, with a view of proceeding to the hospital" but, exhausted, he fell on the bed and died.[26] Immediately blaming chronic alcohol consumption for his poor health, the *Hobart Mercury* on 5 March 1869 reported:

> He was paid off on Saturday last, when he received a balance of wages ... He took up his residence at the 'Dog and Partridge' public-house, at the corner of Goulburn and Barrack streets, and died from a severe attack of English cholera ... His body was removed to the Colonial Hospital on Wednesday night, March 3rd, where it awaits burial, and to-morrow the grave will close over the last male aboriginal of Tasmania.[27]

Lanne's death was significant news indeed. His last breath signalled an invitation for "scientists", on behalf of the so-called Royal Societies, to wrench, in their greedy hands, the freshly severed limbs and lifeless bust from his much-desired corpse. Bonwick relayed the scene, played out like an excerpt from a Victorian Gothic novel, written for his consuming masses, replete with cloak-and-dagger mystery and graphic horror.[28]

One can only speculate as to the effect this had on Mary Ann, Fanny Cochrane and Truganini. A mere glimpse of their devastation, as communicated by Truganini to the author, was published shortly following his mutilation:

> The last of the Aboriginal race of Tasmania, Lallah Rook [sic] [Truganini], who lived with the late King Billy as his wife, has been very low spirited since his death, and when told of the mutilation of his body, she made a vow that nothing would ever induce her to become an inmate of the hospital, where she might be treated as he was after death. Lallah [sic] considers that she has been treated cruelly by the authorities in not allowing her to see the last of one with whom she was associated from his infancy, and wants to know why it is that she has not been supplied with a mourning dress, the same as white women wear.[29]

Truganini's mourning was to be the colony's muse. In only a matter of months a new burlesque, titled *King Billy – The Last of His Race*, made its debut in the Theatre Royal.[30] This tasteless entertainment defies belief, excused by the *Tasmanian Times* as a timely comedy "calculated to soften down much of the bitter feeling which recent events have engendered".

Opening with Lanne and Truganini (named Lalla Rookh) drinking in the Telegraph Hotel, where the actors' makeup "fairly convulsed the house with laughter",[31] the first act has the pair being stalked by characters with names like Dr Scalpel and Jemmy Dismal (an undertaker), the comedy essentially following Scalpel's desire to obtain Billy's head. The second act closed in the so-called Humbug Hospital following Lanne's mutilation, when, with

> a shrill coo-ey from Lalla ... all the characters rush in, and, amidst blue fire and sepulchral music, King Billy rises, attired in a white dress and cap, and carrying a white skeleton umbrella, annihilates Scalpel and Bokell, embraces Lalla, and all join in an amusing medley of nursery rhymes, and amidst which the curtain falls.[32]

Although initially well received by critics and audiences alike, the entertainment was thankfully short-lived.

Just like the burlesque, the mystery of Lanne's mutilation lost significant public interest as the years waned. By 1882, however, Dr Edward Crowther had seemingly grown more comfortable in his admission of direct possession of Indigenous Tasmanian remains, and confessed at this time to being in ownership of Lanne's skeleton.[33] A prized acquisition that was not obtained without a covert surgeon's assistance, "my own uncle got Billy's head", confessed William Blyth four decades later. "Dr. Stokell said Billy was the most muscular man he ever cut up in his life ..."[34]

* * *

Oyster Cove Station was now a squalid testament to the brutality of colonialism. By 1869 only Mary Ann and Truganini remained. Their homes would gradually disintegrate into sorry ruins, and the station's land was divided up and sold off.[35]

In 1870, Mary Ann's self-proclaimed friend, James Bonwick, formally published *The Last of the Tasmanians*. Despite mostly favourable reviews, others were not so kind. Exposing his bias, Joseph Milligan, now the former superintendent of both Aboriginal establishments, wrote to the Royal Society to make known his chagrin, yet this time in defence of the colonists.[36] As evident subscribers to the press, if Mary Ann and Truganini were denied access to this publication, the newspapers would have at least informed them of its content and intent.[37] Declaring their mere portraits as "unsightly", the worst came courtesy of the *Tasmanian Times*:

> These [pages] contain something for several different classes of readers ... The Christianizing colonist meets with an eulogium upon missionaries; the ethnologist discovers numerous illustrative stories of the rude aborigines, with not a few striking portraitures of the same ... ladies will feel awe stricken at the forbidding visage, after a photograph of "Bessy Clark [sic], of Oyster Cove", who assuredly could not have been the result of any process of Natural Selection, unless the selection had been from all the ugliest prototypes developed into one ultimate issue of terrific ugliness ...[38]

So, too, in the article, "the author expresses at length his views on the subject of the general extinction of the aborigines", and one can scarcely comprehend what the pair must have felt reading open discussions concerning their impending deaths.[39] Within these pages, Mary Ann would have further read of herself:

Although she was of superior ability to most white children, and would, if more happily situated, have become a truly distinguished woman, she was thrown by officials among the degraded Blacks of the island, to her own serious moral and intellectual loss. Repelled in cold disdain by her father's blood, she clung to her mother's kind, and ultimately contracted a childless marriage with Walter George Arthur, the most intelligent and educated of the Native race.[40]

Although it cannot be confirmed that Mary Ann read this book, as she was an avid reader it is certainly a possibility. What is assured, however, is that by the year of the book's publication, Mary Ann's chronic sicknesses were taking their final toll, on both mind and body.

Chapter 13

HER VITAL SPARK EXTINGUISHED

Mary Ann had evidently suffered bouts of paralytic numbness for at least a decade prior and it had now begun to take control, the poor mercurial and alcoholic treatments unable to stave off the illness. With her health in rapid decline, she was taken from the home of her husband and into the care of Mr and Mrs Dandridge, who had taken over the management of the establishment in about 1855.[1] Mary Ann was familiar with Maria Dandridge, having sat for a portrait by her father, John Skinner Prout, at Wybalenna in 1845, and the pair evidently became friends, retrospectively sketched in conversation together.[2]

On the evening of Monday 24 July, Mary Ann was taken immediately to Hobart's General Hospital, her faculties rapidly succumbing to the morbid grip of paralysis:

> "THE LAST BUT ONE OF THE ABORIGINALS". – It is well-known that since the death of King Billy, the last survivors of the aboriginal inhabitants of this island are Mary Ann and Lalla Rookh [Truganini], and now it is only likely that in a very few days this small remnant will be reduced to "the last woman". Last night about half-past nine o'clock, Mary Ann was admitted to the hospital from Oyster Cove, suffering from paralysis, and apparently rapidly sinking. The two poor women have been living there for some time with Mr. and Mrs.

Dandridge, and early yesterday it was found that the only hope for Mary Ann was to remove her at once to the hospital. The day was wet but not stormy, and Mr. and Mrs. Dandridge left the Cove with her in an open boat, about half-past nine o'clock; the voyage, therefore, occupied about twelve hours. It rained all but the while; but as soon as the boat reached the wharf a cab was procured, and the sick woman placed in it with her two guardians and friends. Being a heavy woman, she was got into the hospital with some difficulty, and stimulants were at once administered.[3]

Yet it was simply too late. The aforementioned stimulants were to no avail and the next day, on 25 July 1871, Mary Ann died in Hobart's General Hospital, aged approximately 50 years.[4] The cruelty of colonial imprisonment that she had endured throughout her life was mimicked by her very body in her last hours of heartbreaking debility:

Death of Mary Ann. – We regret to learn that poor Mary Ann, the aboriginal, who was conveyed from Oyster Cove to the hospital here on Monday last, has already succumbed to the illness which afflicted her. She died at ten o'clock last night, never having rallied from the time of her admission. Her illness was complete paralysis of the system. She was unable to make any motion whatever with her head or hands, but she remained conscious and intelligent to the last, her clear eye speaking intelligently what [she] could not express otherwise. Mrs. Dandridge had sat with her by her bedside the greater part of the previous night, and throughout the day. She was at the side of the poor creature to the last, when the vital spark was extinguished, and her presence was evidently grateful and soothing to the dying woman.[5]

The media reaction to her passing would prove a stark contrast to that of her contemporary, William Lanne, two years earlier. The public lamentation of his death, and the publicity of his funeral, makes the death of Mary Ann appear irrelevant to the masses by sheer comparison. Lanne's funeral was a rich, if wholly contrived, expression of loss, replete with Union Jacks, possum skins, spears and at least 120 mourners.[6] Despite her apparent celebrity in the previous two decades, Mary Ann's constant relegation to an overweight "half-caste" proved her passing of no great interest to the colony, and the death of "Queen" Mary Ann was poorly lamented by the media and general public alike. In fact, it was not Mary Ann's death that was the main point of reference but the inaccurate declaration of Truganini as now "the last Tasmanian Aborigine" that dominated her obituaries.[7]

The only documentation of her funeral sermon proves equally excruciating. Presided over by the Reverend Gellibrand (in the presence of the undertaker) and Mr C. D. C. Jones on the morning of 27 July 1871, Mary Ann's body was interred:[8]

> Funeral of Mary Ann. – The remains of the half-caste woman Mary Ann, who died of paralysis at the hospital, were interred in St. David's Cemetery yesterday morning. Not a single mourner followed the hearse.[9]

It is not known why her husband and family did not participate in the usual funerary proceedings, instead leaving us with the image of a solitary hearse taking the body of this remarkable woman to her final resting place. For a woman whose life was dedicated to finding a place for herself and her people in a new and wholly prejudiced world; who fought to establish a voice and forge a strength of identity in a culture that deprived her of both; who played by the rules of British "civilisation" and doctrine, despite chaining her to all manner of degradations; and who became one of the most documented faces of Indigenous Tasmania, the funeral of Mary Ann appears a display of almost complete abandonment.

Immediately after her death, her widower, Adam, still residing on their shared land at Oyster Cove, had his licence revoked and was "ordered to quit the station".[10] Her beloved surrogate mother, Truganini, was now the only survivor in this ruinous place, which she left for good with the Dandridges in 1873, passing away five years later.[11]

Eulogy

It is difficult to find an appropriate conclusion to the extraordinary life of Mary Ann. Insultingly, documenters like James Bonwick would lament her unrealised potential, both wholly oppresse-d during her life and denied her in death by the white man himself. "She was a woman who, placed in happier circumstances, could have been the Czarina of Russia and would have emulated the intellectual prowess of a Catharine", he quipped, "though she might have betrayed an equal intensity of passions."[12]

I will close Mary Ann's biography with a single moment in her cruel but important existence. Tucked away in George Augustus Robinson's Wybalenna journals, there is an entry that paints an ominous and prophetic image: a teenage Mary Ann, walking sombrely with Robinson along the outer grounds of the Wybalenna establishment, tracing the earth to show him the unmarked graves of her deceased countrymen and women, telling him the names of those she knew.[13] For me, this moment in time allegorically encapsulates Mary Ann's very life. The young sealer's daughter, among the spindly windswept tea-trees – a mere remnant of the thickets that once stood there, cut down to build the prison walls of the death camp that would wipe out her loved ones – was caught standing between the colonial strength of her father's people (represented by Robinson) and the seemingly unstoppable decimation of her mother's (the graves).

With not an iota of remorse, Robinson would raid these graves for their highly prized treasures, bones he would scatter across his beloved Commonwealth's vast portfolio of appropriated lands, selling them to the most eager collectors.[14] Perhaps due to her paternity, Mary Ann's corpse was spared this fate. Yet, as we witness her solitary journey to her designated plot, absent from the scrutiny of the media and the gaze of her own kin, one cannot be certain her bones were indeed laid to rest.[15]

Three decades after her passing, an elderly woman named Annie Benbow would retrospectively document her childhood years spent at the Oyster Cove establishment, where her father, Sergeant David Macdouall, had worked.[16] Benbow predominantly recounts the captives with affection, telling of their customs and of "singing their wild songs".[17] "Many I was very fond of," she stated, "and used to cry when anyone died."[18] Benbow's naive drawings paint nothing of the despair and degradation suffered by the captives; instead they offer a child's charming memory of an "exotic" youth, featuring jovial activities, peaceful relations between the captives and their oppressors, and Mary Ann herself. My favourite is a colourful sketch, drawn around 1900, of four women in domestic activity with a group of white children watching on (one possibly a small self-portrait of Benbow).[19] The lower right shows a barefoot woman with unbuttoned gown pulled down around her waist cooking over an open fire. Rendered in Mary Ann's likeness with her trademark hairstyle tied with red ribbon, another woman sits beside her with clay pipe and red cap, surely in the likeness of her mother, Tarenootairer. Either formally greeting Benbow's parents or conversing with the administration, Mary Ann is a fixture in the foreground of Benbow's memory, as the veritable "Queen" of the Aboriginal establishment.

Figure 9: Annie Benbow, c. 1900, *Tasmanian Aborigines at Oyster Cove Station*. The likenesses of Mary Ann and Tarenootairer are depicted bottom right.

PART 3

A Vicissitude of Virtue?

Fanny Cochrane, c. 1832–1905

Chapter 14

A PRISON NURSERY

At the Wybalenna Aboriginal establishment on Flinders Island, Fanny Cochrane[1] was born around 1832 under highly enigmatic circumstances. In approximately January or February 1832 Tarenootairer was present at the establishment, and by March G. A. Robinson had noted she was "with child", presumably having already given birth or preparing to do so.

Photographs of Fanny in later years appear to show her to have been born with a cleft palate, also known as a hare lip, which, to 19th-century eyes, may have been a sign of congenital syphilis, a disease that appears to have plagued Tarenootairer during her enslavement by straitsmen in Bass Strait. A highly contagious disease, it would have validated a rapid isolation from the establishment's children until appropriate treatments could be administered to both mother and child. This may also explain the absence of Fanny Cochrane from any records for the majority of her first decade in captivity.

In the 1830s, the childhoods of Indigenous children taken to, or born at, the establishment consisted of almost total institutionalisation.[2] Fanny spent the majority of her infancy relatively undocumented, perhaps going back and forth from her family on Flinders Island to the Queen's Orphan School near Hobart, and then to the household of appointed catechist Robert Clark at around two years old.[3] By January 1836, she is not recorded in the census of "Aborigines at Wybalenna", suggesting she was not physically present for a significant part of George Augustus Robinson's early tenure as commandant.[4]

These tentative years, involving the absences of a family she then scarcely knew, including the death of a grandmother, appear scarred upon Fanny Cochrane's memory. Her infancy was spent predominantly in the care of the Clarks, where she was an alleged "favourite" of the catechist's wife, who subsequently gave her the name Cochrane after one of her own sisters.[5]

* * *

By the early 1840s, Fanny Cochrane was back at Wybalenna, living briefly with her mother, or her sister, Mary Ann, in the main housing complex built for the captives, known as "the square".[6] When old enough – at about 10 years of age – Fanny and two other children, Martha and Jesse, were placed by Dr Joseph Milligan, who was now temporary superintendent, into the Queen's Orphan School in New Town around 1842.[7] Six weeks later she was again sent to live with the catechist in Hobart:

> Robert Clark "the late catechist to the aborigines on Flinders Island", makes application "for permission to receive into his family "an aboriginal child named Fanny, upon his engagement to feed, clothe, and educate her as one of his own children".[8]

Clark enjoyed showing off his so-called juvenile pupils and his successful religious instruction of them. James Bonwick tells of a visit to Clark's home, where the children were "well clothed, with smiling faces, who read to me, with correct intonation, several verses from the New Testament". Further, he wrote, "They looked up to him with the same filial regard which his own children felt for him."[9] Yet such sentiments were transitory. To their dismay, Fanny Cochrane was not becoming the enthusiastic prodigy the Clarks had envisioned.[10] By November 1843, they wanted to absolve themselves of her care and attempted to readmit her into the Orphan School.[11] Instead, under the direction of the lieutenant governor, it was advised that Fanny be returned to Wybalenna.[12]

When the Clarks were themselves relocated back to Flinders Island, Fanny and the other children appear to have been temporarily placed in their care yet again. By their own demand, "the mothers of the various children … were only allowed to see them once a week", usually a Sunday, a method believed to ween both mother and child "from their native habits", and by all appearances it worked.[13] Mary Ann initially claimed a cold relationship with Fanny, stating that her little sister "never liked me"; even her own mother admitted that she did "not often talk to her".[14] This deliberate destruction of Indigenous familial ties resulted in a disconnect between Fanny and her family in these vital stages, and fuelled her apparent volatile behaviour to follow.

* * *

Mrs Clark's strict daily routines for the children centred on domestic training, and saw Fanny tasked with the ironing. Prayers, Bible readings and "family worship" both began and closed their days.[15] The regime included minor schooling for the children during the day, as well as assisting the instruction of adults in the evenings, although the success of these classes was highly exaggerated. "[M]other could just sign her name. Could read just a little, what she had learned herself in her later age," noted one of Fanny's sons.[16]

Life with the Clarks did not reflect their stoic religiosity. The treatment of the children in their care was becoming of great concern to the captives as well as the administration. An earlier weekly report issued to George Augustus Robinson by the medical attendant gives direct insight into the appalling conditions these children were forced to live in:

> The children's dormitory was excessively damp and cold and its cleanliness was not sufficiently attended to … The children were dirty (as natural), which was anything but satisfactory. The girls slept in the catechist's kitchen on a wet brick floor, going to bed without undressing. The children's clothes were in a bad state (the tears due to themselves). Some of the children were suffering from "scald head" (most often caused by lack of cleanliness).[17]

In response to such treatment, the captive children were becoming highly rebellious, with Fanny Cochrane the prime example.[18] Her "unruly" character now marred her already precarious childhood at Wybalenna. In 1843, the Clarks made multiple accusations of attempts at arson on their home, bad language, lies and thievery – even claiming that her own mother "knew Fanny was a bad girl".[19] Despite protesting her innocence, insisting that the other children set her up and she "never stole anything but bread when I was hungry", these acts were met with severe punishments such as locking up, gagging and incessant flogging.[20]

* * *

At approximately 12 to 13 years of age Fanny declared to Robert Clark that she was being visited during the night by a prisoner named Thomas Warham, who would take her into the "wild tobacco" and rape her. Warham, a noted "bad character", had been sentenced to 15 years and transported to the colony for sheep stealing, assault and repeated attempts to escape punishment.[21]

Confirmed through a physical examination by the superintendent, violations of Fanny Cochrane's body had indeed occurred. And Clark's transcription of Fanny's statement, dated 12 August 1845, detailed Warham's coercion, through both verbal and physical violence, as well as blackmail and threats. She well remembered "when he first abused her", wrote Clark. It was a Sunday and Fanny had been in the nursery when most were at chapel. "He rapt at the door," she had stated, and when she opened it, "Warham and Bessy Rue came into the little hall and Bessy Rue took her by the hands". Fanny "screeched loud" as they drew her towards the garden of a Mr Dunn, where Warham "knocked her down" and "pulled up her clothes", proceeding to rape her violently. He "hurt her very much", Fanny pleaded, and Warham "cut her after he got up". He then threatened, while shaking his fist, "If you tell Mr. Clark & Mrs. Clark, I'll …" And this was merely the first time. "The week after, he threw her down and threatened her so in the bush and he forced her against her will," relayed Clark. "[Warham] came into the yard often at night."

With looming threats "not to tell", Fanny was at his mercy. When she "did not hear his whistle", she said, "he always threw a stone at the window". Warham coerced Fanny into stealing supplies for him such as pipes and tobacco, pieces of soap, a wine glass and tumbler, as well as candles, penknives and paper. However, his threats were becoming murderous and no longer directed to just Fanny herself. "Mr. Clark is a wicked man," he told her and expressed his desire to "burn the house when he was repairing the dormitory". Fanny was to be his accomplice and he "showed her how".

On the night of Sunday 10 August 1845, Warham instructed Fanny Cochrane to "burn the house" while he was away in Launceston and that "he would stack the fireworks and she would [take] it up to the roof of the house and burn Mr. and Mrs. Clark in their bed". When this was done she was to "run into the bush & stay there until he would return ... He said he would take care of her".[22]

Yet, when Fanny alerted the Clarks, it was implied these violent episodes were by her own volition and, together with Dr Milligan, they chose to punish *her* for "inappropriate conduct".[23] Clark insisted his method of "fastening her up at night" in a box was for Fanny Cochrane's own safety, as well as for the household's "protection" against her behaviour. The box itself, an "old trunk" a mere "three feet three inches long and fifteen inches broad", was stood upright and used as a makeshift wall "between the wall of the house and the bed":

> It was covered over by a board which left about one fourth of the space open over her head. The board was kept down by a chain and a shot to prevent her throwing it off. The child is 4 foot 7 inches high at present and has grown in stature since the occurrence which was fourteen months ago.[24]

Cited on March 1846, Fanny's own alleged testimony concerning her punishments was recorded by Superintendent Henry Jeanneret:

> I was chained to the bed-post. I slept a good while in the box. I slept partly on the floor and partly in the box. It hurt me when I slept in the box and no bed under me. I had been flogged on the table many a time, and had my hands and feet tied. I used to lie with my knees raised, as the box was too short for me. I was flogged on my naked skin with the stick. I was flogged plenty of times in a week. There was no difference in the manner of my

being flogged. They were not flogged as often as I was. A cannonball was put on the top of a chair, and it fell down and struck me on the forehead. I was turning myself round, and that shook the chair, which made it fall down. This took place when Dr. Milligan was here. Dr. Milligan knew all about it. Had a boil on my knee. Matter came out of it. It was all over my knee. I think it was owing to my sleeping in the box, my feet were cramped. Dr. Milligan said it was of no consequence. I continued to sleep in the box till Dr. Jeanneret came here.[25]

The Clarks' defence was a stoic belief that their abuse was constructive. "Mr. Clark did not deny his having flogged the girls, but declared he had done so in religious anger at their moral offences," defended Bonwick, with a reference to Fanny Cochrane's rape providing further justification. "[O]ne in particular had been seduced [sic] into improper society, and was long kept in rigid seclusion."[26] Responding to these accusations, Jeanneret requested to have Fanny Cochrane removed from the Clarks and into the care of her sister, Mary Ann.[27] Despite the severity of these claims, Clark was ultimately acquitted and the rape accusations, by all appearances, ignored.

Fanny Cochrane's last year on Flinders Island was spent as a household domestic with her sister, and despite her conflict with the Clarks she was coerced into signing an employment contract with Robert Clark, to act "as his servant", for the total sum of "two pounds [and] ten shillings with inclusion of rations and clothes", a further attempt to bring Fanny Cochrane under his oppressive control.[28]

Outside the turbulent home of the Clarks, life was evidently no better. Watching the decimation of her fellow captives, through disease and poor medical aid, was an additional despair to Fanny's already disturbed childhood, and she was not alone. Her brothers, too, were victims of their captivity. Like Fanny, Adam was ushered between institutions and subject to beatings from the catechist, and another brother, known only as "Sarah's Child", was dead from influenza at less than nine months old.

With Robinson long gone and the current administration in total disarray and needing to gain a tighter grip on the colony's purse, a relocation back to the mainland was ordered by 1847; although greeted with much protest from the colonists, the move would lay the foundations for Fanny's burgeoning fame.

Chapter 15

THE ORGAN OF PERCEPTION

Throughout her life, Fanny would show a strength of will and enthusiasm for independence, the origins of which can be clearly found in her earliest years. However, we see that autonomy and empowerment were met with little support from both captive and oppressor. In a great contradiction, the various institutions were raising Fanny Cochrane as a captive's child, yet ensuring she was wholly severed from her cultural and familial ties. The only way she was to survive such institutionalisation was to play by the rules, or at least pretend to, formulating her future relationship with the colonial authority.

Now "practically a woman" and too old to be placed with the other children at the Queen's Orphan School, Fanny was moved into a hut adjacent to the Oyster Cove settlement. This was the household of her sister and brother-in-law, the colonial secretary unable to see how else she could be "satisfactorily disposed of".[1]

The trauma of Wybalenna was to haunt Fanny Cochrane, and her behaviour showed no sign of appeasement. Within a year she was again living "in service", this time with the Dandridge family, who were running a school for the "children of the farmers and labourers outside of the Reserve".[2] However, after a mere few months, her apparent misconduct resulted in her being sent back to her family at the station.[3] Although conditions at Oyster Cove were little improved

– in fact, they were worse than at Wybalenna – this brief period would cultivate the unique traditions that would sustain Fanny Cochrane for the rest of her life.

* * *

This era saw, for the first time, the three women living under one roof. Tarenootairer, Mary Ann and Walter were now Fanny's prime teachers of both the culture of their oppressors and that of their own.[4] With a lapse in "care", the survivors resumed their cultural autonomy. They hunted possum and fished for oysters, with Fanny becoming known as a "great swimmer and diver",[5] and made bonfires to stave off the ever-persistent cold, where they ate, sang and danced in a ring.[6] Now permanently engaged with her own family, Fanny would learn all manner of pre-colonial culture – how to read the weather and the stars; how to catch game with her bare hands; how to find food and medicine among their forest surrounds; how to weave baskets that were given as gifts; and how to understand animals and the complex omens they symbolise.[7] Despite their lives being perpetually fragile, in her later years Fanny reflected on these moments with utter joy:

> … fresh in memory around her, she seemed to rejoice, for she said it was with them [William Lanne, Mary Ann and Walter] she fished, frolicked, and joined in the chase over thickly timbered hills, clapping hands and singing the "Song of Welcome".[8]

Of Annie Benbow's charming illustrations detailing Oyster Cove's early years, the most ambitious depicts almost all the captive population in various forms of activity. Fanny Cochrane is sketched at the central fore standing tall in chignon and day dress just like her sister Mary Ann. Although this alleged representation of Fanny's likeness is not accurate, it showcases a utopian vision of the establishment that was never to be.

In stark contrast to their cultural reprieve, the captives were little attended to and nothing could stop their mortality. Days were spent engaged in remedial labour, sweeping their huts, cooking, collecting wood, "for which they have now to go a considerable distance", and both making and mending their own clothes.[9] Colonial education, so desired by Robinson at Wybalenna, was nonexistent. The adjacent Dandridge school was not extended to the captives, because "instruction was considered hopeless for the Blacks".[10] Mrs Dandridge later exposed her own attitudes towards Indigenous education. "I think the natives were very much better when they were not educated; as soon as they got educated you couldn't trust them," she declared.[11] By December 1848, of the 36 left only "5 could read and write, 10 only could read, and 21 were totally uneducated", noted the *Courier*.[12]

With the youngest children, like Adam, away at the orphanage, Fanny Cochrane and the few remaining teenagers sat shyly watching the stream of visiting curious. Clinging on to some semblance of their former selves while playing the assigned roles of the "civilised savage" that the colony scripted for them, the captives now existed in a type of limbo. Those who survived, like Fanny, were given little choice but to play along with these colonial narratives in an attempt to integrate themselves among their oppressors, or succumb to the despair, disease and inevitable death that were characteristic of the Aboriginal establishment.

Fanny's teenage years were evidently spent weaving back and forth between her own truth and the colonial "guestbook" fiction – like a menagerie to be gawked at, drawn, photographed and novelised.[13] And her life as colonial captive, like a proverbial sitting duck, is never more evident than in the following event.

The Indelible "Dr S.": The Influence of Mesmerism and Spiritism

By the mid-19th century, public and scientific interest in spiritism, phrenology, galvanism (electro-biology) and mesmerism (better known as hypnotism) was gaining momentum. "Public curiosity has been awakened to the mysterious and perplexing subject," stated the *Courier*,[14] and it was buoyed into popular consciousness through the likes of Mary Shelley's *Frankenstein, or the Modern Prometheus* (1818). In 1845, the *Adelaide Observer* declared that in London, "[A] new society 'for the investigation of mesmerism' has been recently established for the purpose of framing its rules and regulations."[15] In the very offices of the *South Australian Register*, a visiting mesmerist from Bristol known as Mr Phillips performed his routine "upon two aboriginal natives", Charley and Harry, who were seated together on a sofa "with their hands clasped". This early exhibition of mesmerism in the colony showcases a predominant "question and answer" routine. A third boy, Jackey, was left seated outside to be used as additional clairvoyant bait. "Where is Jackey?" asked Mr Phillips. "Will Mr [blank] find Jackey?" These are mere examples of the questions asked. With Charley sitting in (allegedly) successful "mesmeric" state, office spectators were asked to hold "different articles" – such as a knife or a pipe – above his head and to ask the boy if he could see these articles with his eyes firmly shut.[16] This case emphasises not only the intent of the mesmerist to induce control over the mental state of the subject, but also the distinct desire to attain a state of astral travel; that is, to be able to "see" beyond walls without the aid of "the organ of perception".[17]

In Melbourne, then known as Port Phillip, one of the premier interests in mesmerism was its perceived symmetry with the cultural and spiritual practices witnessed among Indigenous Australians:

"it may not be uninteresting to our readers to know that mesmerism ... is now, and has been practiced by the aborigines of this and adjacent colonies," wrote the *Geelong Advertiser*.[18] The utilisation of Indigenous subjects as guinea pigs was to become increasingly popular, and the core of this penchant was clearly embedded in Victorian-era racist ideologies. One spectator who considered themselves "rather 'up' in natural history" decreed they "thought that the power of a mesmeriser over a patient, greatly resembled that of a snake over a little bird, or a nigger; both bipeds, feathered and human, being very susceptible to its influence".[19] Other witnesses likened it to outright witchcraft, emanating directly from "the evil one".

One of the most prolific promoters of mesmerism appears to be a man named Mr Gilbert in Port Phillip. So popular were his "biological exhibitions" that select tickets had to be issued to prevent overcrowding.[20] Gilbert was a mesmerist renowned as "free from suspicion or fraud", who defied cries of "shamming" and "took his subjects from among the aborigines without selection".[21] One of Gilbert's exhibitions of August 1850 was relayed to the media, further showcasing his propensity for using Indigenous youths as experimental subjects. "Mr Gilbert delivered his second lecture on mesmerism at the Hall of the Mechanics' Institute, and made experiments on two boys – one an aboriginal black boy. The audience testified their approbation of the proceedings by rapturous plaudits."[22] The poor boy in question is not named and simply described by the *Cornwall Chronicle* as "a young Aborigine, an uneducated, and untutored savage".[23] As well as the belief in their alleged susceptibility to the process of hypnotism, the use of Indigenous youths as subjects was also believed to add an element of "trustworthiness" to the proceedings, their perceived "untutored" intelligence validating the "truths of mesmerism and phrenology" through their "unwitting testimony".[24]

By October 1850, the phenomenon had reached Hobart Town. This time the practitioners kept a humble reserve – no public tickets were sold, not even their full names relayed to the media. In contrast, however, the subject of their exhibition was more clearly made known.[25] A summary of the event was handed to the press as follows:

> **Mesmerism**
>
> An account has been handed to us, with a particular request that it may be published, of mesmeric experiments practiced on an aboriginal female named Fanny. After being thrown into a mesmeric sleep by the usual passes, which we need not repeat, the report goes on in this way:
>
> Now began the third stage, and a most interesting one it was to us spectators. Mr. S. applied the right thumb to the base of the forehead between the eyebrows, and at the same time the left thumb to the occipital protuberance, when a low sepulchral noise issued from Fanny's throat, followed by a terrific howl, which shook the very room we were in. She then rose slowly from her place, walked from one end of the place to the other three times, she then stopped, but on S. making three passes round her head, she made the circuit of the room three times in a most rapid manner – then suddenly stopping, and placing herself in front of S., with her eyes intently fixed on him, and flinging her arms wildly about her, she gave another terrific howl, and fell back into her former place. S. told us then that she was an admirable patient, and that what we know [sic] saw was evidence of her having passed into the transition state, as it is called, and that she would, after a few more passes, be in a perfect state of "clairvoyance". S. then got a small iron pot filled with cold water, and having passed a wooden stick round three times in the pot, and uttering some language we did not understand, told us the water was now mesmerised. S. then sprinkled the water over the woman's face and some into her mouth, presently we heard

a gurgling sort of noise, which S. told us was the decisive sign of her being in a state of "clairvoyance". Fanny then closed one eye, which together with her mouth being wide open, gave her a singular appearance. We spoke to her but she gave no answer. S. said she could not speak before she lay in this state for half-an-hour. At the end of that time, S. pressed both thumbs to her temples, on which she gave a groan, but on S. pressing the left thumb on the shut eye she became silent, but raised her hand and placed it on her mouth, which S. said was a sign that she was ready and prepared to answer any questions we might ask her. The following dialogue then took place: –

D. S.   What is your name?

Native Woman.   Fanny.

S.   Where have you been lately?

N.W.   Oh! In a new country, and very fine.

S.   Who did you see there?

N.W.   De great chiefs of my country.

Dr. M.   Fanny, do you recollect Sir. J. Franklin?

N.W.   Oh, yes, he was de good father, me recollect him well in my country.

Dr. M.   Where is he now?

N.W.   Living on the great waters, and de people in de great country long for to see him; plenty of ships they send for to find him.

D.M.   Where are you now, Fanny?

N.W.   In Hobart Town.

D.M.   Where is your sister now?

N.W.   In de garden.

D.M. What is in her hand?

N.W. A kettle.

D.M. Have I got any flowers in my house?

N.W. Yes, plenty.

D.M. What are they in?

N.W. In a jar (hitherto they were always in a pot.)

D.M. Did anything happen yesterday?

N.W. Yes.

D.M. What was it?

N.W. Some gentlemen and gentlewomens, coming down here, de cart they was in upset and de all thrown head over in de sand, and de gentlemens bruise de ladies badly, and hurt much, for they sink the ladies deep in the sand.[26]

Although vague, the identity of the "aboriginal female named Fanny" is assuredly Fanny Cochrane herself.[27] Other identities worthy of affirmation are that of the "doctors". "Dr M" is likely Dr Joseph Milligan, then superintendent of the Oyster Cove establishment, who lived in Hobart, where the event is said to have taken place. The identity of the mesmerist referred to variously as 'Mr. S.', 'S.' and 'D.S' is especially worth clarifying. A later news article of 1876 makes mention of a spiritualist named Mr Slade.[28] One of the most famed spiritualists of the Victorian era, Henry Slade was an American "slate-medium".[29] Paralleling its popularity in Australia, spiritualism had "swept the United States" in the same period, enjoying maximum popularity "among the upper-class whites and the elite French-speaking free people of colour".[30] However, no reference is made of time he may have spent in Van Diemen's Land.[31] The most logical identity of this person would be the doctor and surgeon to the Oyster Cove establishment, Dr William Smith, who lived at Brown's River.[32] Having direct access to – and established friendships with – the captives at Oyster Cove would have certainly made easy the coercion of Fanny Cochrane as his subject, as well as both the planning and staging of the experiment in Joseph Milligan's home in Hobart. If correct, what is not made evident in the relayed article is the fundamental interest that Drs Smith and Milligan had in mesmerism. However, Mr Gilbert's exhibition in Port Phillip a month prior does give some insight into the alleged science of mesmerism, and its great potential for the mind and the body:

> [A] young gentleman came forward to attest the truth of the science; he had been subjected to a contraction of the knee which has rendered him lame for years; Mr Gilbert, by a few mesmeric passes, had completely cured him; several medical men testified to the truth of this, and several other cures.[33]

The notion of "animal-magnetism" enabled the belief that the mesmerist could "heal diseases of the nerves and other obstinate diseases" by mere suggestive influence, and could "perfect medicines" without the further exposure to their inherent dangers.[34] With the deaths at Oyster Cove seemingly unstoppable, and Dr Smith's administered medicines, such as mercury, only contributing to the mortality, the alleged potential of mesmerism might well have instigated a keen interest. Evidently, the work of many doctors, psychologists and scientists of the 1800s "straddled the line between materialism and spiritualism".[35] If this partially documented event gives any indication, Drs Milligan and Smith were also of this ilk.

A significant area of interest in this event is the clear administrative influence on the spirituality of the captives. Dr Smith would not only influence the health of the captives, to their sheer detriment; he appears to have also instigated the predominance of spiritualism that would be adopted by Fanny Cochrane and subsequent generations of her descendants. Oral history records known as "The Westlake papers" (c. 1908–1910) document both her and her children's unique spirituality, which includes European-style spiritualist methods of "communication". Fanny's eldest son, William, spoke of her clairvoyance through dreams.[36] Her daughter Flora stated her mother both attended and hosted seances, affirmed by a Robert Harvey, who gives richer detail:

> [We] used to sit in séance and ask questions ... waited for sounds and would all hear them. Someone sat in the middle and others used to sit round and waiting for the sounds, just squatting on the ground. Think [sic] asked a question and then waited, and the sounds guided what they were to do and they always did that.[37]

So, too, Fanny Cochrane's son Joseph spoke of this distinct style of seance: "if anyone in the neighbourhood was going to die, you could depend on it if heard three knocks on the door. If heard a rooster crow at night could tell whether good or bad news. Would go and tell the news of the death, giving three knocks on the hive or else the bees would leave."[38]

For the Smith family (that is, Fanny Cochrane's family), these modes of European spiritualism naturally became blended with their own spirituality and its distinctively Indigenous ontology, a unique amalgam that evidently finds its origin in Fanny's unusual experiences at the Oyster Cove establishment.

Chapter 16

PROPAGANDA, PROGENY AND PROSPERITY

At approximately 22 years of age, Fanny met a sawyer, William Smith, a former convict from Kent, England, who was living at North West Bay, and many years older than she. Oral history from relatives claims that, on visiting the Oyster Cove establishment, William witnessed Fanny Cochrane "running along the beach" and by her sheer grace was reminded of the "young deer he had seen in the forests of England".[1] Yet other versions tell a decidedly different story. In conversation with Mary Ann around 1859, Bonwick wrote, "[H]er sister Fanny, many years younger than herself, married a European, after some vicissitudes of virtue."[2] Additional oral histories mention she had first been in a relationship with an unnamed man at Oyster Cove, according to Mrs Alfred Hughes. "Fanny married a black first and ran away to a white man whom the government induced her to marry." Yet this is likely a reference to Plonoopinner (also known as Fanny) and not Fanny Cochrane.[3]

The new couple made an application to be wed, with Fanny granted a pension of £24 in lieu of her keep at Oyster Cove.[4] On 7 October 1854, William Smith and Fanny Cochrane married at the home of Minister Frederick Miller, on Murray Street in Hobart, with the Oyster Cove superintendent, Joseph Milligan, giving her away.[5] This moment marked a brand-new era. Finally shedding the shackles of the Aboriginal establishments, through her marriage Fanny had now secured a facility that would accord her imperfect liberty and, at the very least, the "mobility" that had been denied her kin for the previous two decades.[6]

Within a year the pair moved to Hamilton, "under an engagement to Mr. William Clarke, of Norton Manderville", and after a period of another two years, about 1857, they returned to Hobart, opening a boarding house in Liverpool Street, "two doors above the well-known premises of Perkins and Nephew".[7] Fanny appeared enraptured about her new autonomy and her marriage, and wrote to her sister Mary Ann at Oyster Cove that she was "living perfectly happy with her husband in Hobart Town".[8] On paper, with Fanny's somewhat tenuous background in domestic service, this venture had all signs pointing to success, yet would rapidly prove troublesome, with some believing it was "owing to the visits of natives from Oyster Cove, who apparently received free board with the Smiths".[9] "While the natives were alive," reported the *Mercury* in 1882, "they were constantly with Smith and his wife, who, at great expense to themselves, provided them with every comfort it was in their power to give."[10] The captives would travel miles to visit them. "Adam [Fanny's brother] travelled from Oyster Cove to Hamilton, walking all the way without boots."[11]

Their abandonment of the business could also have been related to Adam's ill-health. Wrapped in the arms of Fanny's husband, he "had been ill on and off", reflected his niece Sarah Bernice. "Father thought it consumption because he had a very bad cough. He died unexpectedly." Tragically he passed away aged a mere 20 years, on 28 October 1857. Sarah Bernice further recalled that they "didn't expect him to go; [that he] was ill through the night and died towards morning. Father had him in his arms and his last words were allegedly, 'Oh Bill, oh Fanny, oh God'."[12] Adam's body was interred at Oyster Cove, and was followed by a period of great mourning for the captives:

> [T]he natives did not know he had died but they came and we found them camped outside next morning. When father asked them how they knew, said their "father had told them". Made the death cry and came up to the house to sympathise.[13]

Adam's death likely prompted Fanny Cochrane's relocation to North West Bay around 1858.

Now back within miles of the Aboriginal establishment, her mother was granted permission to live with the Smiths during Fanny's first pregnancy. On 1 August 1858, a son, William Henry Jr, was born, causing much fuss and excitement for both Fanny and William Sr as well as the Oyster Cove captives.[14] Yet their joy was short-lived. On a visit back to the Aboriginal establishment, Tarenootairer, aged and weak, had taken severely ill with alleged "influenza". One of Fanny Cochrane's daughters narrated second-hand the moment Fanny knew of her mother's impending death:

> On the evening my grandmother was taken bad at Oyster Cove, mother said, "Bill, I can hear the natives calling me". Shortly after a native came with the news. My mother then went to my grandmother's, and when she got there my grandmother said, "Didn't you hear me call you", and my mother said, "Yes".[15]

In a period of one year, Fanny had lost both a brother and her mother, yet gained the first of her six sons. In 1859, the Smiths had once again relocated, this time settling in a small district called Irish Town, where William had leased 100 acres for felling and splitting, and by October Fanny welcomed her first of five daughters, Mary Jane.[16]

Figure 10: Photographer unknown, c. 1870s, *Portrait of Fanny Cochrane and William Smith.*

PROPAGANDA, PROGENY AND PROSPERITY

* * *

This newly settled life for Fanny Cochrane was paralleled by one of the strangest decades yet for the remaining captives at Oyster Cove. Their pre-emptive demise saw them become fodder, almost entertainment, for the colony's propaganda machine, with Mary Ann, Truganini, Pangernowidedic (Bessy Clarke) and William Lanne often paraded before Hobart Town society. By dint of her marriage, Fanny Cochrane had avoided the intensity of such celebrity, yet its effects would not pass her by:[17]

> Mrs. Fanny Cochrane Smith ... should have taken her place at the Queen's birthday balls, when Billy and Truganini, and Wapperty, and the others showed off their white kid gloves and enjoyed the sherry and tarts at Government House, but having married a gentleman following the lucrative industrial employment of a sawyer, she is out of the pale of the "haut ton" of the city.[18]

So, too, in their premature wake, the remaining captives saw a new procession of visiting Quakers and evangelists, all intent on escorting the proverbial "last of their race" to their own monotheistic imperialist "heaven":

> [T]he Bishop was detained a second night in the Cove. This is the little settlement of the Aborigines of whom a solitary example is here to be seen, the second woman being a half-caste, and the last remaining man being again engaged in a whaling expedition. Would it not be well to promote the Superintendent to some other post of trust and to dissolve the establishment? Can no humble Christian household be found willing to take charge of this very last remnant of a race, and make an attempt to let in upon it some Christian light, before it finally succumbs to that mysterious law that bids the savage races melt before the Saxon, like snow before the sun.[19]

A year later, the so-called "last man", William Lanne, died; and by 1871 the nameless "half-caste" noted by the *Tasmanian Times*, Fanny's sister, the matriarch Mary Ann – the last of her own confirmed relatives – was tragically dead too.

There is little direct documentation for this era in Fanny Cochrane's life and the reasons are quite simple. Over a period of 16 years, she gave birth to 11 children, no doubt consuming her days and nights. Oral history documents give privy to a laborious, yet happy, family life. She was a famously good cook – yet thoroughly maintained traditional protocols; she gathered native foods such as white grubs and tooreela, and roasted mullas, willilas and lunna-bunna; she would make her own dresses, a skill learned as a child at Wybalenna; she evolved into a strict but forgiving mother; and she provided regular reprieve for her people from the Aboriginal establishment, who in turn gave additional care and cultural instruction to her children.[20]

Fanny Cochrane's relationship with Truganini intensified to the extent that Truganini became surrogate mother to Fanny and grandmother to Fanny's growing progeny. However, over this period William Sr was gradually succumbing to debility, and by the birth of their last daughter, Isabella Francis, in November 1874 he was unable to work. This particular year marked the couple's 20th anniversary, which was likely celebrated with an official portrait taken in Hobart.[21] Their presence was not unnoticed by the press:

> Something "Aboriginal." – A half-caste native, named "Fanny", was married some quarter of a century since to a person known by the not very uncommon surname of Smith. The bride's dowry at the time of her marriage was an allotment of 100 acres out of the sixteen million now the property of their white and civilized exterminators. "Fanny" has not been an unfruitful hand of

PROPAGANDA, PROGENY AND PROSPERITY

the wide-spreading and reproductive tree, from whose widely-scattered seeds the human harvest springs is garnered. She has now no fewer than a full half-score of sturdy boys and blooming girls, who can legitimately claim closer relationship to the soil of Tasmania than any others now living upon it, with the exception of the aged Lallah [sic] [Truganini] and their own mother. "Fanny's" husband has not for some time past enjoyed the best of health, and is, we believe, at present under medical treatment. There is consequently beginning to arise, in the provident mind of the maternal side of the house some apprehensions lest the loss of health, which would be an irreparable calamity to a family struggling in the bush, might deprive her offspring of the assistance derived from their father's industry. Since her marriage this very excellent and industrious woman has been in the receipt of 9s 4d per week, or of a pension amounting to about 24 pounds per annum. This is not certainly a very bountiful provision, considering who the recipient is, and to what good practical uses this small pittance is applied. In dealing with such an exceptional case as this, we ought to consider it apart from all ideas of parsimony, and even rigid economy, and the fact ought not to be overlooked, that in the generation of which "Fanny" may said to be the source, we have almost the last traces of a remnant of the human family our policy has had the effect of all but extinguishing. We have seen "Fanny", and her Lord walking the last few days in Hobart Town, and we were extremely gratified to find that the industrious couple consistently maintain their character for humble and unobtrusive respectability. We hope to find a proposition submitted to Parliament during the coming session, for taking their claims to an increased pension from the State into consideration.[22]

Although Fanny indeed submitted her proposition to the ministers of parliament, little would happen by way of progress, with the pair returning to their "humble and unobtrusive" country life.

***

With the death of Fanny's sister, the Oyster Cove Aboriginal establishment had now officially closed. Her beloved maternal surrogate, Truganini, had moved to Hobart in the care of the Dandridge family and, having "the presentiment that she was going to die", in only three short years, on 8 May 1876, Truganini succumbed, aged approximately 64 years. In her last days she was afflicted by the veritable incubus called "paralysis" that had stolen the final breaths of Mary Ann and her fellow countrywomen.[23]

What effect this was to have on Fanny Cochrane can only be speculated, but with little doubt she would have been met with an orphan's feelings of grief and solitude. While she had successfully birthed a substantial progeny, she had by now lost most of her known family, both biological and cultural. Of the captives taken to the Oyster Cove establishment she was, quite literally, the only woman left.

Chapter 17

PROVE IT OR LOSE IT!

Since 1854, Fanny Cochrane had been in continuous receipt of her pension, "in lieu of her maintenance at the establishment, so as to provide against her absolute want at any time, and as an inducement to her intended husband to treat her well".[1] The colony's expenditure was regularly made public and pension lists annually published in the newspapers, where in 1860 Fanny is found listed as "Aboriginal Girl, Fanny Cochrane (Smith) 24l".[2]

In July 1874, the aforementioned article in the *Tasmanian Tribune* (quoted on pp. 146–7) not only affirmed the celebrity that Fanny Cochrane had acquired by this decade, but also made privy her precarious marital and financial situation.[3] In August, Fanny made her request to the House of Assembly.[4] Yet, by the 1880s, the petition had stalled, the reasons a matter of conjecture. In April 1882, eight years after her application, a new article appeared in multiple newspapers asserting that there was an Aboriginal (i.e., of full descent) woman still living in Port Cygnet. This retrospective article made public a declaration of Fanny Cochrane's alleged position as the apparent "last of her race":

> In addition to the natives residing at the [Oyster Cove] station there is another woman of about 28 years of age married to a white man of the name Smith. The Government allow her a pension (in lieu of rations and clothing) of about 25l [£25]; she lives with her husband upon a farm granted to them by the Government, near Port Cygnet, and about seven miles from this [Oyster Cove].

After having been married for several years, she, a few months ago, had the happiness to present to her husband a little boy; he is a fine, healthy-looking child, of whom they say all the blacks are very proud ... J.L. Dandridge, Superintendent Aborigines, Oyster Cove, May 25, 1859.

[Editor's Note:] Mrs. Fanny Cochrane Smith (a pensioner of £24 a year) is therefore now the real, live, last of the aborigines of Tasmania.[5]

The revelation to the general colonial public that Truganini, on whose death in 1876 was heralded the "extinction" of the Aboriginal Tasmanian, was not in fact the last drew considerable gasps, curiosity and outright opposition. By June, Fanny Cochrane was a "hot topic". Opinion pieces and letters to the editor ensued.[6] Approximately eight months after the publication of the article, Fanny strategically made her second move on parliament for her still much-needed pension increase. However, exposing what had possibly stifled her original claim of 1874, the concept of "aboriginal" versus "half caste" would explode her case before parliament and public alike, becoming possibly the most famous paternity debate in our history.

In daring to ask for a little bit more, Fanny Cochrane now unexpectedly found herself under threat of losing it all. "It might, at this time, be difficult to prove a matter which was not disputed when the pension was first granted," stated Mr Guesdon before parliament. "It was not fair to go behind the motion and raise a question now which might deprive the woman of her pension altogether."[7]

The "prove it or lose it" trial of the early 1880s forced Fanny and her supporters to find the appropriate evidence that the government of the day would accept, to affirm her claim or risk losing her case.[8] The Aboriginal establishments' archives were scoured by both sides, seemingly to find evidence either for or against. On 14 September, before a public jury of the *Mercury*'s readership, an anonymous author, cited as "one who knows", made the first mention of Eugene (alias Nicermenic), as that much-desired patriarch.[9] This author's knowledge reflects that which James Barnard, claiming to be the one to have searched the records, presented before the Royal Society in 1889, likely identifying his alias.[10] "According to Mr Barnard, Sarah was the name of Mrs Cochrane's mother, and Eugene that of her father, and both were undeniably aboriginals" – the key words here being "according to Mr Barnard", suggesting Nicermenic's patrimony was not Fanny Cochrane's claim but a result of the research Barnard had conducted.[11]

James Barnard, a friend of the former superintendent, Joseph Milligan, who visited the Oyster Cove establishment and claimed to have remembered Fanny well, evidently trawled through the available records and found the only acceptable document. This was a deposition from around 1846 from the Wybalenna Aboriginal establishment, which referred to "Eugene and Sarah being the father and mother of Fanny and Adam" and was signed by multiple witnesses. At last the so-called evidence of Fanny Cochrane's patrimony was at hand and her request could proceed through the House of Assembly.

The September 1882 sitting raised the various agendas that had been bubbling under the surface since the death of Truganini. Although not doubting that Fanny was Indigenous, a Mr Dooley stated that she was not actually the last, "for there was a man, with a wife and nine children, still living, and, when it was last proposed to increase Fanny Cochrane's pension, he was in the House [of Assembly] to see if he could not be placed on the pension list too".[12]

In total contrast, a Mr Lyne insisted that Fanny was a half-caste and had been in his employ some 25 years prior, and that "there were now some 50 half-castes like her, and they might desire to be pensioned likewise". A Mr Douglas also raised his own veritable concerns, whereby he "could not understand on what principle an unfortunate black woman should be better treated than a white woman".[13]

The minister of lands attempted to officially close the case in support of Fanny Cochrane, stating that he "had known Fanny Cochrane for many years". Further, he said, "She had all the appearance of an aboriginal. She and her husband had been hard-working people in their time, but both were now past work. The husband was an invalid. There was a large family to provide for, and he supported the motion."[14] Despite all raised concerns, this particular sitting closed with the motion agreed to grant Fanny her pension increase to £52 per annum.

Responding to Mr Lyne's wrongful assumption, the Smiths stated they "had been residing in Port Cygnet for the past 25 years, and were married in 1857 [sic], so that they could not have been in Swansea at the time Mr Lyne referred to".[15] In a scarcely documented encounter, Fanny had organised a meeting with the politician himself, resulting in an alleged retraction of his statements against her:

> When Fanny Smith met Mr. Lyne face to face, he acknowledged his error, not only to her, but to the House of Assembly, which he had misled; and, in like manner, when Captain Copping confronted him with the truth, he likewise acknowledged the error of his ways, and made the "amende honorable", as far as he could, both in the House of Assembly and through the Press.[16]

In his defence, Lyne retorted that he conceded Fanny Cochrane was not the Indigenous woman named Smith he had presumed (it must be noted that the description given by Mr Lyne befits that of Mary Ann Smith[17]), yet he remained unswayed in his belief that she was a "half-caste".[18] Although not necessarily granted on the grounds of her "caste" (but it must be conceded it certainly played a part), her pension increase was approved on sentiments regarding her poor financial situation. "[H]er husband was now over 60 years of age, and was quite unable to gain his livelihood as in former years. She herself was now beyond her 50th year, and was unable to support herself."[19] The verdict naturally drew outcries from a handful of detractors and those who had been denied their due by dint of a mixed heritage.[20]

However, not all of this trial was full of negatives and doubters; in re-evaluating the case it seems that, for the most part, Fanny's claim was indeed supported. "[I]t suffices that she exists, and, we contend that, whatever may have been the colour of her immediate male progenitor, it is a collateral consideration which should not affect Fanny's claim on the Tasmanian public and Government."[21]

With the case firmly closed, at least in parliament, it became of little public interest once again. However, after two years, Fanny Cochrane was to take things one step further.

* * *

By now, her large family, still so young, was more than she could handle. William was almost totally impaired and unable to share the burden of their hand-to-mouth existence. In 1884, having inhabited, cleared and cultivated the land, the family "looked upon the homestead as their own" and desired to own it, instigating yet another petition to parliament.[22] Not merely the very foundation of colonisation itself, land ownership was also the ingredient by which autonomy and social relevance was (and still is) measured. However, this desire for both charity and autonomy was coming at a price. The maintenance of such independence was a fragile game.

Fanny Cochrane was now applying for 500 acres of land to be granted to her "free of cost".[23] It was immediately noted by ministers that, as stated by a Dr Butler, "the woman had already been treated exceedingly well by the Government, and to go much farther would be to provoke very large demands on the indulgence of Parliament". To the House of Assembly, a small pension increase was one thing; land was evidently another.

The debate over Fanny Cochrane's "caste" was elevated once again, going from a raised eyebrow to a full-blown parliamentary inquiry. It was demanded that all available evidence be laid upon the table of the house, "particularly reports by Superintendents Dr. Milligan and Mr. Dandridge".[24]

Unlike the 1882 "prove it or lose it" trial that, although contested, appears to have run relatively smoothly, now the appointed ministers appeared to be playing a petty, dirty game – the term "half-caste" having a life all its own:

> Mr Reibey moved that the resolution be recommitted, in order to strike out the words "half-caste." He had not intended that they should be inserted.
>
> Mr Gellibrand pointed out that in the motion on the 30th ult ... the woman had been clearly designated as an aboriginal, and he was at a loss to understand how or by what authority the words "half-caste" had been inserted in that day's notice-paper.
>
> Mr Bird said he had been surprised to see the words included. Very few people, he believed, really believed Fanny Smith to be a pure aboriginal, but she had already twice received grants from Parliament, and was given the benefit of the doubt.[25]

So, too, the news media reignited their objections, exposing their own biased agenda. For example, "[T]he late Mr James Simpson, editor of the *Mercury*, opposed the claims of Fanny Smith to any recognition in a pecuniary way by the Government as an aboriginal, with all the vigour and talent at his command."[26] Yet, akin to Minister Lyne of 1882, Simpson had been granted permission to review the various documentations of Milligan and Dandridge and emerged corrected. When "he found out that he was wrong ... he had the manliness to acknowledge his error, and to advocate what he had previously opposed".[27]

Still, both parliamentary and public trepidations ensured her application moved at a glacial pace. In 1888, four years after her land grant request was made public, Fanny Cochrane – who had remained relatively silent – had finally had enough and was forced to publicly defend her stance.[28]

Samuel Dove, a friend of the Smiths and proprietor of the Tattersall's Hotel, wrote to the editors of the *Mercury* on 4 October 1888 on behalf of Fanny and her husband. The letter, published on 9 October, states:

> Sir. – In a local paragraph of your issue on the 5th inst., you refer to Fanny Smith nee Cochrane, who claims to be the last of the aboriginals of this colony, and you further suggest that it is worthwhile for a committee of inquiry to be held as to her alleged claim. I am instructed by Fanny Smith to say that that is what she should like to take place, and further, both Fanny and her husband will pay the full expense of such inquiry should she fail to establish her rights ... If you, Mr. Editor, or any of your various readers are desirous of any further information, I shall be only too pleased to give that same as to establishing Fanny's claim.[29]

Curiously, this statement does not name Fanny's parents. Her defiant challenge, at least for now, went unmatched. Proving that she was indeed the "last Tasmanian" following the death of her maternal surrogate became the least of Fanny Cochrane's many challenges. Of equal importance was her social and moral worthiness of the government's charity she so desperately sought; in summary, she needed to answer the minister's challenge of "why a black woman should be treated better than a white".

This was not unusual for the period. Akin to emancipated black individuals globally (especially in the North and Central Americas), Fanny Cochrane's success in gaining and maintaining her autonomy depended on an ability to prove her value as an industrious citizen, Christian woman, mother and so-called civilised savage.[30]

In response, a counteractive propaganda had to be scripted. Journalists in favour of Fanny Cochrane's petitions promoted the family as no less than salt-of-the-earth people, of overt piousness and moral code, and a veritable example of the benefits of colonialism:

> Fanny Smith is about 55 years of age, and has eleven children and six grand-children. She has had her children educated to read and write, and this has been done almost wholly by her own exertions … All the members of her family are total abstainers – they are good living, God-fearing, law abiding, industrious people. They are no hangers on to charitable institutions …[31]

Their "industriousness" was also deemed in equal measure to that of the white settlers:

> [O]n grounds of more self-interest a Government might, with good reason, make an additional grant of land to the respective member of this uniquely aboriginal or semi-aboriginal family; as they work hard, so they contribute to the general weal. They pay taxes and rent, and in common with the whites, consume dutiable goods, and so add to the revenue.[32]

By the end of 1888, progress was still wanting. In desperation, even poor William, ailing but still very much alive, was now cast as prematurely deceased, with members of parliament painting Fanny as a hard-done-by widow of upstanding character.[33] Collectively these contrived portraits were hardly a reflection of reality.[34] Yet it was all worth the effort when, after five years of dissension and debate, Fanny Cochrane finally won favour. In November 1889, the motion was finally ratified. She was now in ownership of a substantial plot of the Crown's "Waste Lands", totalling a reduced 305 acres, still a significant achievement indeed.[35] The trial was officially over and the case presumed closed.[36]

Her marriage in 1854 had granted her emancipation from the Aboriginal establishments, and now the land she occupied would grant her a unique personal and cultural freedom, yet one purposefully hidden from public view – at least for the time being.

* * *

A positive by-product of the intense political scrutiny of the 1880s is what is possibly the first known photograph of the Smith family. Photographs were an expensive luxury in the late-Victorian era and usually trailed a celebratory event. Although an exact date for the group portrait is unobtainable, by intensive comparative judgements of the youthful appearances of the children (the identities of whom have produced much confusion), it was likely taken sometime between 1885 and 1889. Fanny, now in her mid to late 50s, is dressed in her finest Victorian dress, seated in front of their hand-built wooden cottage replete with shingle and bark roof, a shrub intertwined through a picket fence. Accompanied by her husband, the pair are flanked by some of their children and grandchildren. The photograph is a perfect match for the political and public propaganda of the decade. It showcases a handsome family of humble respectability, Fanny Cochrane in stoic matriarch mode, surrounded by her successful appropriation of European civility, attuned to socio-political tastes and ripe for colonial consumption.

Figure 11: Photographer unknown, c. late 1890s, portrait of Fanny Cochrane Smith.

Chapter 18

RITUALS OF CAPTIVITY

Deconstructing Indigenous "Christianity"

This now-orthodox character portrait of Fanny Cochrane Smith was wholly embraced, dominating her narrative to the present day. Rarely recognised as counteractive propaganda to appease and win favour from the colonial authority, her public image is one of great Victorian piety and charitability – famously polite and generous, a devout Christian who never "forgot that she was Aboriginal".[1] She was a devoted mother and wife, loved by everyone, and was able "to gain the respect of all the Europeans who knew her".[2] One cannot deny she embodied all of these traits, yet her worth appears eternally valued by her ability to seek and obtain respect from the white populace.

As previously discussed, James Bonwick's character profiles of Mary Ann and Walter Arthur have a direct symmetry with the main characters in *Uncle Tom's Cabin* (1852). So, too, the characteristics of Stowe's Topsy, the "pickaninny" – portrayed as a thieving, lying and "unruly" young girl who "goes through various training stages, culminating with her appropriation of good manners at a level commensurate with her racially inherited miming abilities" – are all wholly reflected in Fanny Cochrane's scripted "character portrait".[3] Throughout her childhood and teenage years, she was herself deemed wholly "unruly" and violently protested control by the administration. Yet somehow, through marriage, motherhood and patriarchal generosity, she becomes the respectable figurehead of successful colonialism.

This portrait appears most liberally disseminated after her death. "Fanny Smith used to speak of God as her heavenly parent," noted local storekeeper Robert Harvey, a part-time clerk who signed off on the birth registries of most of Fanny Cochrane's children and some grandchildren (and even a few great-grandchildren). He further stated that "unlike most religious people who do not like to express their beliefs", Fanny openly did so. Harvey stated he had "heard her in meeting[s] and her address was always with a religious strain", and thought a "wonderful change came over her life in her connection with the Methodist Church [and she c]ould express her views in her own way, more vivid than in any persons I have known".[4]

The above is a mere example of the overt or devout Christian image applied to Fanny Cochrane both during her life and after her death, and there appears to be a continued post-colonial pride in Fanny's adopted religiosity. Her public embracement of a Christian image enabled the colony to neatly wrap up the end game for Tasmania's Indigenous peoples in a pious and digestible bow, a singular colonial success story to end a chapter of embarrassing sadistic brutality.

In a continuous "earning" of emancipation from a paternalistic government, Christianity becomes a way for the oppressed to potentially buy their autonomy, if they are "devout" and "skilled" enough in their preaching.[5] Yet, when metaphorically peeling off the veneer of Fanny's Christianity and critically examining her unique "Aboriginal Christian" culture, there emerges a distinct contradiction.

* * *

There is little written on the influence of religion, specifically Christianity, on Indigenous Tasmanians in the early days of contact and colonisation, yet the "Aboriginal Christian" has played a significant role in the historical narrative of Tasmanian colonialism. From George Augustus Robinson's conciliation missions to the religion-focused "education" of the Orphan School and the Aboriginal establishments, the Christianising of Indigenous Tasmanians has been used to both justify and excuse attempted cultural genocide. Yet, although placed strategically at the foreground of colonisation, the actual influence Christianity had on the captive Tasmanians is debatable.[6] Despite his best efforts, Robinson conceded that at any given opportunity most of them remained firmly committed to their culture and their "devils".

From the very beginning, the Christian church was to play a major role in the attempted "civilising" of the Indigenous peoples, and Methodist ministers were present from the outset.[7] One minister, known as Mansfield, was enlisted by Governor Arthur in 1824 to assist in the cause of the "civilization and instruction of the Aborigines of the Island" and so, too, Arthur's appointed conciliator, George Augustus Robinson, was a staunch Methodist.[8] For Robinson, the appeal of Methodist doctrine was a belief in man's equality – that all are "Brothers in Christ".[9] Its strength of influence saw him set up a Christian mission on Bruny Island in 1828, a type of "foundation-stone" for his fateful "friendly mission".

Together with the Baptists, Methodist doctrine was highly influential in the Afro-American south. Its strict policy of anti-slavery proved powerful and essential, and no doubt was its central appeal to Fanny Cochrane.[10] The Methodist theology saw slavery as against the teachings of Jesus and sought to abolish it; in fact, the denomination's founders,

John Wesley, Francis Asbury and Thomas Coke, were so opposed to it, they would only accept members once they had signed emancipation papers.[11]

During their lifetime, the socio-political impact of Christian and Methodist doctrine on the likes of Mary Ann and Walter Arthur was evident, yet it became clear that their Christianity was not one of genuine spirituality, but rather a ritual habit of their enslavement or captivity.[12] The concept of religion as comprising acts of ritual rather than spiritual engagement is highly significant. Religious rituals need not have a spiritual foundation. States Pares, "[R]itual may be seen as the arena in which social contradictions are worked out and systematically subsumed within a reaffirmation of unity".[13] This harkens back to Fanny Cochrane's teenage years at Oyster Cove. Walter George Arthur, perhaps more a political Christian than spiritual, is alleged to have stated that he read from the Bible to his family every night, and the subsequent nightly Bible readings of the 1880s, performed by Fanny and her family in her kitchen, can be viewed as a continuation of this routine.[14]

Despite being slaves themselves (or poverty-stricken emancipated slaves), the so-called Black Churches in North America's Deep South engaged in mission works such as fundraising.[15] This is paralleled by Fanny in the charity fundraisers she would host, such as this event advertised in *The Hobart Mercury* in 1900:

> Mrs Fanny Smith, of Irish Town, promoted a successful tea and concert at her farm on the 14th inst, in aid of the fund for the widows and orphans through the present war. The large barn presented a festive appearance, decorated with ferns and flowers, and the tables bore evidence of Mrs Smith's famed skill in cookery. The spread was one to compare well with the best of its kind.[16]

RITUALS OF CAPTIVITY

Fanny was born directly into an established captive society where regimes of colonialism were her daily culture. The rituals of the Aboriginal establishments consisted of traditions such as hunting, dancing and singing, but these were stifled by domestic duties during the day and then evening school and Bible studies. Through many oral histories we see this "captive culture" continuously practised in the daily lives of Fanny Cochrane and her children in the late 19th and early 20th centuries, painting an alternative view of familial ontology. They are not acting out a supposed cultural and spiritual creolisation born of a hybridised marital union between an Indigenous woman and a white convict, but are literally enacting the identical rituals performed by their relatives in the captive culture of the Aboriginal establishments from the 1830s onward. A mere example of this is found in the aforementioned ritual of charity. The captives at Oyster Cove would take biannual tours for the purpose of gathering charity for the establishment, which was a convention maintained by Fanny Cochrane long after the establishment was closed. For example, "Mrs Smith … used to make a tour every six months and visit houses – and put things in collecting bags."[17]

The early life of Fanny's mother, Tarenootairer, made evident the influence of her own "slave" identity. When researching the varied concepts of slave culture – that is, the culture formed *by* the slaves in response to their enslavement, as opposed to cultures formed by the use of slaves – there is one standout feature: spirituality. It becomes clear in slave cultures that their central foundation is the retainment of a distinct "black spirituality" (pre-Christian) and its varied rituals.[18] This can be explained in relation to the displacement of Indigenous or slave peoples – they can be physically removed from their cultural landscape, stripped of traditional clothing and all visual representations of their former cultures, and even their language restricted or banned; however, an individual's non-tangible spiritual convictions are much harder to break down.

Fanny's global contemporaries[19] contextualised their socio-cultural status through a diverse amalgam of spiritualities, such as European Catholic, African and Indigenous. This formula led to a unique celebration of emancipation through overt spiritual expression.[20] In parallel, Fanny Cochrane blended the eclecticism of the Aboriginal establishments – the socio-political Methodist Christian doctrines of her authorities, the occult sciences of spiritualism and the ancient spirituality of her family – to fashion an adult life devoted to a deep, and unique, spiritual ontology.

The land at Nicholls Rivulet itself also experienced a resurgence of cultural and spiritual customs. The granting of permanent residency replanted the serpentine daily routine of the Aboriginal establishments, and also allowed the family to reinstate their physical relationship to land and land uses, which, in turn, ignited the redevelopment of a deeper spiritual relationship to the land. On becoming land owners (by the colonial European definition at least), the land, wood and fire spirits became active once more, and this is but an example.

Together with the aforementioned spiritualism and spirit possession, Fanny Cochrane is known to have seen spirits conjured from rocks through dance and song, to have an ability to see ghosts and apparitions, and to sense impending sickness or the death of family members.[21] She maintained a deep relationship with the heavens and would pay homage to the skies: "three little stars in the east on a level only once in the year … F[anny] S[mith] thought it a terrible thing if didn't welcome these three little stars." And she reportedly threw ashes from her hearth towards the spring morning star "… to strengthen him and bring warm weather".[22] These are but fragments of her strength of indigeneity – of a woman holding firm the spirits and culture of her people. Can one be both devoutly Christian *and* spirit conjurer, to commune with "God" and with fire? I believe to do both is to be something else entirely – something more, much more.

Unfortunately, anthropological and ethnographical notions of cultural or racial "purity" have denigrated the nature of Fanny Cochrane's diverse and remarkable spiritual culture.[23] The influence of the plantation missions of North and Central America, through the adoption and influence of Methodist Christian paradigms, is a socio-cultural ingredient I believe, in Tasmania, to be unique to Fanny Cochrane and her family, wholly shaping a personal culture as well as a public image for the next century.

Yet this has consistently been used against her. Ignoring the rich and vast "black" experience under the paper-thin veneer of "whiteness", Fanny Cochrane's social and spiritual ideology has consistently been dismissed as diluted or impure. Once again, proving her indigeneity would be at the foreground of a public tug-of-war.

Chapter 19

KING BILLY'S PLAYMATE

A four-room cottage in the remote orcharding district, about seven miles south of Hobart, offered little by way of excitement in the late-colonial period.[1] No doubt, in such intimate confines, privacy was little known, and whispers always heard. With Fanny's husband frail and increasingly confined to a wheelchair, her eldest daughter, Mary Jane, likely attended to most of the maternal duties for the youngest still at home.

One of the only remaining survivors of the Oyster Cove Aboriginal establishment, Fanny Cochrane, as matriarch, would have given her children a childhood that embraced the traditional customs of her maternal world – eating native foods, curing with traditional medicines,[2] weaving fibres, threading shells, singing ancient seasonal songs, and both conjuring and communing with the spirits of the dead.[3] Publicly, however, educating in and engaging with the culture of the paternal coloniser was essential – from kitchen sermons and home-schooling in literacy to felling forests and farming crops. Fabricating an image of colonial appropriation and astute piousness was necessary for continued autonomy and emancipation.

Promoting this estimable late-Victorian exterior, for which the Smiths were now highly regarded, masked much of the inevitable trials and tribulations that such a large family engenders. The onset of public scrutiny throughout the 1880s had transformed them from discreet, humble labourers into the colony's most famous Indigenous family, surely offering little "freedom" for a young child: an upstanding public image was an essential prize for the greater good.

For Fanny's youngest three, namely Laura Martha (b. 1870), Charles Edward (b. 1872) and Isabella Francis (b. 1874), this serpentine regime – of sliding between two cultures – dictated their daily lives. Although objectively offering a cultural and spiritual richness, it evidently couldn't compensate for the stifling isolation of the countryside.

In the early summer of 1885, Laura, now 15 years of age, plotted her escape. Packing a single hat and armed with two dresses, one dark plaid and the other navy blue (one to be worn, the other a spare), she managed to quietly slip away unnoticed – destination Hobart, a hefty but doable nine-hour walk from Cygnet.[4] Described as "dark and swarthy" with raven hair, and with a "stout" build at 5 feet, 1 inch in stature, her visage reflected the strong and determined personality within.[5] If she had thought her plan would unfold with discretion, however, she was sorely mistaken. Her adventure made both the *Police Gazette* and the news media:[6]

> Information is requested respecting Laura Smith, who left her home, Irish Town, near Port Cygnet, about 1 p.m. on the 21st instant. As she was subject to hysterical fits it is feared she may have come to some harm. A search party has been out since, but failed to find any trace of her … If not affected in her mind she may possibly make for Hobart. She is said to be the last of the aboriginals.[7]

After five nervous days, Laura was reported found on 26 December. "We understand that the girl, Laura Smith, who was reported to the territorial police as missing from her home has been found," noted the *Mercury*, yet no further details of her brazen journey were given, nor whether she returned home or made it to Hobart – the latter the most likely.[8]

Back home, co-officiating as witness to her big sister Mary Jane's quaint home wedding was the only discernible excitement for the youngest, Isabella.[9] Like her sister Laura, she was developing an indestructible sense of independence. In 1890, Isabella was in her mid-teens and had met a man by the documented name of James Stirrup.[10] At the tender age of 15 years, Isabella became pregnant, subsequently welcoming a son on 27 May 1891. With her mother the informant, Fanny registered the child five weeks later in the district of Port Cygnet with the elaborate name of Chester James Augustus Stirrup,[11] colloquially shortened to Gus.

As Fanny Cochrane was entering her elderly years with a wheelchair-bound husband and a farm to tend to, a new child was surely not a heartily welcomed addition to her already hand-to-mouth existence, yet it was a development she appears to have taken in her stride.

The day-to-day details of Gus's early childhood with his grandparents require no small amount of conjecture, yet he later gave slight but significant details in his adult conversations. Around 1910, Gus shared with Ernest Westlake the trivial reminiscences of a child, such as his grandmother having "little dumpy toes as wide as long", and a handful of Indigenous vocabulary he no doubt heard most often. It is not difficult to evoke the voice of his grandmother shrilling "Paraway (Get away) pukukana [sic] (little boy) … nina toolabri my carni? (do you understand me, or my talk?)".[12] To this, names of both good and bad spirits were added, and the bulk of Gus's interview details the intense spiritualism embedded in the culture of his family.[13]

* * *

As the Smith family lived in continuous ebb and flow with the seasons, in the aftermath of the political discourse throughout the 1880s, a man named Henry Ling Roth had now taken up the challenge of proving whether Fanny Cochrane was "a pure aborigine".[14] In 1891 he had requested to obtain portraits of Fanny for review and comparison with known photographs of her contemporaries. Fanny was not eager to accommodate. It took a further three years, until around 1894, before she finally granted a series of three photographic portraits (including a family portrait with her husband and two eldest sons), as well as various hair samples requested by Roth.[15] Poorly concluding she was no more than a "half-caste", in 1898 Roth finally presented his dissertation before the Royal Society, publishing it a year later as an appendix to the second edition of *The Aborigines of Tasmania* (1899). Although the edition was initially limited to a mere 225 prints, the influence of Roth's negative conclusion would be far-reaching.

However, Fanny Cochrane had been here before. Perhaps anticipating a third round of public denigration, and mimicking her counteractive actions to the parliamentary inquiry a decade earlier, in 1895 or 1896, she had set aside one acre of her land grant to be held "until the necessity arises for us to erect a church".[16]

Roth's challenge to, and subsequent denial of, Fanny Cochrane's identity had set a new wheel in motion. Likely a direct response to the publication of Roth's book, an event was organised with the Royal Society of Tasmania to showcase, for the first time on record, her strength of "indigeneity".

In 1899, an important trip to Hobart Town beckoned. On 5 August, dressed in their winter finest – Fanny Cochrane in blazered frock with a large silk bow and turtle-shell buttons, and an eight-year-old Gus dressed in a woollen fitted three-quarter suit replete with matching cap and buckled leather shoes – Fanny and her grandson entered the Royal Society Room at the Tasmanian Museum. Fanny was here to record, for the first time on phonograph, traditional Indigenous songs and be coolly interviewed by the awaiting Society Members.[17] What part Gus played in this event is unknown; however, he appears to have been introduced to the gathering as "her nephew Gussie".

Awaiting her were the society's members, consisting of "the Bishop of Tasmania, the Rt. Rev. H. H. Montgomery; Mr. R. M. Johnston, the Registrar-General of Tasmania; Mr. A. Morton, Secretary of the Royal Society and Curator of the Tasmanian Museum; Mr. J. W. Beattie; Superintendent J. Cook; Mr Fisher … and Mr. James Backhouse Walker".[18]

With Fisher operating the phonograph, Fanny confidently began the proceedings: "I'm Fanny Smith. I was born on Flinders Island. I'm the last of the Tasmanians …" This was followed by a short question and answer before she commenced the "Corroboree Song".[19]

The "Corroboree Song" appears to have been a popular, or common, song among Indigenous Tasmanians, especially those of the north-eastern nations. Although this was the first phonograph recording made, it was not the first time the song had been documented.[20] Its popularity, and continual recital, suggests it was sung "in festival" at the Aboriginal establishments. This immediately brings to mind yet another of Annie Benbow's naive sketches of Oyster Cove, detailing a large congregation of Indigenous captives, comprised entirely of women, in a vibrant dance or celebration. In two opposing groups, with legs in motion and arms outreached, their knitted red caps like flaming torches, the women appear to both goad and mirror each other in movement. Their infamous dogs join in the excitement while the ghostly figure of a "white man" appears to keep a safe distance from the bustle. A woman in Mary Ann's likeness sits on the ground watching (like the proverbial queen) with a very young child on her knee, as if the dancers are performing just for them, flanked by two black men and a seated white woman and child.[21]

The second song, known here as the "Spring Song", begins with Fanny's English translation before she sings in the original Indigenous tongue. The brief program closed with various speeches of acknowledgement given by the society members on behalf of "scientific men and all true colonists", with the bishop and society vice-president, Reverend Montgomery, orating:

> It has been my great privilege today ... to have witnessed Mrs Fanny Smith ... sing and speak into the gramophone ... I feel very glad indeed that the aboriginal language of these islands, together with its songs, however fragmentary the results may be, have at least been permanently registered and can be preserved and listened to in future years, when this, and the remaining representatives of the native race have passed away.[22]

Although polite, the bishop's sentiments expose an evident degree of contempt, and other members overtly expressed their predetermined ideology of "caste", as Walker relayed to Roth. "If you could have seen her, you might have made your paper much stronger. She has a pink tinge in her cheeks, and is manifestly a half caste. The Bishop said so at once ..."[23] The dress worn by Fanny Cochrane in Montgomery's group photograph is identical to that worn in an additional three ethnographic-style portraits, identifying that these photographs – which are styled in similar vein to those taken on behalf of Roth in 1894 – were captured at the same sitting (or on the same day) by J. W. Beattie.

For Fanny Cochrane, this session had evidently been intended to preserve her "character" – a response to Roth's denigration of her race with a brief but overt display of her indigeneity before the ever-contemptible "haut ton". However, this renewed ethnographic interest in her life, culture and language had much greater potential.

Figure 12: Photographer unknown (likely J. W. Beattie), c. 1899, portrait of Fanny Cochrane Smith.

KING BILLY'S PLAYMATE

* * *

Fanny Cochrane's personal and financial hardships appeared eternal, so now she took her talents on the road. In the same month as she made the phonographic recordings, August 1899, and with assistance from Horace Watson, who was an avid collector of ethnography, she began a series of advertised public benefit concerts. (It must be noted she was not the first in her family to do this):[24]

> King Billy's Playmate. – At the entertainment given by Mr. Horace Watson at Sandy Bay on Tuesday evening last, "A Night with the Blacks," a very unique and remarkable item was introduced into the programme. Mrs. Fanny Cochrane Smith, the last survivor of the Tasmanian aboriginal race, was present, and at the lecturer's invitation spoke and sang in her native tongue to the audience. She stated that she and King Billy had been brought up together, and appeared quite touched when pictures of many of her old friends amongst the aborigines were shown on the screen. In all probability this sole representative in the whole world of an almost extinct race will appear shortly before the public here.[25]

A second benefit was advertised in October:

> The Last of the Mohicans. – An entertainment for the benefit of Mrs. Fanny Cochrane Smith, the last of the Tasmanian aboriginal race, will be given in the Temperance Hall on Monday evening. Lantern views of Australasian and South Sea natives will be given. There will be an exhibition of native weapons and an instrumental concert.[26]

This particular concert was awarded with a review a fortnight later:

> Mrs. Fanny Cochrane Smith, the last of the Tasmanian aborigines – that is to say a daughter of an aboriginal on the mother's side – has been given a benefit entertainment in the Temperance-hall.

> She made a neat, intelligent and amusing little speech, in good idiomatic English. She vindicated the good character of her race, described their love of honesty, and said that, unlike white people, they disliked kissing, which they looked upon as an insecure method of salutation. Speaking of herself, she said she was 55 years of age [sic], had 11 children, who were all still living, and that, for many years past, her husband (who is a white man) had been disabled by paralysis. She speaks three native languages or dialects, and sang two songs in her own particular tongue, which were simple and melodious.[27]

Further, the popularity of these entertainments even saw requests to have her conduct a tour of Hobart Town schools:

> [W]ith a view of interesting our boys and girls in this important subject, I would like, if arrangements could be made, that our several State schools be visited by Mr Watson and Mrs Smith. I am sure the Minister of Education … whose sympathies are with the children, will give his consent, so that the little ones may have an opportunity of hearing from the lips of Mrs Smith the peculiar chants rendered by the natives in days gone by.[28]

The pinnacle of these concerts was an unprecedented performance at Government House, and an official portrait in commemoration of the event.[29] In these years a new series of photographic portraits of Fanny was also produced. Gone was the humble cottage-style "mammy" of the previous decade – now stood a woman of veritable Indigenous regality. In these photographs, Fanny Cochrane is, for the first time, showcased in traditional dress. She is adorned with wallaby pelts around her waist and wrists, and lengthy strings of famed maireener shells that are draped around her bust (albeit placed over the top of her dark, minimalist, Victorian-esque gown), which are all intended to reflect the nature of her concerts – where she would sing traditional Indigenous songs and orate memories of her culture, family and life at Oyster Cove. One of the four known portraits from this particular session is not a portrait of Fanny Cochrane per se, but an opportunistic rear photograph of her exquisitely decorated headdress. Blending Indigenous and introduced materials, this headdress presents a wreath-like garland of fashioned nouveau-esque peacock feathers, nondescript flowers, a delicately threaded string of rice shells and wide pinstriped ribbon tied in a large bustle at the nape. With her daughter Laura a burgeoning milliner and now living in Hobart, where the photographs were taken (presumed to be at the Beattie Studios), Laura was the prime candidate for both visionary and executioner.

Collectively, such portrayals, as well as the benefit concerts, further aided in solidifying the persona of Fanny Cochrane that we know today. Her measures to publicly showcase her strength of indigeneity, as well as her maternal and moral character, had essentially worked. Yet, as per her style, she would take that one additional step. Essentially picking up where her sister had left off (Mary Ann and Walter had attempted to establish the Flinders Island Bible Society at Wybalenna), construction began on Fanny Cochrane's most enduring legacy, with the foundation stone of the Methodist church at Nicholls Rivulet firmly laid on 6 November 1900.[30]

Chapter 20

GOODBYE, MY FATHER, MOTHER

The church took six months to build, with the benchmark first service held on 5 May 1901, helmed by the Reverend C. W. Atkinson.[1] Hewn from local forest, with a blue-gum exterior and Huon-pine interior, this humble wooden box would become the first active Indigenous congregation in Tasmania since the close of the Aboriginal settlements and the death of Fanny's sister and brother-in-law.[2] She and two of her sons, Joseph Thomas Sears and Tasman Benjamin, were on the board of trustees.[3] Importantly, Methodist ministries allowed black men to serve as lay preachers, with Fanny's eldest, William Henry Jr, appointed the first lay preacher of this refurbished Nicholls Rivulet parish.[4] The turn of the new century also saw Fanny Cochrane play host to a Sunday-school picnic on her farm, with a large group portrait taken of the Nicholls Rivulet community.[5] Only a few of Fanny Cochrane's children are present, along with their spouses, a handful of her grandchildren and local associates. Standing centre stage is Fanny herself, with William Sr seated beside her.

* * *

With the trials of the previous decade now relegated to the last century, the year of Federation in Australia marked a new beginning for Fanny

Cochrane. Reaching her late 60s, a less public and more settled life beckoned; however, enjoying the benefits she had both sacrificed and fought for was short-lived:

> On Wednesday 26th [November 1902], Mr Wm Smith, of Nicholas's Rivulet [sic], passed over to the great majority, at the ripe age of 81 years, after having been a great sufferer for the last 30 years. By his death the State loses one of the links in the early history of Tasmania, he having married Fanny Cochrane, the last of the aborigines, who survives him, and whose kindly face is so familiar in the Port Cygnet district. He also leaves 6 sons and 5 daughters, each of them commanding the respect of the community. The deceased was buried in the Wesleyan churchyard, the Rev. Mr Atkinson officiating, his funeral being largely attended, many residents coming from long distances to pay their last respects.[6]

What cultural impact William Sr was to have on the evolving culture of the Smith family and Nicholls Rivulet is hard to ascertain. As a sort of spectral figure, paralysed for many decades by an unspecified impairment, his legacy appears one of mutual devotion between him and his famed wife.[7]

This blow was followed by another. Oral history states the personal turmoil of her youngest daughter, Isabella (Gus's mother), had reached its crescendo around 1902.[8] Her vague and mysterious death was but a silent tragedy rife with rumour and continued hearsay.[9] No exact date of death can be determined for Isabella. There is simply no death record at all – no official certificate, no log-book record or even a concise timeframe can be ascertained.[10] Her eldest brother, William Henry, in a letter dated 1924, enigmatically noted that she had died "some few years" after the birth of her son Augustus.[11]

* * *

These tragic losses no doubt took their toll. Fanny would escape into her friends' company expressing great "worry over her children".[12] The year of 1903 shows a Fanny Cochrane drastically aged from the photographs of the 1890s. Having lost substantial weight, she is frail and small.

What was no doubt a great distraction from her grief, on 8 and 10 October, at Horace Watson's home, known as Barton Hall, in Sandy Bay, Fanny was now making new records on phonograph.[13] "Mr. Horace Watson …", noted the *Mercury* in 1909, "an ardent student of aboriginal life, had shown much kindness to Mrs. Fanny Cochrane Smith, one of the direct descendants of the Tasmanian Aboriginals, and she had to show her gratitude to him by singing two of the native songs into a phonograph."[14] The "kindness" this article speaks of is retold by Miss Emily Keene, who stated, "Mr. Watson had organised a concert for Fanny Cochrane Smith's benefit when financial troubles arose, and the recordings were made out of appreciation for Mr. Watson's services."[15]

Watson's records contain longer, more complete versions of the songs originally recorded by the Royal Society in 1899.[16] Despite her jovial disposition, akin to the earlier Royal Society session – where Fanny can be heard expressing her grief for her parents, saying "Goodbye, my father, mother" – so, too, a deep melancholy imbues Watson's recordings, described as "tuneful, and somewhat sad".[17] Likely sung in chorus, "in antiphonal, or responsorial style", all that is present is her solitary and poorly preserved voice.[18]

The phonograph records of 1903 were to be her last hurrah. "Cylinder 8", as the recording was known, concluded the day with the last haunting words from Fanny Cochrane herself: "Fanny Smith now commences to sing this hymn but quickly reverts to the aboriginal style of singing. The only recognisable phrase is 'Praise the Lord'."[19]

Figure 13: A. A. Rollings, 1903.
Fanny Cochrane Smith Recording Aboriginal Songs for Horace Watson.

* * *

The last year of Fanny Cochrane's extraordinary life is little known. In April 1904, she appointed a new Methodist minister to her church, the Reverend T. Roberts. Hosting a "concert and coffee social", she welcomed him with "one of the songs of the Tasmanian Aborigines", her son Tasman following with his own "vocal number".[20]

With an organ purchased and donated by a daughter-in-law, sermons became "services of song" and were much enjoyed.[21] Although a vibrant place of harvest where you "could see drays laden with apples wending their way to the wharf", a newspaper article of 1904 makes ominous mention of the ill-health plaguing this small community. "[S]ickness is exceedingly prevalent here just now; typhoid fever has made its appearance. Dr Bernard Thomas has a case under his care, which is doing fairly well."[22]

Fanny had divided up portions of her land grant among a few of her surviving children, keeping 100 acres for her own use. By her last year, the homestead comprised her four-room cottage, with barn and stable. She had cultivated three acres of still-healthy orchards, keeping 80 acres of natural forest.[23] It is easy to imagine solitary moments perched on the porch of Fanny's home, built by her and her late husband's very own hands, at times accompanied by her surviving children and many grandchildren.

As the apparent last of her original family, she kept the lines of communication with the dead very much open – the twinkling stars she, and her mother before her, would acknowledge in the crystal-clear night sky perhaps the celestial residencies of her loved ones, a comfort to an old woman who had lost so many.[24] Seated in the chair William Sr had spent the last three decades of his life confined to, either singing her personal hymns or silently surveying the vast lands she had acquired, but not without a hefty price.

* * *

At approximately 74 years of age (most media reports saying 74), Fanny Cochrane was tired. According to her eldest daughter, Mary Jane, her mother was only ill "at the very last fortnight, [with] pleurisy, then pneumonia".[25] At the home of Charles Batge, in Wattle Grove, she was attended to by Dr Thomas, who "did all medical skill could do".[26]

Like Truganini, she had sensed her own demise: "[S]he was only ill 8 or 9 days and used to say she wouldn't get better," recalled her friend

Mrs Batge.[27] The captive Indigenous people's belief that when they died they would return to their own country, reuniting with family and friends, left most at the Aboriginal establishments willingly embracing the inevitable. "[N]o you cry for me Mother, I go back to my people" is one anonymous quote (provided by Mrs Dandridge, so possibly from Truganini).[28] When Fanny was dying, the minister's wife was sent to pray with her, yet phrases of God or heaven are not to be found. Instead she was witnessed in conversation with her long-deceased mother, Tarenootairer, before allegedly saying, "I'm going home."[29]

* * *

Publicly, the fame Fanny had acquired during her later life saw her death elicit a mixture of testimonials. "The Last of the Tasmanian Aboriginals" headlined the *Mercury*, inciting chagrin from other Indigenous communities, incensed at a denial of their existence in her obituaries.[30] Other articles expressed a manner so nonchalant she could have been anybody:

> Fanny C. Smith, last half-caste [sic] survivor of the Tasmanian Aboriginals, is dead.[31]

In contrast, unlike her sister's sad, solitary journey, Fanny Cochrane was ushered to the grave by a large congregation. At Wattle Grove on a Sunday afternoon, her body began its journey to the Methodist Cemetery "and by the time it reached [there] it was estimated fully 400 persons attended".[32] The Reverend Roberts officiated an additional memorial in the Nicholls Rivulet Methodist Church on 6 March 1905, though his eulogy was unfortunately saturated with the imperialist attitudes of the times:

The preacher said the deceased was endowed with a sound mind in a sound body, and her character proved that Tasmanian aboriginals were capable of taking on a high degree of civilisation. The grace of Christianity in her life was beautifully exemplified. He took his text from Genesis iv. 24 …[33]

Off-handed recommendations that her skeleton be acquired and studied were thankfully never entertained.[34] Her friends called for the government to erect a memorial in her honour, but to no avail.[35] For the objective and ignorant, the "closing scene in respect to the Tasmanian Aboriginal race" was finally over.[36]

For Fanny's remaining children, her fame had been a blessing, a burden and a buffer. The turn of the century had marked a new identity for the burgeoning Commonwealth nation, introducing policies that would politically rob the children of their Indigenous and cultural identities for decades. With Fanny Cochrane's passing, they would be exposed to the full force of this imperialist dogma, and a new era of socio-political battles awaited them.

Eulogy

In early 1906, Fanny's daughter Flora was living with her husband and children in her late parents' homestead, which had been advertised for sale in June 1905, yet their residency was violently cut short.[37] The summer bushfires were outnumbering the residents and conjuring an ominous atmosphere. As reported in the *Mercury*, "The horizon is quite dark with smoke, and the strong, northerly wind is doing considerable damage to the apples and pears."[38] Already on edge, Flora was at home with her young children, soldiering through the day like any other, when "she thought something was burning" but could not locate the source.[39] A fire had indeed begun in the loft, only becoming visible when its flames appeared, lapping at the open air from the shingle roof. By then it was too late. With only enough time to muster her children to the safety of the fields, all she and the children could do was stand dolefully and watch. On 28 January 1906, the cottage, hand-crafted by William Smith and Fanny Cochrane themselves, was utterly consumed. In her will, Fanny Cochrane bequeathed all her furniture and personal belongings to her son Walter George, so named after Mary Ann's beloved and highly influential husband, Walter George Arthur.[40] How many of Fanny Cochrane's heirlooms had been previously removed to the safety of Walter's abode cannot be known, yet, aside from a few handwoven baskets, given as gifts to prestigious acquaintances, nothing of hers survives to the present, denoting a lifetime's accumulation reduced to mere ashes.

But this was not her legacy. Fanny Cochrane's hard-won autonomy is surely her greatest achievement. Her most immediately recognisable legacies are her richly diverse and deep-seated spirituality, immortalised by the small Methodist church at Nicholls Rivulet, and of course her music.

Invaluable artefacts, the 1899 phonograph cylinders spent many decades in the archives of the Tasmanian Museum. Along with her portrait, framed regally by a large fan of spears, the 1903 records sat relegated among Horace Watson's "Cabinet of Curiosities":

> Amongst the Tasmanian ethnological specimens, there is a lock of the hair of William Lanney, the last male survivor of the aboriginal Tasmanians. It was presented by Mrs. Stakell. There are also some native baskets, some of which are unfinished. There is only one Tasmanian spear. It is a very plain, harmless-looking thing, made from the native tea-tree. Mr. Watson possesses some excellent phonographic records of native songs, by Fanny Smith, who was the last link between the lost Tasmanian race and modern times.[41]

The rediscovery of the wax cylinders at the Hobart Museum in 1949 made news across the continent. Headlines such as "Voice of Extinct People Lives on in Memory and Wax!" were blazoned across the *Mercury*. Mrs Emily Keene (who was present at the time of the recordings in Sandy Bay) later, and dramatically, remarked, "[W]hen Mr. Watson played the recordings back to Fanny Cochrane Smith, she cried, 'My poor race. What have I done?'" and said that Fanny "thought the voice she had heard was that of her mother".[42] Yet this is in stark contradiction with the news report of the time, which concluded, "[W]ith a hearty shake of the hand she said to Mr Watson, 'I'm glad you have my people's language, so that it will still live'."[43]

What has been newly learned from this re-examination of Fanny Cochrane's life is that she had a strength of will equalled only by her mother and sister. She rarely allowed herself to remain a victim of circumstance. Even as a child she fearlessly fought her oppressors and abusers. Just like her sister, she effectively played the colony at its own game, but the hurdles Mary Ann struggled to clear Fanny Cochrane soared over. She wilfully pampered parliament's paternalism, gaining the politicians' sentiment for her own advancement. Her utilisation of the media to gain further socio-political advantage was both brave and brilliant.

Fanny's richly complex legacy continues through the survivors of her extremely large family, a rarity for so many Indigenous Tasmanians of the period. In 1908 and 1910, Ernest Westlake conducted his round of interviews with Fanny's children, grandchildren and friends, gathering indispensable anecdotes and oral histories. Of all the nostalgic reminiscences and dedications to Fanny Cochrane Smith, few lamented more simply, elegantly and appropriately than her own daughter, Sarah Bernice Laurel, who quipped, "There was nothing dull about her."[44]

EPILOGUE

> … there was a peculiar yellow glow in the light cast
> by the sun, like that seen when bushfires are about …
> [Some ladies] went outside to investigate, and saw
> that the sun was enveloped in a saffron coloured
> mist of circular shape, the outer rim of which was
> prismatic, like the colours of the rainbow. On
> placing themselves so that the sun was obscured by
> an intervening chimney, they saw a small white spot
> slowly approaching the sun. This disappeared
> as it touched the sun's disc …[1]

The above description given by the *Mercury* of Halley's Comet as it passed over the sun on 25 May 1910 is a beautiful evocation of the apocalyptic theatre of the skies and of Mother Nature in the first half of the 20th century.[2] George Augustus Robinson's documentation of the Cape Portland vocabulary shows him interpreting the word for the sun as the same word for the "good spirit ([or]God)" – "noi.heen.ner".[3] Like most Indigenous cultures globally, relationships to both celestial and earthly bodies are deeply spiritual in nature, yet colonisation had not only incurred a literal war between coloniser and colonised, it had introduced a new, and devastating, ideological war between humans and nature. Fire, so essential to traditional land maintenance, food harvesting, hunting and warmth from the bitter cold, had now become an enemy to their homes, farms and livelihoods; the rivers that fed their new crops also destroyed them in equal measure. These are mere examples of a new, conflicting relationship to the world.

A strange new relationship between the Smiths and their immigrant cohabiters had also taken root. As Fanny Cochrane's portrait hung in Horace Watson's room of ethnography, her children, grandchildren and great-grandchildren were also metaphorically placed in the annals of the colony's own "Cabinet of Curiosities". Her "whitey-brown" progeny of the 1880s were now the "Port Cygnet half-castes" of the 1910s.[4] Obituaries such as Walter George Smith's in December of 1912, lamenting a son of the "last real half-caste [sic] survivor of the lost Tasmanian race", are but early examples of the strange new attitudes towards them.[5] Tensions would gradually blister to the surface, and the struggling Nicholls Rivulet School was to be both its protagonist and its battleground.

"The Nigger Night-School", 1913

It seemed no one wanted to be there.[6] From 1908 the staffing of the school had been a constant battle.[7] "It has given me no end of trouble," stated a local councillor:

> [N]ot a single teacher has been there without some of the parents had a grievance. If the teacher happened to have Liberal views the Labourites were up in arms against her. If she was a Labourite the other side objected. If she was Catholic she still met with opposition, and if she belonged to the Church of England complaints came from other religious sects. It seems as if it is impossible to satisfy the people there.[8]

Poverty would be a principal contributor. "[P]arents pleaded that their children had no boots to go to school in, and they could not afford to buy them any."[9] Appropriately symbolic, the school grounds were under encroachment from blackberry brambles, and parents were called to do maintenance drives, spending days clearing them. Ironically,

EPILOGUE

blackberry-, apple- and hop-picking seasons would also be earmarked as one of the main reasons for a distinct absence of pupils. "[T]he present all-round drop is ascribed to the demands for child labour for apple and blackberry picking."[10] The excuse became so prevalent it eventually entailed accusations of outright slavery: "[T]he children are kept at home to pick blackberries, apples, or anything. This sort of child slavery has been going on here for years."[11] Declared the worst in Tasmania, the Nicholls Rivulet School was under constant threat of closure.[12]

"Entertainments" became the new fad to attract local parents, raise much-needed funds and simply keep the doors open for its scarcely existent curriculum. On the evening of 13 December, the school's young and patriotic teacher had planned a Christmas holiday pantomime, principally to raise money for a library.[13] With a local councillor as guest chairman, a "lengthy programme" was directed, but attendance was poor.[14] The possible reason became all too clear. After the youngest pupils had kickstarted the event with a "hoop drill and march", the older girls gave a brief recital named "Merry Widow Hat", from a popular Viennese operetta.[15] A "fancy dance" evoked "loud applause" and more "amusing" recitals continued the proceedings. In the era before mains electricity had reached the town, a lamp-lit room was likely set to usher the finale of the evening's entertainments:[16]

> The programme closed with a very jovial nigger farce, "The Nigger Night School", which was much enjoyed and warmly applauded.[17]

The stage directions provided by the script paint a clear picture of proceedings. A blackboard made from a yard of black paper, a bench, desk, stool and hatstand were all that was required for the set. "[N]o special costumes need be worn", the notes advise, and "all of the characters [are to] 'make-up' with burnt cork and carmine, and wear short woolly negro wigs".[18] The skit, "full of comic business and darkey jokes", revolved around a teacher, Dr Sloe, struggling to control his young pupils (all boys, who conspire against him) and give them an "eddicashun", as well as dealing with a hysterical parent who clearly wants her child working for her at home (Mrs Deborah White, "to be played by a male actor"). The sketch closed with misogynistic musings and slapstick high jinks, where Deborah gets her revenge by slamming the blackboard over Dr Sloe's head, who then proceeds to chase all his pupils, one by one, out of the classroom. Rendered entirely in spoken "niggerisms", at the time it was scribed, Thomas Barne's 1896 "nigger farce" was one in a number of his mocking "black face sketches".[19] Culturally, the class of 1913 was relatively even – equal parts the progeny of settlers, the other half Indigenous children.[20] Espousing every possible stereotype, it invokes a tasteless insensitivity to a small congregation of families so racially denigrated on a public scale since the 1870s.

As a product of its times, the staging of such a play was likely not intended to offend.[21] Yet, with life imitating art, or vice versa, one can evidently see a reflection between the characters in the play itself and the relationship between the council, the school and the parents – as well as the teacher's relationship with her own class. She had met her match with the boys, who by her own words "were a constant source of annoyance", and she demanded not one year later that they "are either expelled or removed to the training school".[22] A mere perusal of newspapers of the period also reveals the guest councillor's family had been, since the 1880s, avid proprietors of the minstrel concert, buoying its popularity in Port Cygnet. If this event is representative of anything, it is a prime example of how, within Indigenous, black or multi-ethnic communities – and at the whim of a councillor, a

EPILOGUE

teacher or a journalist – the proverbial "colour-line" could be rendered painfully vivid.

For the affected families, the entertainment achieved little by way of its not-so-subliminal purpose. Their relationship to the Nicholls Rivulet School would only further sour. "[W]hether it is the fault of the children, the parents, or the teachers, is equally difficult to determine," absolved the council.[23] By 1915 attendance was so low the Secretary for Education recommended that "unless some people were gaoled he did not believe they would comply".[24] Further threats of imprisonment for parents, as well as accusations of physical abuse by teachers against students, would dramatically round off this tumultuous decade.[25]

Yet the threats instigated little action and the 1920s saw no improvement. "[S]ome of them can't read or write," declared another councillor. "If the truant inspector is told to take proceedings, why are they not taken?" The constable in charge evidently had his hands full: "I have seen him [the constable] take children out of carts on the streets and take them to their parents."[26] No doubt strengthened by the councillor's enquiry, action was indeed taken. Either unwittingly or by an outright refusal to send his youngest, Gordon (Gus), to school, Joseph Thomas Sears Smith instigated Gus's removal by the warden to a "children's home" in New Norfolk. Ironically, according to Gus, education was little imposed in this asylum, where strict discipline and both domestic and commercial labour were the order of the day.[27] The punishment temporary – and the lesson painfully learned – Gus was eventually returned to his family.

By 1929, some efforts were being made by the community to embrace the school. Working bees were set up to clear the grounds and raise ever-necessary funds, and saw the Smiths now actively involved – Joseph's wife, Tilly, providing the refreshments.[28] Yet it all seemed too little, too late. The storm cloud that had hung over the tiny school could not be lifted. By 1940, the parents themselves now called for the problematic school's closure and for the council to bus their children to Cygnet.[29]

* * *

Yet, it must be stated, all was not tension and conflict. There were some ground-breaking achievements too. Akin to the Aboriginal establishments, for the Smiths the battle for autonomy was at the fore. The men – such as William, Fredrick and Tasman – had evidently grown tired of being at the mercy of industrial profit and they entered politics, assisting in the founding of the Tasmanian Liberal League, a union to ensure that their farms were protected. This was surely a first in Indigenous political history, at least in Tasmania.[30]

The charity drives instigated by Fanny Cochrane continued well into the new century. Held in their barns, the families raised money for the very wars that claimed the lives of some of their beloved sons,[31] and dances and socials funded the Methodist church.[32] Fanny Cochrane's friend Mrs Batge and family had taken charge of the Sunday school.[33] And with Fanny's eldest daughter, Mary Jane, as benefactor, the church held on into the early 1950s.[34] But it could not hold on forever.

Anecdotes of poverty, desperation and destitution dominate my family's memory archive. Among the banter of my elders and their rich reminiscences of Nan Casey[35] and "Apple Fairs", and of life back home, I'm told of feral rabbits strung up on open fires and weeds becoming staple fair, even offcuts of livestock their only fodder for fun, Pa (Gordon, Gus) Smith making balloons from pig's bladders, for example. Their memories of Grandpa Joe, Fanny's son,[36] are some

EPILOGUE

of the most cherished – a strong, funny and loyal figure.[37] In his 70s, Joseph helped pull apart a cottage he had built and reconstructed it on an adjacent property in preparation for the birth of Gordon's first child (of five) in 1935, my grandmother, Brenda Jean.[38] And it's through such rare reminiscences as these that one can envision Grandpa Joe in his waning decade, sitting on his porch, shotgun in hand, smoking a pipe, devoted to protecting his prized orchard of cherry trees from an arch nemesis – the "dickie bird".[39] His peaceful death on 17 August 1948, as an 86-year-old widower, left an unfillable void.[40] His small wake was held at home on a cool winter afternoon, before the half-hour journey along the shallow inclining road lined with white cottages to St Mark's Cemetery in Cygnet.

By the late 1940s the children of Fanny Cochrane and William Smith Sr were now but a few. Despite their best efforts, as a result of the economic devastation of war and nature's volatile elements continually destroying their livelihoods, many were forced to seek new beginnings elsewhere.

As the community thinned, the famed Methodist church became inactive, a shell. Yet, its value was always above and beyond its physical use. For over a century, it has stood humbly in the landscape of both geography and memory. Its hidden knowledge encompasses decades of family life – from the slumbering skeleton of my own recollections in the 1990s, and reaching as far back as those first brutal steps of invasion in the early 19th century. It is an enduring and interactive monolith to a much-valued heritage, and a symbolic answer to my original questions.

NOTES

Introduction

1. For this particular discussion relating to the "caste" or paternity debate of Fanny Cochrane Smith, the term "half-caste" related (politically and scientifically) to specifically an Aboriginal mother of "full-descent" and an alleged "white" or European father. In the 20th century, however, the definition of "half-caste" has been manipulated and redefined by successive governments and "protectorates" (Reynolds, Henry 2005b, *Nowhere people*, Penguin, Melbourne, p. 140).
2. See Appendix I and II in Birnie, Joel 2019, "A song of welcome: the first century of the British colonisation of Van Diemen's Land in three Indigenous biographies", PhD thesis, Monash University, Melbourne.
3. Banivanua Mar, Tracey 2016, *Decolonisation and the Pacific: Indigenous globalisation and the ends of empire*, Cambridge University Press, Cambridge, p. 188.
4. Briscoe, Gordon 1993, "Aboriginal Australian identity: the historiography of relations between Indigenous ethnic groups and other Australians, 1788 to 1988", *History Workshop*, no. 36, Autumn, Colonial and Post-Colonial History, pp. 157–58.
5. Daniels, Dennis 1995, *The assertion of Tasmanian Aboriginality from the 1967 referendum to Mabo*, Coursework Master thesis, University of Tasmania, Hobart, p. 44, https://eprints.utas.edu.au/3585/.
6. Daniels 1995, p. 44.
7. Brenda Jean Smith, born in Nicholls Rivulet in 1935 (married names a.k.a Tatnell and Campbell); correspondence, George Menham to Brenda Latnell [sic], Office of the Minister for Aboriginal Affairs, 25 July 1983 (no reference number stated).
8. G. M. Brownbill to Brenda Tatnell (nee Smith), Department of Aboriginal Affairs, 8 August 1983, Reference Number: Min.1187.
9. D.C. Griffiths to B.J. Campbell (nee Smith/Tatnell), Australian Heritage Commission, 4/6/1986, Nominator Name & Reference Number: Campbell, B.J., 6042.
10. R. Webb to B.J. Campbell (nee Smith/Tatnell), Australian Heritage Commission, 23/10/1991, Reference Number: 8851 RB.
11. My great-grandfather Gordon "Gus" Smith was the son of Lilian Frances "Theresa" Smith, eldest daughter of Joseph Thomas Sears Smith and Harriet "Tilly" Sculthorpe. Gordon was raised by Joseph and Tilly, his grandparents, as their son.

12 Reid, Kirsty & Paisley, Fiona (eds.) 2017, *Sources and methods in histories of colonialism: approaching the imperial archive*, Routledge, New York, p. 3.
13 Cameron, Patsy & Miller, Linn 2009, "Carne neemerranner – telling places and history on the ground", *The Australian Journal of Indigenous Education*, vol. 38, no. S1, p. 3.
14 Johnston, Anna 2009, "George Augustus Robinson, the 'Great Conciliator': colonial celebrity and its postcolonial aftermath", *Postcolonial Studies*, vol. 12, no. 2, p. 161, DOI: 10.1080/13688790902887155.
15 Russell, Lynette 2012, *Roving mariners: Australian Aboriginal whalers and sealers in the Southern Oceans, 1790–1870*, SUNY Press, New York, p. 108.
16 Plomley, N. J. B. 1991, "The Westlake Papers: Records of Interviews in Tasmania by Ernest Westlake, 1908–1910", *Occasional Paper No. 4*, Queen Victoria Museum & Arts Gallery, Tasmania., pp. 59–69.
17 Anon 1896, *Photograph album containing views of Horace Watson's Tasmanian Cabinet of Curiosities and Watson family photographs, ca. 1896–1903*, IE Number: IE8871700, Mitchell Library, State Library of New South Wales, https://archival.sl.nsw.gov.au/Details/archive/110374730.

Chapter 1: Saltwater Country

1 Plomley, N. J. B. 2008, *Friendly mission: the Tasmanian journals and papers of George Augustus Robinson, 1829–1834*, 2nd edn, Queen Victoria Museum and Art Gallery, Launceston, pp. 444.
2 I have chosen to maintain this version of spelling as it appears most prevalently in the colonial texts that reference her. Her name is spelt in various publications as Tibb, Tanganuturra, Tangernuterrer, Tingnerterrer, Tingnooterrunne, Tingernotareher, Ploorernelle, Dinudara, Jackanoothara, Sarah.
3 All evidences point to Tarenootairer being a Pinterairrer woman from layrappenthe country on the island's north-eastern cape. For clarity on Tarenootairer's tribe/clan/nation see: Birnie, Joel (2019). "A Song of Welcome": The British Colonisation of Van Diemen's Land in Three Indigenous Biographies", PhD Thesis, Monash University, Victoria.
4 Ryan, Lyndall 2012, *Tasmanian Aborigines: a history since 1803*, Allen & Unwin, Sydney, p. 22.
5 See Plomley 1987b, p. 224; and Plomley & Henley 1990, p. 53.
6 Plomley 1991, p. 60.
7 Plomley 2008, p. 282.
8 Merry, Kay 2003, "The cross-cultural relationships between the sealers and the Tasmanian Aboriginal women at Bass Strait and Kangaroo Island in the early nineteenth century", Counterpoints 2003: celebrating diversity in research, *The Flinders University Online Journal of Interdisciplinary Conference Papers*, vol. 3, no. 1, p. 80.
9 *The Voice*, 13/6/1936, p. 5.

NOTES

10 *The Mercury*, 6/7/1874, p. 3.
11 *The Mercury*, 6/7/1874, p. 3.

Chapter 2: Nummer-Lore (White Devil's Wife)

1   Ryan, Lyndall 2008, "List of multiple killings of Aborigines in Tasmania: 1804–1835", *Mass violence and resistance – research network*, https://www.sciencespo.fr/mass-violence-war-massacre-resistance/fr/document/list-multiple-killings-aborigines-tasmania-1804-1835, p. 3; *The Mercury* 6/07/1874 p. 3; *Hobart Town Gazette* 27/03/1819 p. 1; *Hobart Town Gazette* 20/03/1819 p. 2; *Hobart Town Gazette* 13/03/1819, p. 1; *Hobart Town Gazette* 28/11/1818, p. 1.
2   Plomley 2008, p. 91. However, Johnson & McFarlane imply that Aboriginal participation in the slavery of their women has been greatly exaggerated (Johnson, Murray & McFarlane, Ian 2015, *Van Diemen's Land, an Aboriginal history*, UNSW Press, Sydney, p. 134).
3   *The Mercury*, 6/7/1874, p. 3.
4   Clements, Nicholas 2014, *The Black War: fear, sex and resistance in Tasmania*, University of Queensland Press, St. Lucia, p. 172.
5   This particular name "nummer lore" is found in G. A. Robinson's journals to the west coast circa March–July 1832. In conversation with Kit (alias Kittewar) he records, "Kit informed me that when she got to the natives at Moonderhercowdim [sic?] – that the natives was frightened of her and asked her where was the Nummer i.e. white men". Further conversation with Kit and these unnamed West Coast natives notes, "She was accompanied by the Sealers and they have styled her – Nummer Lore – White Man's Wife" (George Augustus Robinson, 1832. ML A7030, Item 5, pp. 56–57).
6   This period was also known for the abduction of Indigenous children by settlers of the inland, eastern and central eastern districts (*Hobart Town Gazette*, 27/03/1819, p. 1).
7   Merry 2003, p. 81.
8   *Circular Head Chronicle*, 30/11/1938, p. 4.
9   What we know of Tarenootairer's earliest years comes from her own testament via George Augustus Robinson's notes taken at the temporary Aboriginal establishment on Gun Carriage Island c. 1831 (Robinson 1831a; 1831b). Collectively, the locations of these three men in western Bass Strait during the years 1813 to 1822 validate Tarenootairer's own statement of her early captivity in Bass Strait and their respective "possession" of her during this time.
10 Robinson 1831a, p. 16.
11 There are substantial accounts of the sealers' and boatmen's coastal abduction of Indigenous women. Accounts documented as early as the 1820s describe often violent altercations between Indigenous people, settlers and straitsmen (Brady, McCabe, Perry, Geffreys and Britton

1826–1851. *Echoes of Bushranging Days in Van Diemen's Land*, Box 2, Volume 5, National Library of Australia Manuscripts Collection MS3251, https://manuscript3251.wordpress.com, p. 217).
12 Robinson 1831a, pp. 31–32.
13 *The Mercury*, 6/7/1874, p. 3.
14 Voice, 10/12/1932, p. 2. The original article, from which this information derives, is detailed in the *Hobart Town Gazette* and the *Australian*, 28/10/1824, p. 2.
15 Stuart, Iain 1997, "Sea rats, bandits and roistering buccaneers: what were the Bass Strait sealers really like?", *Journal of the Royal Australian Historical Society*, vol. 8, no 1, p. 55.
16 Robinson 1831a, p. 6.
17 Plomley & Henley (1990).
18 *Tasmanian News*, 11/11/1910, p. 1.
19 McGowan, Angela 2000, "On their own: towards an analysis of sealers' sites on Heard Island", *Papers and Proceedings of the Royal Society of Tasmania*, vol. 133, part 2, p. 61.
20 Plomley 2008, p. 305.
21 Plomley 2008, pp. 401–402.
22 *The Tasmanian*, 26/3/1892, p. 30.
23 Robinson 1831a, p. 16.
24 Elder, Bruce 1988, *Blood on the wattle: massacres and maltreatment of Australian Aborigines since 1788*, Child and Associates, Frenchs Forest, NSW, p. 32.
25 These accounts of brutality towards the enslaved women are found throughout the journals and diaries of colonial administrators, like George Augustus Robinson, recounting in detail their daily torture (Elder 1988, p. 30).
26 Shakespeare, William 1803, *The plays of William Shakespeare*, vol. 21, Johnson, J. (ed.), 5th edn, University of California, California, p. 345.
27 Rivington, J. & F. C. 1821, *Plays and poems of William Shakespeare*, University of Michigan, Michigan, p. 370.
28 Lumby, Jonathan 1995, *The Lancashire witch craze: Jennet Preston and the Lancashire witches, 1612*, Carnegie Publishing, Lancaster, pp. 35–36.
29 This timeframe confirms Tarenootairer spent only a year (most likely less) with John Smith, the bulk of her captivity in service to Robinson.
30 Plomley 2008, p. 291.
31 It must be noted that all ages (for the involved parties) are approximations only and are usually based on their assumed ages when they died, which were also approximations (see Plomley 1987b, p. 795).
32 Plomley 2008, p. 245.
33 Plomley 2008, p. 304.
34 *Hobart Town Gazette*, 01/07/1826 p. 4.
35 *Hobart Town Gazette*, 25/3/1826 p. 2.

NOTES

36 *The Australian*, 9/3/1826, p. 2. The name difference is likely a mere error of Skelton's or of the journalist who translated the letter to newsprint.
37 *The Examiner*, 13/9/1926, p. 6.
38 Robinson 1831a, p. 6.
39 Plomley 2008, p. 304.
40 Plomley 2008, p. 304.
41 Plomley 2008, p. 335.
42 Plomley 2008, p. 304.
43 Plomley 2008, pp. 304–305. G. A. Robinson's original name for Tarenootairer was Ploorernelle, and is most likely how either he first heard the name or how the sealer Robinson told it. There is no indication that G. A. Robinson spoke to the women himself. Once Tarenootairer was removed from the servitude of sealer Robinson, the name Ploorernelle is never mentioned again and she is referred to only as Tarenootairer or Tibb (Plomley 2008, p. 324).
44 Robinson quoting Tarenootairer's recollection of an incident of murder on Woody Island, 29 July 1831 (Plomley 2008, p. 424).
45 Plomley 2008: p. 91.

Chaper 3: A Token of Grief

1 Plomley 1991, pp. 19–20.
2 Harman, Kristyn 2018b, *Explainer: the evidence for the Tasmanian genocide*, University of Tasmania, 17 January, viewed 12 October 2018, http://www.utas.edu.au/news/2018/1/18/513-explainer-the-evidence-for-the-tasmanian-genocide.
3 Rae-Ellis, Vivienne 1992, *Black Robinson: protector of Aborigines*, Melbourne University Press, Melbourne, p. 20.
4 Plomley 1987b, p. 15.
5 Plomley 2008, p. 324.
6 Ritz, Hermann 1909, "The speech of the Tasmanian Aborigines", *Papers and Proceedings of the Royal Society of Tasmania*, Hobart, p. 58.
7 Plomley 1987b, p. 28.
8 Ryan 2012, p. 181.
9 Plomley 2008, p. 397.
10 Plomley 2008, pp. 381 & 397.
11 *The Courier*, 23/10/1830, p. 2.
12 Plomley 2008, pp. 284, 413 & 549.
13 Plomley 2008, p. 416.
14 Plomley 2008, pp. 432–433.
15 Ryan, Lyndall 1982, *The Aboriginal Tasmanians*, University of Queensland Press, Brisbane, p. 154.
16 Plomley 1987b, p. 886; Plomley, N. J. B. 1983, *The Tasmanian tribes & cicatrices as tribal indicators among the Tasmanian Aborigines*, Queen Victoria Museum and Art Gallery, Launceston, p. 37; Ryan: 1982, p. 139.

17 De Vries, Susanna 1995, *Strength of spirit: pioneering women of achievement from First Fleet to Federation*, Millennium Books, Alexandria, NSW, pp. 111–131; Matson-Green, Vicki Maikutena 2005, "Tarenorerer (1800–1831)", *Australian dictionary of biography*, supp. vol., National Centre of Biography, Australian National University, Canberra (published first in hardcopy 2005, Melbourne University Press), https://adb.anu.edu.au/biography/tarenorerer-13212/text23923, p. 376.
18 Roberts, Jan 1986, *Jack of Cape Grim*, Greenhouse Publications, Melbourne, p. 97.
19 Plomley 2008, p. 517.
20 Ryan: 1982, p. 157.
21 Ryan 1982, p. 131.
22 Elder 1988, p. 36.
23 Plomley 2008, p. 513.
24 Ryan 2012, p. 187.
25 Boyce, James 2014, *God's own country: the Anglican Church and Tasmanian Aborigines*, Anglicare Tasmania, Hobart, p. 21.

Chapter 4: "Black Man's Houses"

1 Backhouse, James & Walker, George W. 1834, *Extracts from the letters of James Backhouse, now engaged in a religious visit to Van Diemen's Land, and New South Wales, accompanied by George Washington Walker*, Harvey and Darton, London, p. 71.
2 Elder 1988, p. 37.
3 From the *Surveyor Generals Report* (Plomley 1987b, p. 21).
4 Plomley 1987b, p. 49.
5 *Launceston Advertiser*, 3/4/1834, p. 2.
6 Plomley 1987b, pp. 36, 39.
7 Elder 1988, p. 38.
8 Plomley 1987b, pp. 955, 974.
9 Plomley 1987b, pp. 264–265.
10 Elder 1988, p. 38.
11 Walker, James Backhouse 1897, "Some notes on the tribal divisions of the Aborigines of Tasmania & notes on the Aborigines of Tasmania, extracted from the manuscript journals of George Washington Walker, with an Introduction by James B. Walker, F.R.G.S.", *Papers and Proceedings of the Royal Society of Tasmania*, Hobart, p. 179.
12 Plomley 1987b, p. 264.
13 Robinson was always busying himself with statistics and administrative information, even recording Tarenootairer's height, as 4 feet, 11¼ inches (Plomley 1987b, p. 869).
14 Plomley 1987b, p. 25.

NOTES

15. Turner, Sir William 1908, "The craniology, racial affinities, and descent of the Aborigines of Tasmania", *Transactions of the Royal Society of Edinburgh*, vol. XLVI, part II, no. 17, Robert Grant & Son, London, p. 374.
16. Coad 2010, pp. 2–3.
17. Boyce 2014, p. 38.
18. Coad 2010, p. 6.
19. Plomley 1987b, p. 346.
20. Plomley 1987b, pp. 222 & 445.
21. Plomley 1987b, p. 884.
22. As stated by G. A. Robinson on 15 January 1836 (Plomley 1987b, p. 878). So, too, these new names possibly became an important statement for the Indigenous captives, acquiring the same rules and uses that their Indigenous traditions dictated (Ryan 2012, pp. 224–225).
23. Johnson & McFarlane 2015, pp. 246–247.
24. Elder 1988, p. 40.
25. Marks, Claude 1975, *Pilgrims, heretics, and lovers: a medieval journey*, MacMillan, New York, p. 307.
26. Haebich, Anna 2000, *Broken circles: fragmenting Indigenous families 1800–2000*, Fremantle Arts Centre Press, Fremantle, p. 83.
27. George Augustus Robinson's "Examination of Eugene" at the school c. 1838 (Lushington, Charles & Labouchere, L. 1839, *Australian Aborigines, copies or extracts of despatches relative to the massacre of various Aborigines in Australia, in the year 1838*, British Parliamentary Papers, House of Commons, vol. 34, paper 526, London, p. 14).
28. Jeanneret 1854, p. 38.
29. Plomley 1987b, p. 463.
30. Plomley 1987b, p. 947.
31. Dean 2000, p. 45.
32. Jeanneret 1854, p. 48.
33. Jeanneret 1854, p. 55.
34. Elder 1988, p. 39.
35. *Austral-Asiatic Review*, Tasmanian and Australian Advertiser, 10/04/1838, p. 7.
36. Eberhard, Adrienne 2004, *Jane, Lady Franklin*, Black Pepper Publishing, Melbourne, p. 53.
37. Note: There are a number of poorly rendered entries in relation to this list of victims. Plomley notes that "this list of burials, which is associated with a chart of the burial ground, is in the handwriting of Charles Robinson" (Plomley 1987b, p. 911).
38. Plomley 1987b, p. 786.
39. Plomley 1987b, p. 101.
40. Plomley 1987b, p. 113.

41 Plomley 2008, p. 658.
42 Johnson & McFarlane 2015, p. 252.
43 Plomley 1987b, p. 378.
44 Plomley 1987b, p. 27.
45 Plomley 1987b, p. 657.
46 Ryan 2012, pp. 226–227.
47 Robinson 1838, p. 12.
48 Plomley 1987b, p. 426.
49 Ryan 2012, p. 227.
50 Elder 1988, p. 40.
51 An example of this can best be summed up in a petition to Queen Victoria written by the captives themselves and led by Tarenootairer's own daughter Mary Ann and son-in-law Walter George Arthur.

Chapter 5: Dinudară (Sarah)
1 Felton 1984, p. 9.
2 Harman, Kristyn 2018a, "'As much as they can gorge': colonial containment and Indigenous Tasmanian mobility at Oyster Cove Aboriginal Station", in *Indigenous mobilities: across and beyond the Antipodes*, ANU Press, Canberra, p. 156.
3 Harman 2018a, p. 157.
4 Harman 2018a, p. 159.
5 Plomley 1991, p. 18.
6 Harman 2018a, p. 168.
7 Plomley 1991, pp. 71–72.
8 Harman 2018a, p. 157.
9 Denison, William 1870, *Varieties of a vice-regal life*, vol. 1, Longmans, Green and Co, London, pp. 68–72.
10 *The Courier*, 29/12/1847, p. 2.
11 Elder 1988, p. 41.
12 Ryan 2012, p. 260.
13 Harman 2018a, pp. 160–161.
14 Harman 2018a, p. 161.
15 *The Mercury*, 11/4/1882, p. 1.
16 Ryan 2012, p. 260.
17 Elder 1988, p. 41.
18 McFarlane, Ian 2002, *Aboriginal society in North West Tasmania: dispossession and genocide*, University of Tasmania, Hobart, p. 253.
19 Harman 2018a, p. 162.
20 Tarenootairer herself is alleged to have told a Mrs Elmer, "[They] had divisions for the different families so they [Bessy Clarke and Sarah] told us" (Plomley 1991, p. 19). However, whether these divisions were European or Indigenous in origin cannot be ascertained.

NOTES

21 Harman 2018a, p. 164. Further evidence is found in the Oyster Cove Visitors Book, which records Tippo and William were hired to clear and cultivate land (August 1855).

22 Oyster Cove Visitors Book: "Jack Allen and the two youths, Adam and William have left on board a Whaling vessel, 'The Jane' ... 31 January 1857" (CSO89/1/1, formerly available from https://librariestas.ent.sirsidynix.net.au).

23 Plomley 1991, p. 23.

24 Harman 2018a, p. 167.

25 Plomley 1991, p. 12.

26 Plomley 1991, p. 62.

27 Plomley 1991, p. 68.

28 For further examples see Plomley, N. J. B. 1991, "The Westlake papers: records of interviews in Tasmania by Ernest Westlake, 1908–1910", *Occasional Paper No. 4*, Queen Victoria Museum & Arts Gallery, Launceston, p. 68).

29 Plomley 1991, p. 69.

30 Plomley 1991, p. 19.

31 Plomley 1991, p. 19.

32 Plomley 1991, pp. 28–29.

33 Coslovich, Gabriella 2011, "Rare portraits of Tasmanian Aborigines up for sale", *The Age*, viewed 12 March 2012, https://www.theage.com.au/national/victoria/rare-portraits-of-tasmanian-aborigines-up-for-sale-20110515-1eoah.html.

34 Tipping, Marjorie J. 1969, "Becker, Ludwig (1808–1861)", *Australian dictionary of biography*, vol. 3, National Centre of Biography, Australian National University, Canberra, published first in hardcopy 1969, viewed 23 June 2019, http://adb.anu.edu.au/biography/becker-ludwig-2961/text4309.

35 Plomley 1991, p. 123.

36 Harman 2018a, pp. 165–169.

37 As Sarah Bernice Laurel Smith had not yet been born when Tarenootairer passed away, this quote is likely passed down from her mother, Fanny, or father, William Smith. This too could mean that the Billy in reference is her father and possibly not William Lanne. Further, the reference to a grandmother may also be to Truganini, who became a prominent surrogate grandmother to Tarenootairer's grandchildren (Plomley 1991, p. 122).

38 Harman 2018a, p. 167.

39 Birnie 2019, pp. 155–156.

40 Plomley 1987b, p. 944.

41 McFarlane 2002, p. 254.

42 Felton 1984, p. 12.

43 Plomley 1991, pp. 11–12.

44 Plomley 1991, p. 58.

Chapter 6: Her Feeble Pulse

1. *The Mercury*, 14/9/1882, p. 2.
2. Ryan 2012, p. 262.
3. *The Mercury*, 10/9/1889, p. 4. Excerpt from the Oyster Cove Visitors Book: "I have this day visited the Station and School and Find all well except Adam Who has not been well since His return from Whaling – He is now recovering –" 14 October 1857, Edward Fissman AM (CSO89/1/1, formerly available from https://librariestas.ent.sirsidynix.net.au, as well as Plomley 1987b, p. 837).
4. Others were Wapperty, daughter of Mannalargenna, who was the mother of Bessy Myete (Lydon, Jane (ed.) 2014, *Calling the shots: Aboriginal photographies*, Aboriginal Studies Press, Canberra, pp. 37–47); and Harriett, alias "Wot", mother of Mary Ann Thompson and Thomas Thompson.
5. *The Mercury*, 11/04/1882, p. 1, article titled "Tasmanian in 1882", written by J. L. Dandridge (published in 1882 but dated as written at Oyster Cove, May 25, 1859).
6. Rae-Ellis, Vivienne 1976, *Trucanini: queen or traitor*, OBM Publishing Company, Hobart, p. 130.
7. *The Mercury* 11/04/1882, p. 1.
8. Plomley 1991, p. 61.
9. Plomley 1991, p. 21.
10. Dr. William Smith, Oyster Cove Visitor's Book, September 25th 1858, CSO89/1/1, formerly available from https://librariestas.ent.sirsidynix.net.au.
11. Dowling, Peter 2006, "Mercury poisoning at Oyster Cove? Suspected cases of unintentional poisoning of Tasmanian Aboriginal internees", *Tasmanian Historical Studies*, vol. 11, p. 67.
12. Dowling 2006, p. 62.
13. Kutlubay, Zekayi and Serdaroglu, Server (eds.) 2017. *Fundamentals of sexually transmitted infections*, InTech, Books On Demand, Croatia, p. 116.
14. Plomley 1987b, p. 945.
15. Ryan 2012, p. 262.
16. *The Courier*, 6/10/1858, p. 3.
17. Bonwick 1870, pp. 357–358.
18. Sarah Laurel Smith to Westlake: "Truc [Truganini] told a story of some soldiers who roused them from a corroboree, and she saw one of them stick an infant on his bayonet and put it in the fire" (Plomley 1991, p. 60).
19. *The Courier*, 11/09/1855 p. 2.
20. Turnbull, P. 2017, *Science, museums and collecting the Indigenous dead in colonial Australia*, Palgrave Macmillan, Cham, Switzerland, p. Turner 134.
21. Petrow, Stefan 1997, "Aboriginal skulls in the nineteenth century", *Papers and Proceedings: Tasmanian Historical Research Association*, vol. 44, no. 3, September, p. 93.

22　Turner, Sir William 1908, "The craniology, racial affinities, and descent of the Aborigines of Tasmania", *Transactions of the Royal Society of Edinburgh*, vol. XLVI, part II, no. 17, Robert Grant & Son, London, p. 374.
23　Turner, Sir William 1910, "The Aborigines of Tasmania, part II: the skeleton", *Transactions of the Royal Society of Edinburgh*, vol. XLVII, part III, no. 16, Robert Grant & Son, London, p. 412.

Chapter 7: A King's Island Daughter

1　Also known as Queen Mary Ann(e), Mary Ann Cochrane, Mary Ann Arthur, Marianne, Maryann and Mary Ann Booker.
2　*Tasmanian News*, 11/11/1910 p. 1.
3　Fornasiero J, Monteath, P. & West-Sooby, J. 2004, *Encountering Terra Australis: the Australian voyages of Nicolas Baudin and Matthew Flinders*, Wakefield Press, Adelaide, p. 218.
4　Fornasiero, Monteath &West-Sooby 2004, pp. 218–229.
5　Fornasiero, Monteath &West-Sooby 2004, p. 228.
6　Fornasiero, Monteath &West-Sooby 2004, p. 229.
7　*The Australian*, 9/3/1826, p. 2.
8　Bonwick 1870, p. 282.
9　Haebich 2000, p. 83.
10　*The Independent Launceston*, 20/4/1833, p. 3.
11　*Sydney Gazette* and *New South Wales Advertiser*, 5/11/1828, p. 2.
12　*Hobart Town Gazette*, 4/11/1826, p. 1.
13　The identity of the second man who drowned is not stated in the article. *Hobart Town Courier*, 1/1/1831, p. 2.
14　Plomley 1987b, pp. 349 & 477.
15　*Launceston Advertiser*, 18/4/1832, p. 123; *Launceston Advertiser*, 27/12/1832, p. 414.
16　*Sydney Gazette* and *New South Wales Advertiser*, 5/9/1827, p. 1.
17　*Hobart Town Courier*, 21/3/1829, p. 2.
18　Sherrow, Victoria 2006, *Encyclopedia of hair: a cultural history*, Greenwood Publishing Group, Connecticut, p. 386.
19　*Austral-Asiatic Review*, 29/10/1833, p. 2.
20　Haskins, Victoria 2001, "On the doorstep: Aboriginal domestic service as a 'contact zone'", *Australian Feminist Studies*, vol. 16, no. 34, p. 17, DOI: 10.1080/08164640120038881.
21　Haebich 2000, p. 83.
22　Robinson, Shirleene, 2015. "'Always a good demand': Aboriginal child domestic servants in nineteenth- and early twentieth-century Australia", in, Victoria K. Haskins & Claire Lowrie (eds.), *Colonization and domestic service: historical and contemporary perspectives*, vol. 14, Routledge international studies of women and place, Routledge, London, pp. 104–105.

23 Jones, Bernie D. 2011, *Fathers of conscience: mixed-race inheritance in the antebellum South*, University of Georgia Press, Athens, Georgia, pp. 1–20.
24 Plomley 2008, p. 517.
25 *Independent*, 3/9/1831, p. 3.
26 Parry, Naomi 2007, "'Such a longing': Black and white children in welfare in New South Wales and Tasmania, 1880–1940", PhD thesis, University of New South Wales, Sydney, p. 103.
27 *The debates in Parliament session 1833 on the resolutions and bill for the abolition of slavery in the British Colonies: with a copy of the Act of Parliament*, 1834, Maurice & Co., Fenchurch, London. See also *Hobart Town Courier*, 6/9/1833, p. 2; Mount Lyell Standard and Strahan Gazette, 27/4/1901, p. 2.
28 Boyce 2014, p. 37.
29 Meredith, Louisa Anne 1852 (2010), *My home in Tasmania, during a residence of nine years*, vols. 1–2, Cambridge University Press, Cambridge, p. 25.
30 Parry 2007, p. 103.
31 Boyce 2014, p. 38.

Chapter 8: The Bride and Bridegroom

1 Ryan 2012, p. 225.
2 Stevens, Leonie 2017, *"Me write myself": the free Aboriginal Inhabitants of Van Diemen's Land at Wybalenna*, Monash University Publishing, Melbourne, p. 80.
3 Plomley 1987b, p. 343.
4 Haebich 2000, p. 87.
5 Plomley 1987b, p. 516.
6 Dammery, Sally 2001, *Walter George Arthur: a free Tasmanian?*, Monash Publications in History, School of Historical Studies, Monash University, Melbourne, p. 1.
7 Dammery 2001, p. 1.
8 Dammery 2001, p. 7.
9 Dammery 2001, p. 12.
10 Dammery 2001, p. 8.
11 "Selling for two pence a copy, this publication has historical significance as Australia's first Aboriginal newspaper", Johnson & McFarlane 2015, p. 246.
12 Raabus, Carol 2011, "Australia's Indigenous publishing pioneer, Walter George Arthur", ABC Local, viewed 12 October 2018, https://www.abc.net.au/local/audio/2011/02/17/3141671.htm.
13 Stevens 2017, pp. 138–139.
14 Dammery 2001, p. 12.
15 There is an entry in G. A. Robinson's journal where he clearly forces a couple to marry despite their obvious disinterest (Plomley 1987b, p. 470).
16 Plomley 1987b, p. 543.
17 Plomley 1987b, p. 551.

NOTES

18 Reynolds, Henry 2005a, "Arthur, Walter George (1820–1861)", *Australian dictionary of biography*, National Centre of Biography, Australian National University, Canberra, published first in hardcopy 2005, accessed online 21 November 2018, http://adb.anu.edu.au/biography/arthur-walter-george-12775/text23047; Plomley 1987b, p. 551.
19 Plomley 1987b, p. 570; Dammery 2001, p. 15; Stevens 2017, p. 193.
20 Plomley 1987b, p. 551.
21 Plomley 1987b, p. 570.
22 Dammery 2001, p. 15.
23 Robinson's letter to the Superintendent of Port Phillip, dated 17th December 1839: http://access.prov.vic.gov.au/public/veo-download?objectId=090fe273 8091d2c3&format=pdf&docTitle=00010P00000000010250pdf&encoding Id=Revision-3-Document-1-Encoding-1-DocumentData.
24 Roberts 1986, p. 11.

Chapter 9: "Your Humble Aborigine Child"

1 *Hobart Town Courier*, 20/02/1835, p. 2.
2 Roberts 1986, p. 14.
3 Plomley 1987b, p. 786.
4 Dammery 2001, p. 16. Additionally, G. A. Robinson's letter to the superintendent dated 20 December 1839 references Mary Ann in a list of his own "servants". "My servants are four – a woman/halfcaste/ and her husband, a boy/halfcaste/ and David one of the lads originally selected", http://access.prov.vic.gov.au/public/component/daPublicBaseContainer?com ponent=daViewItem&entityId=1164259547.
5 Plomley 1987b, p. 786.
6 Port Phillip Patriot and Melbourne Advertiser, 3/4/1839, p. 5.
7 Stevens 2017, p. 245.
8 Plomley 1987b, p. 445.
9 *Launceston Examiner*, 10/8/1843, p. 3.
10 Dammery 2001, p. 17.
11 Reynolds 2005b.
12 G. A. Robinson's letter dated 26 December 1839, discussing the difficulty in matching rations to "work performed by the natives", http://access.prov. vic.gov.au/public/component/daPublicBaseContainer?component=daViewIt em&entityId=4164259574.
13 Robinson's journal, Port Phillip, Saturday 22 August 1840 (Clark 1998, p. 349) and a letter from the colonial secretary to the superintendent, dated 29 October 1841. http://access.prov.vic.gov.au/public/veo-download?o bjectId=090fe2738090614b&format=pdf&docTitle=00010P00000000020 380pdf&encodingId=Revision-3-Document-1-Encoding-1-DocumentData.
14 Roberts 1986, pp. 87–88.
15 Roberts 1986, p. 42.

16 Robinson's journal, Port Phillip, Saturday 10 August 1839 (Clark 1998, p. 66) and G. A. Robinson's letter to the superintendent dated 20 December 1839. (http://access.prov.vic.gov.au/public/component/daPublicBaseContainer?component=daViewItem&entityId=1164259547).

17 Letter from Colonial Secretary approving Robinson's request to set up the establishment at "Narre Narre Warren" dated 12 November 1840, http://access.prov.vic.gov.au/public/component/daPublicBaseContainer?component=daViewItem&entityId=6164259994.

18 G. A. Robinson's letter to W. Thomas, 30 September 1841: "… Many of the Children by consent of their parents have permitted me that they will return and attend to school with respect to Mrs R. [Robinson]", http://access.prov.vic.gov.au/public/component/daPublicBaseContainer?component=daViewItem&entityId=4167696952.

19 Plomley 1987b, p. 787.

20 Robinson offers a description of the said gifts, "a good handkerchief each, two beads each, knives, fireworks, fish hooks, needle cases and pictures" (Clark 1998, p. 73).

21 Dammery 2001, p. 24.

22 *The Examiner*, 31/10/1942, p. 4.

23 Reynolds 2005b.

24 Stevens 2017, p. 228.

25 Walker, George Washington 1839–44, *George Washington Walker's letter book, 1839–44*, University of Tasmania Open Access Repository, Hobart, pp. 26–290, https://eprints.utas.edu.au/2844/. Formerly available from http://www.utas.edu.au/library/exhibitions/quaker. Letter Books 1831–1844, mainly relating to Society of Friends, dated 16 September 1842.

26 Lawson, Tom 2014, *The last man: a British genocide in Tasmania*, IB Tauris, London, p. 116.

27 McFarlane 2002, p. 265.

28 Jeanneret 1854, p. 45.

29 Jeanneret 1854, p. 49.

30 Jeanneret 1854, p. 40.

31 CSO11/1/124 658, pp. 71–72.

32 Jeanneret states that "all the Aborigines" but Walter called him "Papa" (Jeanneret 1854, p. 48).

33 Grossman, Michele 2012, *Blacklines: contemporary critical writing by Indigenous Australians*, Melbourne University Publishing, Melbourne, p. 17.

34 Banivanua Mar 2016, p. 51.

35 *Petition to Her Majesty Queen Victoria*, dated 17th February 1846 (CSO 11/26/378, AJCP Microfilm 280/195, Reel 544, SLV).

36 Reynolds, Henry 1991, "Walter George Arthur, pioneer Aboriginal activist", *Island*, no. 49, Summer, p. 38.

37 Reynolds 1991, p. 38.

NOTES

38 Jeanneret 1854, p. 23.
39 In 1854 he compiled a dossier to the Crown in defence of his actions and to hold them accountable for the grants of land he was promised for his time in the colony that he had yet to receive (Jeanneret 1854, p. 4–6).
40 Jeanneret 1854, p. 10. Jeanneret's claims were further supported by Plomley who suggested that there was direct influence of Joseph Milligan and Robert Clark in the writing of the petition: "Further emphasizing Milligan's involvement in instigating the petitions, before leaving Flinders Island he awarded certificates of 'good conduct' to Walter, Mary Ann, Davy Bruny [sic] and his wife Matilda, 'the most vociferous among the Aborigines'" (Plomley 1987b, p. 151).
41 Johnson & McFarlane 2015, p. 259.
42 Jeanneret 1854, pp. 33–35.
43 King Tippo's statement: "Cannot write, but Mr. Clark pencilled his name, and being sick at the time, Walter George Arthur guided his hand while he wrote over it" (Jeanneret 1854, p. 34).
44 "Eugene states: 'Dr. Jeanneret never threatened to shoot him, not put him in gaol, not stop his rations nor clothing, nor refused medical aid. Never asked him to fight the soldiers'" (Jeanneret 1854, p. 34). Another non-signatory, Frederick, further declared, "He [Jeanneret] never did shoot me. Sarah told doctor I was fighting Eugene [her husband]. Sarah told me Dr. Jeanneret would shoot me" (Jeanneret 1854, p. 38).
45 Jeanneret 1854, p. 41.
46 *Mary Ann, Kings Island*, by John Skinner Prout, Wybalenna, 1845. The British Museum provides the following description: "It depicts Mary Ann, a Tasmanian Aboriginal woman, sitting with her hands together. She is wearing necklaces, a dress, and a shawl. 1845". (British Museum, https://www.britishmuseum.org/collection/object/E_Oc2006-Drg-22).
47 "Neptune: 'Mr Clark told me to write the petition. Mary Ann tell me to go to Mr Clark's house and write the petition'." (Jeanneret 1854, p. 43).
48 Jeanneret 1854, pp. 44–45; and also Reynolds 1995a, p. 9.
49 Heiss, Anita & Minter, Peter 2014, *Macquarie PEN anthology of Aboriginal literature*, Allen & Unwin, Crows Nest, NSW, pp. 11–12.
50 Mary Ann Arthur's Letter, dated 16/6/1846 (CSO 11/26/378, AJCP 280/195, Reel 544, 318–319)/ Heiss & Minter 2014, p. 12.
51 Stevens 2017, p. 280.
52 Robert Clark, letter to George Washington Walker, 27th May 1846, UTAS Library, Quaker Collection, S&RMC, W7/36, pp. 3–4.

Chapter 10: Her Majesty, the Queen

1 Bonwick 1870, p. 284.
2 Ryan 2012, p. 260.
3 Plomley 1987b, p. 183.

4   Plomley 1987b, p. 183.
5   *Tasmanian Daily News*, 10/7/1856, p. 2.
6   Bonwick 1870, p. 276.
7   Dowling, Peter 2006, "Mercury poisoning at Oyster Cove? Suspected cases of unintentional poisoning of Tasmanian Aboriginal internees", *Tasmanian Historical Studies*, vol. 11, p. 60.
8   Prior to antibiotics and penicillin, the treatment for syphilis was the use of arsphenamine or mercury, the latter utilised to a fatal degree at the Oyster Cove Aboriginal establishment.
9   Coad 2010, p. 8.
10 Jeanneret, Henry 1854, *The vindication of a colonial Magistrate from the aspersion of His Grace the Duke of Newcastle: by official documents and attestations, with a remonstrance; and exposure of a colonial conspiracy, whereby Her Majesty the Queen has been imposed upon in a petition against Henry Jeanneret, M. D., late superintendent of the Aborigines of Van Diemen's Land*, Hope and Co., London, p. 46.
11 The mystery surrounding the young boy's origins and what became of him may place Mary Ann's childlessness into question. The possibility that George is a child of Mary Ann and Walter Arthur cannot be discounted entirely. There has been an assumption, due to a lack of documentation, that Mary Ann and Walter had no children; yet it is clear from this research that the absence of documentation does not mean that this assumption is correct.
12 Lydon 2014, p. 25.
13 Birnie, Joel 2014, *Pakana Maleetye: art and the survival of Indigeneity within the Aboriginal community of Nicholls Rivulet, Tasmania*, Masters thesis, Monash University, Melbourne, p. 25.
14 Denison, William 1870. *Varieties of a Vice-Regal Life*, Volume 1, Longmans, Green and Co, London, pp. 80, 83–84.
15 Denison 1870, p. 68.
16 Denison 1870, p. 68.
17 Denison 1870, pp. 68–72.
18 Hobarton Guardian, 29/12/1847, p. 2.
19 Denison 1870, p. 103.
20 Bonwick 1870, p. 274.
21 Clark was tasked with conducting an official census for January 1848 – one for the Aboriginal inhabitants, not including the children at the Orphan Asylum, and a separate census for his own family (Tasmanian Archives Office, Robert Clark's Census of Aborigines at Oyster Cove 1st January 1848, CEN1/1/91/55B). Of the Indigenous captives, totalling 38 in all, there is only one child – a boy between the age of 2 and 7 (this would be Little George), one male and one female between the ages of 7 and 14 (Fanny Cochrane likely to be the aforementioned female), 13 men and 14 women between the ages of 21 and 45, 6 women between the ages of 45 and 60, and two women

NOTES

of ages 60 and upwards. However, come the census of March 1851, the Indigenous captives were now 33 individuals – 10 couples, 2 single males and 11 single females, ages unspecified (Tasmanian Archives Office, March 1851 Census, Dr Joseph Milligan, CEN1/1/106/88B). Milligan's census is reduced to a mere list of numbers and is difficult to decipher. At the top of the ledger, he made an additional categorical note labelled "Aborigines". Although crossed out, it is under this heading that an account of the Indigenous captives is numbered, totalling 33. The erasing of this category suggests that the subsequent tables of numbers contain both the Aboriginal captives and the non-Indigenous administrators for the total sum of the inhabitants of the establishment; this renders it impossible to differentiate the Aboriginal men, women and children from the white administrators.

22 *Australasian*, 1/6/1872, p. 6.
23 Johnson & McFarlane 2015, pp. 278–279.
24 *Britannia and Trades' Advocate*, 26/12/1850, p. 3.
25 *The Mercury*, 25 July 1939, p. 8.
26 *The Courier*, 6/12/1853, p. 2.
27 This particular reference to "youngsters" is vague. There were practically no young children at the establishment at this time. Most recorded children at the settlements were by now young adults or in their late teens. If "young adults" is meant, it adds further validity to their account of this meeting; if it means "children", it could possibly be a reference to only three known children of the early period of the 1850s, George, Charley and Billy, meaning that they were still alive at the time of this meeting (Plomley 1987b, p. 945).
28 Douglas, Ann 1986, "Introduction", in Harriet Beecher Stowe, *Uncle Tom's cabin; or, life among the lowly*, Penguin Books, Harmondsworth, pp. 10–11.
29 Lowance, Mason, Westbrook, Ellen & De Prospo, R. C. 1994, *The Stowe debate: rhetorical strategies in Uncle Tom's cabin*, University of Massachusetts Press, Massachusetts, p. 247.
30 Lowance, Westbrook & De Prospo 1994, pp. 205–247.
31 Lowance, Westbrook & De Prospo 1994, p. 223.
32 Lydon, Jane 2016, *Photography, humanitarianism, empire*, Bloomsbury Publishing, London, p. 57.

Chapter 11: Uncle Walter's Hut

1 Oyster Cove Visitors Book, CSO89/1/1; https://stors.tas.gov.au/CSO89-1-1, 24/12/1855; Reynolds 1995, p. 19.
2 Boyce 2014, p. 49.
3 Excerpt from the Oyster Cove Visitors Book (CSO89/1/1, https://stors.tas.gov.au/CSO89-1-1): "I have this day visited the Station and find all well except Mary Ann who has a bad cold but is said to be better – the women appeared in the Chapel with their new dresses and all conducted themselves with great propriety" Nov. 30th 1855.

4   Bonwick, James 1884, *The lost Tasmanian race*, Low, Marston, Searle & Rivington, London, p. 181.
5   However, Reynolds finds no reason to disbelieve this statement (Reynolds 1991, p. 38).
6   Dammery 2001, p. 11.
7   Boyce 2014, p. 27.
8   Reynolds 1995a, p. 172.
9   Smithers, Gregory 2017, *Science, sexuality, and race in the United States and Australia, 1780–1940*, Routledge, New York, p. 206.
10 Fenton 1884, p. 379. The last line indicates that these are the expressions of Mary Ann, but are recorded in Bonwick's words and are not necessarily the words of Mary Ann herself.
11 *The Mercury*, 11/4/1882, p. 1.
12 Tasmanian Archives Office, RGD35/1/3P3.
13 Bonwick 1870, pp. 278–279.
14 Featherstone, Guy 1968, "Life and times of James Bonwick", MA thesis, University of Melbourne, Melbourne; Featherstone, Guy 1969, "Bonwick, James (1817–1906)", *Australian dictionary of biography*, vol. 3, National Centre of Biography, Australian National University, Canberra, viewed 15 July 2019, http://adb.anu.edu.au/biography/bonwick-james-3022/text4429.
15 Bonwick 1870, p. 285.
16 Stowe 1852, p. 24.
17 Bonwick 1870, p. 282.
18 Bonwick 1870, p. 284.
19 Stowe 1852, pp. 25–31.
20 Bonwick 1870, p. 280.
21 Featherstone 1968, http://adb.anu.edu.au/biography/bonwick-james-3022/text4429.
22 Bonwick 1870, p. 285.
23 Plomley 1987b, p. 183.
24 Reynolds 1995a, p. 20.
25 Bonwick 1870, p. 317.
26 Dammery 2001, p. 45.
27 Plomley 1987b, p. 183.
28 Oyster Cove Visitors Book: "By 20th October Mary Ann was in town still ill, and Walter was away on a Whaling voyage, by November she was suffering an attack of Jaundice. In July 1860 Mary Ann is again struck down with Influenza (along with Jack Allen)" (CSO89/1/1, https://stors.tas.gov.au/CSO89-1-1, pp. 21, 23).
29 Oyster Cove Visitors Book, 20th April 1862 (CSO89/1/1, https://stors.tas.gov.au/CSO89-1-1).
30 *Launceston Examiner*, 25/6/1886, p. 1.
31 *The Mercury*, 13/5/1861, p. 3.

NOTES

32 Oyster Cove Visitors Book, 9th June 1861 (CSO89/1/1, https://stors.tas.gov.au/CSO89-1-1, p. 29).
33 Casson, Marjory Rose (n.d.), "The last years", in *Tasmania's Aboriginal people*, unpublished manuscript circa 1950s, p. 192, https://www.samuseum.sa.gov.au/collection/archives/provenances/series/aa-55-1.
34 Harman 2018, p. 171.
35 *The Mercury*, 2/5/1865, p. 2.
36 *The Voice*, 6/6/1931, p. 3. Dates of Mathinna's death vary – some sources say 1852, others 1856. She is believed to have been 18 years old at the time of her death.
37 Stanfield, Rachel 2018, *Indigenous mobilities across and beyond the Antipodes*, ANU Press, Canberra, p. 151.

Chapter 12: Mary Ann and Her Countrywomen

1   Boyce 2014, p. 53.
2   Harman 2018, p. 171.
3   Plomley 1987b, p. 180.
4   Casson n.d., p. 192.
5   *The Mercury*, 7 October 1865, p. 1.
6   *The Mercury*, 25 May 1866, p. 4.
7   Barnard, James 1866, *Catalogue of the contributions made by Tasmania to the Intercolonial Exhibition of Australia at Melbourne in 1866*, Government Printer, Hobart Town, p. 19.
8   Births Deaths and Marriages Registry, D'Entrecasteaux Channel, Tasmania.
9   "December 13th 1867, Visited the Station – the Aborigines well – The Superintendent complained of Adam Booker, Mary Ann's husband, having made use of obscene & threatening language, on the Station to Mrs Dandridge" (Oyster Cove Visitors Book, CSO89/1/1, https://stors.tas.gov.au/CSO89-1-1).
10 Plomley 1991, p. 18.
11 Plomley 1987b, p. 189.
12 Oyster Cove Visitors Book (CSO89/1/1, https://stors.tas.gov.au/CSO89-1-1), p. 57.
13 *Cornwall Chronicle*, 15/1/1868, p. 5.
14 *The Hobart Mercury*, 10/1/1868, p. 2.
15 *Launceston Examiner*, 18/1/1868, p. 4 & *The Mercury*, 24/1/1868, p. 2.
16 There are multiple examples of this published in the newspapers of the period, such as *Tasmanian Times* 6/11/1869, p. 3 and *Launceston Examiner* 25/6/1866 p. 1.
17 Dowling 2006, p. 63.
18 Oyster Cove Visitors Book (CSO89/1/1, https://stors.tas.gov.au/CSO89-1-1), p. 26.
19 Oyster Cove Visitors Book (CSO89/1/1, https://stors.tas.gov.au/CSO89-1-1), p. 38.

20 Oyster Cove Visitors Book (CSO89/1/1, https://stors.tas.gov.au/CSO89-1-1), p. 49.
21 Oyster Cove Visitors Book (CSO89/1/1, https://stors.tas.gov.au/CSO89-1-1), p. 45.
22 Oyster Cove Visitors Book (CSO89/1/1, https://stors.tas.gov.au/CSO89-1-1), p. 48.
23 "February 25th 1867 – Visited & inspected the Station. Saw 'Mary Ann' who has been suffering for some days from bilious Diarrhoea but is now better – The Superintendent reports that 'Bessy' died of dysentery on the ... 11th instant – Recommended that 'Mary Ann' should have two half glasses of brandy per diem for a few days and some medicine – Billy [William Lanne] has gone to Port Cygnet with letters for 'Fanny' the three females are out hunting" (Oyster Cove Visitors Book, CSO89/1/1, https://stors.tas.gov.au/CSO89-1-1).
24 Dowling 2006, p. 66.
25 Bonwick 1870, p. 394; *The Voice*, 6/6/1931, p. 3.
26 Bonwick 1870, p. 395.
27 Bonwick 1870, p. 395.
28 Bonwick 1870, pp. 395–400.
29 *The Mercury*, 31/3/1869 p. 2.
30 *Tasmanian Times*, 25/5/1869, p. 2.
31 *Tasmanian Times*, 27/5/1869, p. 2.
32 *Tasmanian Times*, 25/5/1869, p. 2.
33 Plomley stated that there was "an extensive file of papers dealing with the post-mortem mutilation of the body of the Aboriginal 'Billy' by Dr. Crowther at the Colonial Hospital" (CSD 7/23/127; Plomley 1987b, p. 199). Further particulars found in *The Mercury*, 11/4/1882, p. 1.
34 Plomley 1991, p. 122.
35 Allen, Jim & Jones, Rhys 1980, *Oyster Cove: Archaeological traces of the last Tasmanian and notes on the criteria for the authentication of flaked glass artefacts*, Papers and Proceeding of the Royal Society of Tasmania, vol. 114, p. 226, https://eprints.utas.edu.au/14165/.
36 *Launceston Examiner*, 23/08/1870, p. 3.
37 There is small – possible – evidence of their keen interest in the news (*The Mercury*, 22/10.1870 p. 2).
38 *Tasmanian Times*, 25/2/1870, p. 3.
39 *The Mercury*, 17/2/1870, p. 2.
40 Bonwick 1870, p. 317.

Chapter 13: Her Vital Spark Extinguished

1 Dowling 2006, p. 61.
2 Stanfield 2018, pp. 155–156.
3 *The Mercury*, 25/7/1871, p. 2.

NOTES

4   Death Registry of Mary Ann Booker, Hobart General Hospital. Tasmanian Archives Office.
5   *The Mercury*, 26/7/1871, p. 2.
6   *The Mercury*, 8/3/1869, p. 2.
7   Further articles reporting the death of Mary Ann: *The Sydney Morning Herald* (19/8/1871, p. 7) reads: "'Mary Ann,' one of the two remaining aboriginal inhabitants, died in the Hobart Town Hospital recently from paralysis. 'Lalla Rookh' is now the only survivor of the Tasmanian aboriginals. She is living at Oyster Cove"; *The Mercury*, 10/8/1871, p. 4 noted: "The Tasmanian half-caste woman, Mary Ann, who has for many years resided at the aboriginal station, Oyster Cove, died from paralysis, at the General Hospital, on the 23th ult [sic]. There is but one genuine aboriginal of this colony left – the woman Lalla Rookh – who is now about sixty-five years of age."
8   *The Mercury*, 27/7/1871, p. 2.
9   *The Mercury*, 28/7/1871, p. 2.
10 Plomley 1987b, p. 189.
11 Plomley 1987b, p. 190.
12 Bonwick 1870, p. 282.
13 Plomley 1987b, p. 500.
14 Plomley 1987b, pp. 530, 537.
15 Sir William Turner's 1910 Royal Society paper noted the presence of a number of "half-caste" crania and skeletons in museum collections (Turner, Sir William 1910, "The Aborigines of Tasmania, part II: the skeleton", *Transactions of the Royal Society of Edinburgh*, vol. XLVII, part III, no. 16, Robert Grant & Son, London, pp. 373–374). Although it is implied that the remains of racially mixed Tasmanians were considered generally of no great scientific interest, Mary Ann's celebrity may have meant her remains were more desirable.
16 Dictionary of Australian Artists Online, no date given, *Annie Benbow*: https://www.daao.org.au/bio/anne-benbow/.
17 Plomley 1991, p. 96.
18 Plomley 1991, p. 126.
19 Digitised item from: W.L. Crowther Library, Tasmanian Archive and Heritage Office, https://stors.tas.gov.au/AUTAS001124870148w800.

Chapter 14: A Prison Nursery

1   Also known as Fanny Smith, Fanny Cochrane Smith, Fanny Corkren, Fanny Catherine, Fanny Coughlin, Fanny Coughlan and Jenny Coughran.
2   Dean 2000, p. 9.
3   Boyce, James 2014, *God's own country: the Anglican Church and Tasmanian Aborigines*, Anglicare Tasmania, Hobart, p. 46.
4   However, Plomley does state that "the records seldom name the children" (Plomley 1987b, p. 144).

213

5   Coad, David 2010, *Port Cygnet 1860–1900*, vol. 2, History of Tasmania, D. Coad, Kingston, Tasmania, p. 4.
6   Coad 2010, p. 6.
7   *Aboriginal Historical Places*, www.aboriginalheritage.tas.gov.au.
8   Skye, Lee Miena 2007, *Kerygmatics of the new millennium: a study of Australian Aboriginal women's Christology*, ISPCK, Delhi, p. 68.
9   Bonwick 1870, pp. 258–259.
10 Coad 2010, pp. 4–6.
11 Felton, Heather 1984, *On being Aboriginal – Book 2: Fanny Cochrane Smith*, Aborigines of Tasmania, Education Department, Hobart, p. 9.
12 Colonial Secretary's Office 17 November 1843 (CSO8/1/72 1642); Coad 2010, p. 3).
13 *The Mercury*, 14/9/1882, p. 2.
14 Coad 2010, p. 6.
15 Ryan 2012, p. 226.
16 Plomley 1991, pp. 65–67.
17 Plomley 1987b, p. 701.
18 Haebich 2000, p. 85.
19 Colonial Secretary's Office, CSO11/1/124 658, pp. 76–77 & Coad 2010, p. 6.
20 Coad 2010, p. 5.
21 Tasmanian Archives Office Online/CON31-1-48, p. 46.
22 Colonial Secretary's Office, CSO11/1/124 658, pp. 91–95; Coad 2010, pp. 6–7.
23 Colonial Secretary's Office, CSO11/1/124 658, pp. 91–95.
24 Coad 2010, p. 5.
25 Jeanneret 1854, p. 47.
26 Bonwick 1870, p. 269.
27 Jeanneret 1854, p. 43.
28 Coad 2010, p. 3.

Chapter 15: The Organ of Perception

1   Coad 2010, p. 8.
2   Bonwick 1884, p. 178.
3   Plomley 1987b, p. 858; Haebich 2000, pp. 122–123.
4   Plomley 1991, pp. 62–63.
5   Plomley 1991, pp. 10–11.
6   Moyle 1960, p. 74.
7   Plomley 1991, pp. 10–11, 30, 60–62, 63–64.
8   Mitchell Library, State Library of New South Wales, File Number: FL8871840 http://digital.sl.nsw.gov.au/delivery/DeliveryManagerServlet?embedded=true&toolbar=false&dps_pid=IE8871700&_ga=2.226814493.1888928521.1564738722-35057762.1564738722.

NOTES

9 *The Mercury*, 11/4/1882, p. 1.
10 Bonwick 1884, p. 178.
11 Plomley 1991, p. 46.
12 *The Courier*, 19/9/1849, p. 3.
13 Novels include *Younah! A Tasmanian Aboriginal Romance of the Cataract Gorge*, by W. I. Thrower (1894), which was published as a serial by the Mercury Office.
14 *The Courier*, 23/11/1850, p. 2.
15 *Adelaide Observer*, 20/9/1845, p. 6.
16 South Australian Register, 24/10/1850, p. 3.
17 *Geelong Advertiser*, 19/8/1850, p. 2.
18 *Geelong Advertiser*, 28/10/1850, p. 2.
19 *Geelong Advertiser*, 27/8/1850, p. 2.
20 *The Argus*, 19/8/1850, p. 2.
21 *Leader*, 9/12/1876, p. 5.
22 *The Courier*, 31/8/1850, p. 4.
23 *Cornwall Chronicle*, 7/9/1850, p. 586.
24 *Geelong Advertiser*, 19/8/1850. p. 2.
25 *Cornwall Chronicle*, 26/10/1850, p. 736.
26 Britannia and Trades Advocate, 17/10/1850, p. 2.
27 There were two Aboriginal women by the name of Fanny living at the Oyster Cove Aboriginal establishment, one known as Plonoopinner (alias Wortabowigee, Jock or Fanny), the other Fanny Cochrane. However, Plonoopinner had no documented sister, living or deceased, and only had a brother called Titterrarpar, alias Ajax (Plomley 1987b, p. 858). Additionally, there was a distinct penchant for using Aboriginal youths as subjects, believing they were more "susceptible". Plonoopinner was approximately 45–46 years old, whereas Fanny Cochrane was approximately 18 years of age at this time.
28 *Leader*, 9/12/1876, p. 5.
29 Doyle, Arthur Conan 1926, "Chapter XIII: Henry Slade and Dr. Monck", in *The history of spiritualism*, vol. I, Cassell & Co., London.
30 Long, Carolyn Morrow 2001, *Spiritual merchants: religion, magic, and commerce*, University of Tennessee Press, Knoxville, p. 53.
31 Doyle 1926.
32 *The Courier*, 6/10/1858, p. 3.
33 *Cornwall Chronicle*, 7/9/1850, p. 586.
34 DeLong, Anne 2018, *Classic horror: a historical exploration of literature*, Greenwood, Santa Barbara, p. 179.
35 DeLong 2018, p. 119.
36 Plomley 1991, p. 67.
37 Plomley 1991, pp. 21, 137.
38 Plomley 1991, p. 65.

Chapter 16: Propaganda, Progeny and Prosperity

1. Felton 1984, p. 11.
2. Bonwick 1870, p. 317.
3. Plomley 1991, pp. 22–24.
4. *The Mercury*, 8/9/1882, p. 3.
5. *The Mercury*, 14/9/1882, p. 2.
6. Harman 2018, p. 171.
7. *The Mercury*, 14/9/1882, p. 2.
8. Bonwick 1870, p. 317.
9. Longman 1960, p. 85.
10. *The Mercury*, 14/9/1882, p. 2.
11. Plomley 1991, p. 69.
12. Plomley 1991, p. 60.
13. Plomley 1991, p. 60, and *Tasmanian Tribune*, 13/8/1874, p. 3.
14. Tasmanian Archives Office, *William Henry Smith* birth and baptism register/ RGD32/1/4 p. 2.
15. Plomley 1991, p. 61.
16. Tasmanian Archives Office, Birth registry of *Mary Jane Smith*/RGD33-1-37, p. 562.
17. Harman 2018, p. 170.
18. *The Mercury*, 11/4/1882, p. 1.
19. *Tasmanian Times*, 29/4/1868, p. 2.
20. Plomley 1991, pp. 61, 62, 64 & 65.
21. Portrait photography usually marked a relatively special occasion in Victorian-era colonies, and I believe their portrait must have been taken to commemorate a milestone. Their official 20th wedding anniversary was in October 1874, yet Fanny Cochrane was eight months pregnant with Isabella at that time, placing the couple's portrait as likely taken earlier that year. The newspaper article discussing their presence in Hobart in July 1874 likely coincides with this.
22. *Tasmanian Tribune*, 10/7/1874, p. 2.
23. *Australasian Sketcher with Pen and Pencil*, 10/6/1876, p. 43.

Chaper 17: Prove It or Lose It!

1. *The Mercury*, 8/9/1882, p. 3.
2. *Launceston Examiner*, 3/11/1860, p. 2.
3. *Tasmanian Tribune*, 10/7/1874, p. 2.
4. *Tasmanian Tribune*, 13/8/1874, p. 3.
5. *The Mercury*, 11/4/1882, p. 1.
6. *The Mercury*, 15/6/1882, page 3.
7. *The Mercury*, 8/9/1882, p. 3.
8. *The Mercury*, 10/9/1889, p. 4.
9. *The Mercury*, 14/9/1882, p. 2.

NOTES

10 *The Mercury*, 10/9/1889, p. 4.
11 *Critic*, 27/3/1914, p. 2.
12 The identity of this man is not stated and further investigation would be necessary to identify him.
13 *The Mercury*, 8/9/1882, p. 3.
14 *The Mercury*, 8/9/1882, p. 3.
15 *The Mercury*, 15/9/1882, p. 3.
16 *The Mercury*, 6/11/1884, p. 3.
17 One year after Fanny Cochrane Smith's land claim, c. 1884, a land or financial claim was made by a woman named Mary Ann Smith, in 1885. The claim was relayed in *The Mercury* on 6 November 1885 (pp. 3–4). Mary Ann Smith is likely to actually be Mary Ann Thomson, who was abducted from Wybalenna c. 1839 by the Reverend Thomas Dove (d. 1882) and wife (Dora Kay Dove) and taken to the main island, "but later returned". She was subsequently removed by M. L. Smith in September 1841 (aged about 12 years), and "probably remained with him for some years" (Plomley 1987b, p. 865).
18 *The Mercury*, 10/11/1884, p. 4.
19 *The Mercury*, 8/9/1882, p. 3.
20 *Launceston Examiner*, 6/11/1882, p. 3.
21 *Tasmanian News*, 18/4/1884, p. 2.
22 *Tasmanian News*, 14/9/1888, p. 4.
23 *The Mercury*, 7/11/1884, p. 3.
24 *The Mercury*, 7/11/1884 p. 3.
25 *The Mercury*, 7/11/1884, p. 3.
26 *Tasmanian News*, 31/10/1884, p. 2.
27 *Tasmanian News*, 31/10/1884, p. 2.
28 *The Mercury*, 14/9/1882 p. 2.
29 *The Mercury*, 9/10/1888, p. 4.
30 Pares, Luis Nicolau 2013, *The formation of Candomblé: Vodun history and ritual in Brazil*, University of North Carolina Press, North Carolina, p. 86.
31 *Tasmanian News*, 31/10/1884, p. 2.
32 *Tasmanian News*, 18/4/1884, p. 2.
33 *Tasmanian News*, 14/9/1888, p. 4.
34 *Launceston Examiner*, 24/12/1885, p. 3.
35 Tasmanian Parliamentary Library, 5/6/2003, No.4730, pp. 2–3.
36 *The Queenslander*, 23/11/1889, p. 48.

Chapter 18: Rituals of Captivity

1 Felton 1984, p. 16.
2 Felton 1984, p. 16.
3 Lowance, Mason, Westbrook, Ellen & De Prospo, R. C. 1994, p. 223.
4 Plomley 1991, pp. 21–22.

5 Raboteau, Albert, 2004. *Slave religion: the "invisible institution" in the antebellum South*, Oxford University Press, New York, p. 151.
6 Plomley 1987b, p. 97.
7 Boyce 2014, p. 11.
8 Boyce 2014, p. 12; O'Brien, Glen & Carey, Hilary M. 2016, "Introduction: Methodism and the Southern World", in Glen O'Brien and Hilary Carey (eds.), *Methodism in Australia: a history*, Routledge Methodist studies Series, Routledge, London, p. 1.
9 Boyce 2014, p. 16.
10 The Methodists also play a prominent role in Stowe's *Uncle Tom's Cabin*: "'Amen,' was the murmured response from the lips of Tom and Mammy, and some of the elder ones, who belonged to the Methodist Church" (Stowe 1852, p. 221).
11 Raboteau 2004: p. 161.
12 "[T]he slaves did not simply become Christians; they creatively fashioned a Christian tradition to fit their own peculiar experience of enslavement" (Raboteau 2004, p. 226).
13 Pares 2013, p. 79.
14 Australian Heritage Commission, 20/9/91, ref. 6042.
15 Raboteau 2004, p. 196.
16 *The Mercury*, 16/2/1900, p. 3.
17 Plomley 1991, pp. 71,72.
18 Raboteau 2004, p. 21.
19 Such as Marie Catherine Laveau (c. 1801–1881) and Mother Leafy Anderson (1897–1827) in New Orleans (Long 2001, p. 54).
20 Apter, Andrew & Derby, Lauren 2010, *Activating the past: history and memory in the Black Atlantic world*, Cambridge Scholars Publishing, Newcastle, p. 99.
21 Plomley 1991, pp. 10–11 & 30.
22 Plomley 1991, pp. 63–64 & 68–69.
23 Raboteau 2004, p. 97.

Chapter 19: King Billy's Playmate
1 Birnie 2019, pp. 207–208.
2 Plomley 1991, p. 30–31.
3 Plomley 1991, p. 21.
4 *The Mercury*, 15/11/1937, p. 4.
5 *The Mercury*, 24/12/1885, p. 2; *Launceston Examiner*, 24/12/1885, p. 3; *Tasmanian News*, 24/12/1885, p. 3.
6 *The Mercury*, 24/12/1885, p. 2; *Launceston Examiner*, 24/12/1885, p. 3; *Tasmanian News*, 24/12/1885, p. 3.
7 *Tasmanian Police Gazette*, Friday 25th December 1885, Vol. XXIV, no. 1379, p. 207.

NOTES

8 *The Mercury*, 26/12/1885, p. 2.
9 Wedding Registry of Mary Jane Smith and William Miller, 28/2/1889, ref. no. RGD37/1/48P100.
10 Births, Death and Marriages, Tasmanian Archives Office, ref. no. RGD/1/72P813.
11 Plomley 1991, p. 63.
12 Plomley 1991, p. 64.
13 For example:

> "Three little stars in the east on a level only once in the year. Thought a lot of them, just to see them blinking. FS thought it a terrible thing if didn't welcome these three little stars. Would sprinkle the ashes from the hearth very early in the morning before the sun had risen, when the stars are bright." (Plomley 1991, p. 63)

> "Used to believe that if anybody bad they would knock. Sometimes would hear a knock while at home and would say, 'Someone going out', and would be right too. Sometimes would sit and wait for the knock, sometimes let it come of itself." (Plomley 1991, p 63)

> "Would whistle up the wind to blow. They would take a pointed stick with a large fan of gum leaves and wave it in the air, and at the same time whistle. Would also do this when at sea. If fell out with one another would whistle up the wind." (Plomley 1991, p. 63)

14 Taylor, Rebe 2016, "The first stone and the last Tasmanian: the colonial correspondence of Edward Burnett Tylor and Henry Ling Roth", *Oceania*, vol. 86, no. 3, p. 333.
15 Taylor 2016, p. 333.
16 Australian Heritage Commission, 20/9/1991, ref. 6042.
17 Longman 1960, p .80.
18 Longman 1960, p. 80.
19 Longman 1960, p. 80.
20 Moyle 1960, p. 74.
21 State Library of Tasmania (ref: SD_ILS:140802).
22 Longman 1960, pp. 80–81.
23 Taylor, R. 2016, p. 334.
24 One of her sons evidently gave public recitals almost a decade earlier, with the *Mercury* in 1890 documenting a benefit containing "two songs in Tasmanian blacks' language [sung] by Mr. Smith" *The Mercury*, 9/5/1890, p. 3.
25 *The Mercury*, 31/8/1899, p. 3.
26 *The Mercury*, 28/10/1899, p. 2.
27 *The Mercury*, 11/11/1899, p. 2.
28 *Tasmanian News*, 1/11/1899, p. 3.

29   *The Mercury*, 28/3/1949, p. 9. It is difficult to place when this event occurred. The portrait allegedly taken in Government House appears to have been "air-brushed", as was common then, making her age in the photograph difficult to determine. However, such a performance would have logically occurred in 1899, instigated by her Royal Society Session and Benefit concerts.
30   Australian Heritage Commission, 20/9/1991, ref. 6042.

Chapter 20: Goodbye, My Father, Mother

1   Australian Heritage Commission, 20/9/1991, ref. 6042.
2   Findlay (2015) notes William Henry Smith, Fanny Cochrane Smith, Joseph Thomas Sears Smith and Tasman Benjamin Smith as four of the eight given as Certificate of Title (Vol. 121, Folio 70) holders for this property (Finlay, Grant 2015, *Always crackne in heaven*, PhD thesis, University of Tasmania, Hobart, pp. 307–308).
3   Finlay 2015, p. 309.
4   Raboteau 2004. pp. 150–151.
5   *The Mercury*, 16 February 1900, p. 3.
6   *The Mercury*, 1/12/1902, p. 6.
7   Plomley 1991, p. 19.
8   Coad, David 2011, *Port Cygnet 1900–1914*, vol. 3, History of Tasmania, D. Coad, Kingston, Tasmania, p. 130.
9   Friend 1992, p. 82–83.
10 Unable to obtain any confirmation of this event, I contemplated omitting it from the text; however, if true, it cannot be ignored.
11 William Henry Smith, dated 1/10/1924, National Archives of Australia, No.1763924, p. 63–64.
12 Plomley 1991, p. 126.
13 Longman 1960, p. 81.
14 *The Mercury*, 15/6/1909, p. 6.
15 *The Mercury*, 23/3/1949, p. 5.
16 Moyle 1960, p. 73.
17 *The West Australian*, 14/1/1949, p. 15.
18 Moyle 1960, p. 75.
19 Longman 1960, p. 84.
20 *The Mercury*, 27/4/1904, p. 3.
21 *The Mercury*, 1/12/1904, p. 2.
22 *The Mercury*, 27/4/1904, p. 3.
23 *The Mercury*, 12/6/1905, p. 8.
24 Taylor, Rebe 2017, *Into the heart of Tasmania: a search for human antiquity*, Melbourne University Press, Melbourne, p. 103.
25 Plomley 1991, pp. 62–63.
26 *The Mercury*, 27/2/1905, p. 6.

27 Plomley 1991, p. 101.
28 Quote from Mrs Knowles (nee Dandridge) regarding attitudes to death (Plomley 1991, p. 103).
29 Plomley 1991, pp. 10–11, 13–14.
30 *North Western Advocate* and the *Emu Bay Times*, 17/3/1905, p. 4.
31 *The Mercury*, 27/2/1905, p. 6.
32 *Tasmanian News*, 1/3/1905, p. 3.
33 *The Mercury*, 6/3/1905, p. 5.
34 Taylor 2016, p. 331; Coad 2010, p. 20.
35 *The Mercury*, 10/3/1905, p. 7.
36 *The Mercury*, 27/2/1905, p. 6.
37 *The Mercury*, 12/6/1905, p. 8.
38 *The Mercury*, 2/2/1906, p. 2.
39 *The Mercury*, 2/2/1906, p. 2.
40 Tasmanian Archives Office, Last Will and Testament of Fanny Smith, AD960/1/27/6590, pp. 1–3.
41 *Daily Post*, 10/6/1908, p. 2.
42 *The Mercury*, 23/3/1949, p. 5.
43 Anon 1896, *Photograph album containing views of Horace Watson's Tasmanian Cabinet of Curiosities and Watson family photographs, ca. 1896–1903*, IE Number: IE8871700, Mitchell Library, State Library of New South Wales, https://archival.sl.nsw.gov.au/Details/archive/110374730.
44 Plomley 1991, pp. 60–62.

Epilogue

1 *The Mercury*, 30/5/1910, p. 2.
2 As witnessed by a John Cotton, from Cambridge, north-east of Hobart.
3 Plomley 1976, pp. 242 & 417.
4 *Tasmanian News*, 18/4/1884, p. 2; Plomley 1991, p. 12.
5 *The Mercury*, 27/12/1912, p. 5.
6 In defence of both the school and its teacher, Frederick Smith wrote to the *Daily Post*:

> Sir – My attention having been drawn to a letter in your issue of "the *Daily Post*" of July 29, under the above heading and signed "Irishtown", as a parent of children attending this school, I feel it my duty to contradict the references made to our teacher by the writer. Those who are sufficiently intelligent cannot but recognise Miss Harris's qualities as a lady, and patient, competent teacher. For the sake of my own and other children I hope that she may long remain here. – Yours, etc. F. J. Smith (*Daily Post*, 10/8/1908, p. 3).

7 *Daily Post*, 4/8/1908, p. 2.
8 *Huon Times*, 5/9/1914, p. 3.
9 *Huon Times*, 6/3/1915, p. 2.

10 *Huon Times*, 8/4/1914, p. 7; *Huon Times*, 5/11/1920, p. 5.
11 World, 14/3/1921, p. 8.
12 *The Mercury*, 7 /2/ 1922, p. 4 & *Daily Post*, 27/6/1913, p. 4.
13 *Huon Times*, 24/12/1913, p. 4.
14 *The Mercury*, 23/3/1887, p. 4.
15 Schweizer, Marlis 2009, "'Darn that *Merry Widow Hat*': The on- and offstage life of a theatrical commodity, circa 1907–1908", *Theatre Survey*, vol. 50, no. 2, pp. 189–221, doi:10.1017/S0040557409990044.
16 *The Mercury*, 11/2/1924, p. 80.
17 *Huon Times*, 24/12/1913, p. 4.
18 Barnes, Thomas 1896, *The Nigger Night-School: A Farce in One Act*, Dick & Fitzgerald Publishers, New York, p. 2.
19 *Pickles and Tickles: A Farce in One Act* was another notable "nigger farce" (Barnes, James 1898, *The darkey breach of promise case: a nigger mock trial*, Fitzgerald Publishing, New York).
20 Mostly the children of Joseph, Flora, Mary Jane and Tasman Smith.
21 *Huon Times*, 15/12/1916, p. 5.
22 *Huon Times*, 12/8/1914, p. 2.
23 *Huon Times*, 11/4/1922, p. 2.
24 *Huon Times*, 6/3/1915, p. 2.
25 *Huon Times*, 15/9/1916, p. 2.
26 *Huon Times*, 5/11/1920, p. 5.
27 Birnie 2009, p. 13.
28 *Huon Times*, 22/2/1929, p. 2.
29 *The Mercury*, 30/11/1940, p. 5.
30 *The Mercury*, 21/9/1909, p. 3.
31 *The Mercury*, 25/12/1906, p. 2.
32 *The Mercury*, 9/9/1949, p. 6.
33 *Huon Times*, 12/2/1924, p. 3.
34 *The Mercury*, 21/3/1949, p. 11.
35 Lilian Frances "Theresa" Smith, eldest daughter of Joseph Thomas Sears Smith and Harriet "Tilly" Sculthorpe.
36 Joseph Thomas Sears Smith.
37 An example of Joseph's "loyalties" (*The Mercury*, 9/10/1883, p. 1).
38 Brenda Jean Smith.
39 Birnie 2009, p. 10.
40 *The Mercury*, 18/8/1948, p. 8.

BIBLIOGRAPHY

Allen, Jim & Jones, Rhys 1980, *Oyster Cove: Archaeological traces of the last Tasmanian and notes on the criteria for the authentication of flaked glass artefacts*, Papers and Proceeding of the Royal Society of Tasmania, vol. 114, pp. 225–233, https://eprints.utas.edu.au/14165/.

Anon 1896, *Photograph album containing views of Horace Watson's Tasmanian Cabinet of Curiosities and Watson family photographs, ca. 1896–1903*, IE Number: IE8871700, Mitchell Library, State Library of New South Wales, https://archival.sl.nsw.gov.au/Details/archive/110374730.

Apter, Andrew & Derby, Lauren 2010, *Activating the past: history and memory in the Black Atlantic world*, Cambridge Scholars Publishing, Newcastle.

Backhouse, James & Walker, George W. 1834, *Extracts from the letters of James Backhouse, now engaged in a religious visit to Van Diemen's Land, and New South Wales, accompanied by George Washington Walker*, Harvey and Darton, London.

Banivanua Mar, Tracey 2016, *Decolonisation and the Pacific: Indigenous globalisation and the ends of empire*, Cambridge University Press, Cambridge.

Barnard, James 1866, *Catalogue of the contributions made by Tasmania to the Intercolonial Exhibition of Australia at Melbourne in 1866*, Government Printer, Hobart Town.

Barnes, James 1898, *The darkey breach of promise case: a nigger mock trial*, Fitzgerald Publishing, New York.

Barnes, Thomas 1896, *The nigger night-school: a farce in one act*, Dick & Fitzgerald Publishers, New York.

Birnie, Joel 2009, "A biography of Gordon Ronald Wilfred Smith", unpublished essay, University of South Australia, Adelaide.

Birnie, Joel 2014, "Pakana Maleetye: art and the survival of Indigeneity within the Aboriginal community of Nicholls Rivulet, Tasmania", Masters thesis, Monash University, Melbourne.

Birnie, Joel 2019, "A song of welcome: the first century of the British colonisation of Van Diemen's Land in three Indigenous biographies", PhD thesis, Monash University, Melbourne.

Bonwick, James 1870, *The last of the Tasmanians: or, the Black War of Van Diemen's Land*, Sampson Low Publishers, London.

Bonwick, James 1884, *The lost Tasmanian race*, Low, Marston, Searle & Rivington, London.

Boyce, James 2014, *God's own country: the Anglican Church and Tasmanian Aborigines*, Anglicare Tasmania, Hobart.

Brady, McCabe, Perry, Geffreys & Britton 1837–1851, *Echoes of bushranging days in Van Diemen's Land*, box 2, vol. 5, National Library of Australia Manuscripts Collection MS3251, https://manuscript3251.wordpress.com.

Briscoe, Gordon 1993, "Aboriginal Australian identity: the historiography of relations between Indigenous ethnic groups and other Australians, 1788 to 1988", *History Workshop*, no. 36, Autumn, Colonial and Post-Colonial History, pp. 133–161.

Brown, P. L. 2006. "Learmonth, Thomas (1818–1903)", *Australian dictionary of biography*, vol. 2, National Centre of Biography, Australian National University, Canberra (published first in hardcopy 1967), https://adb.anu.edu.au/biography/learmonth-thomas-2835/text3059.

Cameron, Patsy & Miller, Linn 2009, "Carne neemerranner – telling places and history on the ground", *The Australian Journal of Indigenous Education*, vol. 38, no. S1, pp. 3–9, doi:10.1375/S1326011100000764.

Casson, Marjory Rose (n.d.), "The last years", in *Tasmania's Aboriginal people*, unpublished manuscript circa 1950s, pp. 183–198, https://www.samuseum.sa.gov.au/collection/archives/provenances/series/aa-55-1.

Clements, Nicholas 2014, *The Black War: fear, sex and resistance in Tasmania*, University of Queensland Press, St. Lucia.

Coad, David 2010, *Port Cygnet 1860–1900*, vol. 2, History of Tasmania, D. Coad, Kingston, Tasmania.

Coad, David 2011, *Port Cygnet 1900–1914*, vol. 3, History of Tasmania, D. Coad, Kingston, Tasmania.

Coslovich, Gabriella 2011, "Rare portraits of Tasmanian Aborigines up for sale", *The Age*, viewed 12 March 2012, https://www.theage.com.au/national/victoria/rare-portraits-of-tasmanian-aborigines-up-for-sale-20110515-1eoah.html.

Dammery, Sally 2001, *Walter George Arthur: a free Tasmanian?*, Monash Publications in History, School of Historical Studies, Monash University, Melbourne.

Daniels, Dennis 1995, "The assertion of Tasmanian Aboriginality from the 1967 referendum to Mabo", Coursework Master thesis, University of Tasmania, Hobart, https://eprints.utas.edu.au/3585/.

The debates in Parliament session 1833 on the resolutions and bill for the abolition of slavery in the British Colonies: with a copy of the Act of Parliament, 1834, Maurice & Co., Fenchurch, London.

DeLong, Anne 2018, *Classic horror: a historical exploration of literature*, Greenwood, Santa Barbara.

Denison, William 1870, *Varieties of a vice-regal life*, vol. 1, Longmans, Green and Co, London.

De Vries, Susanna 1995, *Strength of spirit: pioneering women of achievement from First Fleet to Federation*, Millennium Books, Alexandria, NSW.

Douglas, Ann 1986, "Introduction", in Harriet Beecher Stowe, *Uncle Tom's cabin; or, life among the lowly*, Penguin Books, Harmondsworth.

Dowling, Peter 2006, "Mercury poisoning at Oyster Cove? Suspected cases of unintentional poisoning of Tasmanian Aboriginal internees", *Tasmanian Historical Studies*, vol. 11, pp. 59–68.

BIBLIOGRAPHY

Doyle, Arthur Conan 1926, "Chapter XIII: Henry Slade and Dr. Monck", in *The history of spiritualism*, vol. I, Cassell & Co., London.

Eberhard, Adrienne 2004, *Jane, Lady Franklin*, Black Pepper Publishing, Melbourne.

Elder, Bruce 1988, *Blood on the wattle: massacres and maltreatment of Australian Aborigines since 1788*, Child and Associates, Frenchs Forest, NSW.

Featherstone, Guy 1968, "Life and times of James Bonwick", MA thesis, University of Melbourne, Melbourne.

Featherstone, Guy 1969, "Bonwick, James (1817–1906)", *Australian dictionary of biography*, vol. 3, National Centre of Biography, Australian National University, Canberra (published first in hardcopy 1969), viewed 15 July 2019, http://adb.anu.edu.au/biography/bonwick-james-3022/text4429.

Felton, Heather 1984, *On being Aboriginal – Book 2: Fanny Cochrane Smith*, Aborigines of Tasmania, Education Department, Hobart.

Felton, Heather 2006, "Mathinna", *The Companion to Tasmanian History*, Centre for Tasmanian Historical Studies, http://www.utas.edu.au/library/companion_to_tasmanian_history/M/Mathinna.htm.

Fenton, James 1884, *A history of Tasmania, from its discovery in 1642 to the present time*, Macmillan & Co., London.

Finlay, Grant 2015, "Always crackne in heaven", PhD thesis, University of Tasmania, Hobart.

Fornasiero J, Monteath, P. & West-Sooby, J. 2004, *Encountering Terra Australis: the Australian voyages of Nicolas Baudin and Matthew Flinders*, Wakefield Press, Adelaide.

Grossman, Michele 2012, *Blacklines: contemporary critical writing by Indigenous Australians*, Melbourne University Publishing, Melbourne.

Haebich, Anna 2000, *Broken circles: fragmenting Indigenous families 1800–2000*, Fremantle Arts Centre Press, Fremantle.

Harman, Kristyn 2018a, "'As much as they can gorge': colonial containment and Indigenous Tasmanian mobility at Oyster Cove Aboriginal Station", in *Indigenous mobilities: across and beyond the Antipodes*, ANU Press, Canberra.

Harman, Kristyn 2018b, *Explainer: the evidence for the Tasmanian genocide*, University of Tasmania, 17 January, viewed 12 October 2018, http://www.utas.edu.au/news/2018/1/18/513-explainer-the-evidence-for-the-tasmanian-genocide.

Harnan, Kristyn 2018c, "Explainer: how Tasmania's Aboriginal people reclaimed a language, palawa kani, *The Conversation*, 19 July 2018: http://theconversation.com/explainer-how-tasmanias-aboriginal-people-reclaimed-a-language-palawa-kani-99764.

Haskins, Victoria 2001, "On the doorstep: Aboriginal domestic service as a 'contact zone'", *Australian Feminist Studies*, vol. 16, no. 34, pp. 13–25, DOI: 10.1080/08164640120038881.

Haskins, Victoria K. & Lowrie, Claire (eds.) 2015, *Colonization and domestic service: historical and contemporary perspectives*, vol. 14, Routledge international studies of women and place, Routledge, London.

Heiss, Anita & Minter, Peter 2014, *Macquarie PEN anthology of Aboriginal literature*, Allen & Unwin, Crows Nest, NSW.

Jeanneret, Henry 1854, *The vindication of a colonial Magistrate from the aspersion of His Grace the Duke of Newcastle: by official documents and attestations, with a remonstrance; and exposure of a colonial conspiracy, whereby Her Majesty the Queen has been imposed upon in a petition against Henry Jeanneret, M. D., late superintendent of the Aborigines of Van Diemen's Land*, Hope and Co., London.

Johnson, Murray & McFarlane, Ian 2015, *Van Diemen's Land, an Aboriginal history*, UNSW Press, Sydney.

Johnston, Anna 2009, "George Augustus Robinson, the 'Great Conciliator': colonial celebrity and its postcolonial aftermath", *Postcolonial Studies*, vol. 12, no. 2, pp. 153–172, DOI: 10.1080/13688790902887155.

Jones, Bernie D. 2011, *Fathers of conscience: mixed-race inheritance in the antebellum South*, University of Georgia Press, Athens, Georgia.

Kenny, Anna 2013, "*Geist* through myth: revealing an Aboriginal ontology", in *The Aranda's Pepa: an introduction to Carl Strehlow's masterpiece Die Aranda- und Loritja-Stämme in Zentral-Australien (1907–1920)*, ANU Press, Canberra, pp. 135–168: https://library.oapen.org/handle/20.500.12657/33507.

Kutlubay, Zekayi and Serdaroglu, Server (eds.) 2017. *Fundamentals of sexually transmitted infections*, InTech, Books On Demand, Croatia.

Lawson, Tom 2014, *The last man: a British genocide in Tasmania*, IB Tauris, London.

Long, Carolyn Morrow 2001, *Spiritual merchants: religion, magic, and commerce*, University of Tennessee Press, Knoxville.

Lowance, Mason, Westbrook, Ellen & De Prospo, R. C. 1994, *The Stowe debate: rhetorical strategies in Uncle Tom's cabin*, University of Massachusetts Press, Massachusetts.

Lumby, Jonathan 1995, *The Lancashire witch craze: Jennet Preston and the Lancashire witches, 1612*, Carnegie Publishing, Lancaster.

Lushington, Charles & Labouchere, L. 1839, *Australian Aborigines, copies or extracts of despatches relative to the massacre of various Aborigines in Australia, in the year 1838*, British Parliamentary Papers, House of Commons, vol. 34, paper 526, London.

Lydon, Jane (ed.) 2014, *Calling the shots: Aboriginal photographies*, Aboriginal Studies Press, Canberra.

Lydon, Jane 2016, *Photography, humanitarianism, empire*, Bloomsbury Publishing, London.

McFarlane, Ian 2002, *Aboriginal society in North West Tasmania: dispossession and genocide*, University of Tasmania, Hobart.

McGowan, Angela 2000, "On their own: towards an analysis of sealers' sites on Heard Island", *Papers and Proceedings of the Royal Society of Tasmania*, vol. 133, part 2, pp. 61–70.

Marks, Claude 1975, *Pilgrims, heretics, and lovers: a medieval journey*, MacMillan, New York.

BIBLIOGRAPHY

Matson-Green, Vicki Maikutena 2005, "Tarenorerer (1800–1831)", *Australian dictionary of biography*, supp. vol., National Centre of Biography, Australian National University, Canberra (published first in hardcopy 2005, Melbourne University Press), https://adb.anu.edu.au/biography/tarenorerer-13212/text23923.

Meredith, Louisa Anne 1852 (2010), *My home in Tasmania, during a residence of nine years*, vols. 1–2, Cambridge University Press, Cambridge.

Merry, Kay 2003, "The cross-cultural relationships between the sealers and the Tasmanian Aboriginal women at Bass Strait and Kangaroo Island in the early nineteenth century", Counterpoints 2003: celebrating diversity in research, *The Flinders University Online Journal of Interdisciplinary Conference Papers*, vol. 3, no. 1, pp. 80–88.

Moyle, Alice 1960, "Two native song-styles recorded in Tasmania (with six musical examples)", *Papers and Proceedings of the Royal Society of Tasmania*, vol. 94, pp. 73–78.

Moyle, Alice 1968, *Tasmanian music, an impasse?*, Australian Institute of Aboriginal Studies, Monash University, Melbourne.

O'Brien, Glen & Carey, Hilary M. 2016, "Introduction: Methodism and the Southern World", in Glen O'Brien and Hilary Carey (eds.), *Methodism in Australia: a history*, Routledge Methodist studies Series, Routledge, London.

Pares, Luis Nicolau 2013, *The formation of Candomblé: Vodun history and ritual in Brazil*, University of North Carolina Press, North Carolina.

Parry, Naomi 2007, "'Such a longing': Black and white children in welfare in New South Wales and Tasmania, 1880–1940", PhD thesis, University of New South Wales, Sydney.

Petrow, Stefan 1997, "Aboriginal skulls in the nineteenth century", *Papers and Proceedings: Tasmanian Historical Research Association*, vol. 44, no. 3, September, pp. 174–186.

Plomley, N. J. B. 1976, *A word-list of the Tasmanian Aboriginal languages*, N. Plomley in association with the Government of Tasmania, Hobart.

Plomley, N. J. B. 1983, *The Tasmanian tribes & cicatrices as tribal indicators among the Tasmanian Aborigines*, Queen Victoria Museum and Art Gallery, Launceston.

Plomley, N. J. B. 1987a, "The Tasmanian Aborigines: a research report", *Bulletin of the Centre for Tasmanian Historical Studies*, vol. 1, no. 3, pp. 4–16.

Plomley, N. J. B. 1987b, *Weep in silence: a history of the Flinders Island Aboriginal settlement*, Blubber Head Press, Hobart.

Plomley, N. J. B. 1991, "The Westlake papers: records of interviews in Tasmania by Ernest Westlake, 1908–1910", *Occasional Paper No. 4*, Queen Victoria Museum & Arts Gallery, Launceston.

Plomley, N. J. B. 2008, *Friendly mission: the Tasmanian journals and papers of George Augustus Robinson, 1829–1834*, 2nd edn, Queen Victoria Museum and Art Gallery, Launceston.

Raabus, Carol 2011, "Australia's Indigenous publishing pioneer, Walter George Arthur", ABC Local, viewed 12 October 2018, https://www.abc.net.au/local/audio/2011/02/17/3141671.htm.

Raboteau, Albert, 2004. *Slave religion: the "invisible institution" in the antebellum South*, Oxford University Press, New York.

Rae-Ellis, Vivienne 1976, *Trucanini: queen or traitor*, OBM Publishing Company, Hobart.

Rae-Ellis, Vivienne 1992, *Black Robinson: protector of Aborigines*, Melbourne University Press, Melbourne.

Reid, Kirsty & Paisley, Fiona (eds.) 2017, *Sources and methods in histories of colonialism: approaching the imperial archive*, Routledge, New York.

Reynolds, Henry 1991, "Walter George Arthur, pioneer Aboriginal", *Island*, no. 49, Summer, pp. 36–39.

Reynolds, Henry 1995a, *Fate of a free people*, Penguin, Melbourne.

Reynolds, Henry 1995b, *The other side of the frontier: Aboriginal resistance to the European invasion of Australia,* Penguin, Melbourne.

Reynolds, Henry 2005a, "Arthur, Walter George (1820–1861)", *Australian dictionary of biography*, National Centre of Biography, Australian National University, Canberra (published first in hardcopy 2005, Melbourne University Press), viewed online 21 November 2018, http://adb.anu.edu.au/biography/arthur-walter-george-12775/text23047.

Reynolds, Henry 2005b, *Nowhere people*, Penguin, Melbourne.

Ritz, Hermann 1909, "The speech of the Tasmanian Aborigines", *Papers and Proceedings of the Royal Society of Tasmania*, Hobart, pp. 44–81.

Rivington, J. & F. C. 1821, *Plays and poems of William Shakespeare*, University of Michigan, Michigan.

Roberts, Jan 1986, *Jack of Cape Grim*, Greenhouse Publications, Melbourne.

Robinson, George Augustus 1831a, "1831 Tasmania on the sealers located on the Islands in the Straits Expd in 1831", in *Robinson, George Augustus – correspondence and other papers, both official and private, Van Diemen's Land, 1829–1833*, Mitchell Library, A 7059 part 5, vol. 39, State Library of New South Wales, Sydney, http://archival-classic.sl.nsw.gov.au/_transcript/2017/D00007/a1148.html.

Robinson, George Augustus 1831b. *Item 5: George Augustus Robinson, notes relating to the sealers in Bass Strait and their native women, May–June 1831*, A 7059, item 5, State Library of NSW, Sydney, http://archival.sl.nsw.gov.au/Details/archive/110618321.

Robinson, Shirleene, 2015. "'Always a good demand': Aboriginal child domestic servants in nineteenth- and early twentieth-century Australia", in, Victoria K. Haskins & Claire Lowrie (eds.), *Colonization and domestic service: historical and contemporary perspectives*, vol. 14, Routledge international studies of women and place, Routledge, London.

Russell, Lynette 2012, *Roving mariners: Australian Aboriginal whalers and sealers in the Southern Oceans, 1790–1870*, SUNY Press, New York.

BIBLIOGRAPHY

Ryan, Lyndall 1982, *The Aboriginal Tasmanians*, University of Queensland Press, Brisbane.

Ryan, Lyndall 2008, "List of multiple killings of Aborigines in Tasmania: 1804–1835", *Mass Violence and Resistance – Research Network*, https://www.sciencespo.fr/mass-violence-war-massacre-resistance/fr/document/list-multiple-killings-aborigines-tasmania-1804-1835.

Ryan, Lyndall 2012, *Tasmanian Aborigines: a history since 1803*, Allen & Unwin, Sydney.

Schweizer, Marlis 2009, "'Darn that *Merry Widow Hat*': The on- and offstage life of a theatrical commodity, circa 1907–1908", *Theatre Survey*, vol. 50, no. 2, pp. 189–221, doi:10.1017/S0040557409990044.

Shakespeare, William 1803, *The plays of William Shakespeare*, vol. 21, Johnson, J (ed.), 5th edn, University of California, California.

Shelley, Mary 1818, *Frankenstein; or, the modern Prometheus*, Lackington, Hughes, Harding, Mavor & Jones, London.

Sherrow, Victoria 2006, *Encyclopedia of hair: a cultural history*, Greenwood Publishing Group, Connecticut.

Skye, Lee Miena 2007, *Kerygmatics of the new millennium: a study of Australian Aboriginal women's Christology*, ISPCK, Delhi.

Smithers, Gregory 2017, *Science, sexuality, and race in the United States and Australia, 1780–1940*, Routledge, New York.

Stanfield, Rachel 2018, *Indigenous mobilities across and beyond the Antipodes*, ANU Press, Canberra.

Stevens, Leonie 2017, *"Me write myself": the free Aboriginal Inhabitants of Van Diemen's Land at Wybalenna*, Monash University Publishing, Melbourne.

Stowe, Harriet Beecher 1852, *Uncle Tom's cabin; or, life among the lowly*, Bliss, Sands and Foster, London.

Stuart, Iain 1997, "Sea rats, bandits and roistering buccaneers: what were the Bass Strait sealers really like?", *Journal of the Royal Australian Historical Society*, vol. 8, no 1, pp. 47–58.

Taylor, Rebe 2016, "The first stone and the last Tasmanian: the colonial correspondence of Edward Burnett Tylor and Henry Ling Roth", *Oceania*, vol. 86, no. 3, pp. 320–343.

Taylor, Rebe 2017, *Into the heart of Tasmania: a search for human antiquity*, Melbourne University Press, Melbourne.

Thrower, W. I. 1894, *Younah! A Tasmanian Aboriginal romance of the Cataract Gorge*, Mercury Office, Hobart, https://nla.gov.au:443/tarkine/nla.obj-42942584.

Tipping, Marjorie J. 1969, "Becker, Ludwig (1808–1861)", *Australian dictionary of biography*, vol. 3, National Centre of Biography, Australian National University, Canberra (published first in hardcopy 1969), viewed 23 June 2019, http://adb.anu.edu.au/biography/becker-ludwig-2961/text4309.

Turnbull, P. 2017, *Science, museums and collecting the Indigenous dead in colonial Australia*, Palgrave Macmillan, Cham, Switzerland.

Turner, Sir William 1908, "The craniology, racial affinities, and descent of the Aborigines of Tasmania", *Transactions of the Royal Society of Edinburgh*, vol. XLVI, part II, no. 17, Robert Grant & Son, London.

Turner, Sir William 1910, "The Aborigines of Tasmania, part II: the skeleton", *Transactions of the Royal Society of Edinburgh*, vol. XLVII, part III, no. 16, Robert Grant & Son, London.

Walker, George Washington 1839–44, *George Washington Walker's letter book, 1839–44*, University of Tasmania Open Access Repository, Hobart, https://eprints.utas.edu.au/2844/.

Walker, James Backhouse 1890, *Reminiscences of life in Hobart 1840s to 1860s*, University of Tasmania Open Access Repository, Hobart, https://eprints.utas.edu.au/1865/.

Walker, James Backhouse 1897, "Some notes on the tribal divisions of the Aborigines of Tasmania & notes on the Aborigines of Tasmania, extracted from the manuscript journals of George Washington Walker, with an Introduction by James B. Walker, F.R.G.S.", *Papers and Proceedings of the Royal Society of Tasmania*, Hobart.

Correspondence

Port Phillip Correspondences courtesy of https://prov.vic.gov.au:
Colonial Secretary (addressed to), 9 August, 1840.
C. J. La Trobe to G. A. Robinson, 28 February 1842.
E. J. Newton to C. J. La Trobe, 18 December 1839.
G. A. Robinson to La Trobe, 7 October 1839.
G. A. Robinson to Colonial Secretary's Office, 8 November 1839.
G. A. Robinson to Superintendent (Port Phillip), 17 December 1839.
G. A. Robinson to La Trobe, 26 December 1839.
G. A. Robinson to C. J. La Trobe, 11 March 1841.
G. A. Robinson to Mr. Thomson, 30 September 1841.
G. A. Robinson to La Trobe, 23 December 1841.
G. A. Robinson to La Trobe, 5 July 1842.
G. A. Robinson to La Trobe, 6 July 1842.
G. A. Robinson to Charles Joseph La Trobe, 14 July 1842.
G. A. Robinson to La Trobe, 27 July 1842.
G. A. Robinson to La Trobe, 23 August 1842.
G. A. Robinson to Charles Joseph La Trobe, 1 September 1842.
G. A. Robinson to La Trobe, 12 October 1842.
Superintendent (Port Phillip) *to Colonial Secretary*, 7 August 1840.
William Thomas to G. A. Robinson, 6 October 1840.
E. Thomson to Colonial Secretary's Office, 25 July 1840.
E. Thomson to Colonial Secretary's Office, 29 October 1840.
E. Thomson to Colonial Secretary's Office, 7 March 1842.
E. Thomson to Colonial Secretary's Office, 15 July 1843.

BIBLIOGRAPHY

Newspaper Articles courtesy of National Library of Australia
http://trove.nla.gov.au.

Additional Web References
"Bessy Clark: 1825–1867". National Portrait Gallery, https://www.portrait.gov.au/people/bessy-clark-1825.

"Collections – Quaker collection", University of Tasmania, https://eprints.utas.edu.au/view/collections/quaker.html.

"Dr Henry Jeanneret". *The Australian Churchman*, 2 July 1886, cited in Stray Dog Photos, http://straydogphotos.com/family/henry-jeanneret.html.

"Early free settlers". Maritime Museum of Tasmania, http://www.maritimetas.org/collection-displays/displays/over-seas-stories-tasmanian-migrants/early-free-settlers.

"History". Cygnet, https://cygnet.org.au/history/.

"History resources – members of Parliament: John Lyle" [sic] (John Lyne). Parliament of Tasmania, https://www.parliament.tas.gov.au/history/members/lynej177.html.

"Launceston", Anne McLaughlin. The Companion to Tasmanian History, http://www.utas.edu.au/library/companion_to_tasmanian_history/L/Launceston.htm.

"Letters from Robert Clark, Catechist of Flinders Island, to George Washington Walker, Van Diemen's Land, 1845–1846", University of Tasmania, https://eprints.utas.edu.au/2847/.

"Orphan Number 4694. Orphan: Mary Ann Robinson", Friends of the Orphan Schools, St John's Park Precinct New Town, Tasmania, http://www.orphanschool.org.au/showorphan.php?orphan_ID=4694.

"Portraits of Tasmanian Aborigines. From Francois Péron's *Voyage de découvertes aux Terres Australes*". *The LaTrobe Journal*, no. 41, Autumn 1988, http://latrobejournal.slv.vic.gov.au/latrobejournal/issue/latrobe-41/fig-latrobe-41P003b.html.

"Robinson, George Augustus (1791–1866)". *Australian dictionary of biography*, National Centre of Biography, Australian National University, http://adb.anu.edu.au/biography/robinson-george-augustus-2596.

"Tasmanian Aborigines at Oyster Cove Station", Libraries Tasmania, https://linctas.ent.sirsidynix.net.au/client/en_AU/library/search/detailnonmodal/ent:$002f$002fSD_ILS$002f0$002fSD_ILS:140803/one.

Tasmanian communities online, LaTrobe Online Access Centre, formerly available from http://www.tco.asn.au/oac/community_history.cgi?oacID=24&articleID=181302, date viewed 29/04/10.

"Van Diemen's Land: island colony, Tasmania, Australia (1642–1855)". *Britannica*, https://www.britannica.com/place/Van-Diemens-Land.

"Walter George Arthur". AustLit, https://www.austlit.edu.au/austlit/page/A106424.

ABOUT THE AUTHOR

Joel Stephen Birnie is an academic, visual artist and filmmaker. Raised predominantly by his Indigenous Tasmanian family, he proudly embraces a multi-ethnic heritage from across the globe. Joel's creative work has been exhibited in galleries and festivals across Australia, including in Darwin, Sydney, Adelaide and at the Koori Heritage Trust in Melbourne. He holds a Bachelor of Arts in Indigenous Studies and a Master of Fine Arts, and in 2019 completed a PhD at Monash, which focused on deconstructing and reconstructing the 150 years of European colonisation in Tasmania from a familial (Indigenous) perspective.

Lightning Source UK Ltd.
Milton Keynes UK
UKHW012218050922
408363UK00005B/374